Forgiven

VINCE RUSSO

FOREWORD BY ED FERRARA

ECW PRESS

Published by ECW Press
2120 Queen Street East, Suite 200, Toronto, Ontario, Canada M4E 1E2

LIBRARY AND ARCHIVES CANADA CATALOGUING IN PUBLICATION

Russo, Vince
Forgiven : one man's journey from self-glorification to
sanctification / Vince Russo.

ISBN 1-55022-704-1

1. Russo, Vince. 2. Wrestling promoters — United States-
Biography. 3. Christian biography — United States. I. Title.

GV1196.R87A3 2005   796.812'092   C2005-904300-8

Editor: Michael Holmes
Cover and Text Design: Tania Craan
Production: Mary Bowness
Cover Photo: Scott Finkelstein
Printing: Friesens

This book is set in Minion and Akzidenz Grotesk

DISTRIBUTION

Canada: Jaguar Book Group, 100 Armstrong Ave., Georgetown, ON L7G 5S4
United States: Independent Publishers Group, 814 North Franklin Street,
Chicago, IL, U.S.A. 60610

PRINTED AND BOUND IN CANADA

ECW PRESS
ecwpress.com

Contents

Acknowledgements

First and foremost, this book is dedicated to Jesus Christ for saving my life. His love, guidance and patience are still, to this day, beyond my human comprehension. Every word written in this book is dedicated to Him and the glorification of His being and His Kingdom.

To my wife Amy: you had every reason in the world to leave me . . . but you never did. Your unconditional love was not of this world. Regardless of how many years I live, I will never be able to repay you for your faithfulness.

To my three kids, Will, VJ and Annie: you mean the world to me. I hope this book serves as my legacy in an effort to show you how not to let your priorities ever get away from you as you someday raise families of your own.

To my father, Jim: to this day you have the biggest heart I have ever seen. You instilled God-like qualities in me when I was so far away from the truth.

To my sister Debbie: I apologize for not being there as much as I should have. Maybe I haven't shown it over the years — but you are in my heart every single day.

To my niece Chloe and my nephew Greg: even though I wasn't there physically — my spirit was always with you. I hope this book serves as an inspiration to you both — showing that through the love of Christ there is hope for us all.

To my best friend in the world, Jeff Iorio: you have been on this wild ride for almost 30 years — and you've never once gotten off. From the bottom of my heart, I love you. There, I said it!

To my Sigma Tau Gamma Fraternity brothers, for being my family when I was a thousand miles away from home: Beans, Flounder—you will never be forgotten!

To my mother-in-law, Alta: thank you for allowing that punk kid from New Yawk to marry your daughter. I hope I've done good.

To ECW Press's Michael Holmes for seeing my dream through: your patience and guidance were a true blessing. I could never thank you enough.

And, oh yeah, one last thing: NO THANKS goes to the San Francisco Giants for giving me a lifetime of sheer grief and disappointment. How more loyal do I have to be in order to get just one lousy championship?

Did I forget anyone? Of course I didn't.

Last . . . but not least . . . my mother, Terry.

I've kidded and teased for 44 years because the situations have just lent themselves. But with God now as my witness—there is no one else on earth that could have raised me the way you did. Are you crazy? Perhaps you had to be, in order to put up with me. But you know what, Ma? I wouldn't have had it any other way. I love you . . . and I thank you.

Foreword

What you're about to read isn't a book about wrestling, although there's a lot of wrestling in it. It isn't about Christianity, either, although Christian faith plays a large part in it as well.

The book you're holding in your hands right now is about perspective.

More than anything else, it's about the need to take a step outside ourselves from time to time and look at our surroundings from an alien point of view. When we fail to do this, we sometimes find ourselves trapped in hostile environments — unsure of how we got there, and equally unsure as to how we might escape.

But before I go getting all heavy on you, let me back up a bit. . . .

Vince Russo and I have had a long history, and I consider him one of my oldest and dearest friends — not too shabby, considering we only met in 1998. Consider it a testament to the environment we were in at the time: the WWF.[1] We were literally thrown together in a working relationship that could have ended (and, in some ways, did) in disaster. But something clicked between the two of us, almost from moment one.

Perhaps it was because we were both Italian guys from the Northeast (Vince from Long Island, myself from New Jersey). Or maybe it was that we had been wrestling fans ever since we were kids. Or it could have been our frighteningly similar taste in just about everything: from movies (*Raging Bull* and anything with the Marx

---

[1] Yeah, yeah, I know it's "WWE" now . . . but I never worked for World Wrestling Entertainment. Vince and I worked for the World Wrestling Federation. Ergo, my use of "WWF" isn't a typo. Look elsewhere, typo-geeks — I'm not gonna make it that easy for you.

Brothers) to television (*The Honeymooners* and *All in the Family*) to music (we're both avowed Beatles and John Lennon freaks). My being a few years his junior didn't stop us from both having grown up watching the same Abbott & Costello movies WPIX (New York's channel 11) would air every Sunday morning at 11:30. Similarly, the age difference didn't stand in the way of us both knowing the sheer bliss a "Sack o' Castles"[2] would mean to a growling stomach . . . not to mention the nightmare that same bliss could become an hour after the Castles were gone (trust me, it was never pretty).

You see, we shared similar backgrounds, and that played a huge part in how quickly and intensely we bonded. At the time in the WWF, we only had each other to look out for, we only had each other to depend on, we only had each other to trust. We quickly went from acquaintances to friends and partners, only to find ourselves just as quickly on the bitter outs with one another. There was a time, shortly after our friendship and partnership dissolved in WCW, when the mere mention of Vince's name would elicit nothing but an audible groan and look of disgust from me. And I know Vince's feelings toward me were no different.

Needless to say, a lot of water has passed under the bridge since those dark days, and we buried the hatchet long ago. We somehow emerged from the ugliness of the wrestling business as better, happier men, and rediscovered the friendship that we once enjoyed, only to cherish it all the more.

When Vince asked me to write the foreword to his book in early 2005, I was honored. I had just finished reading a rough draft of the latest version of his manuscript, and I had been corresponding with him about it via phone and E-mail. He had taken my suggestions and criticisms with an eagerness that showed his new perspective and outlook on life. This was a different Vince Russo from the man I had

---

[2] If you get this reference, good on ya. If you don't, read on . . . Vince goes into more detail in the body of the book.

spent all those hours on the road with, all those hours working side-by-side with and, for a good couple of years, all those hours disliking.

Vince has always been an extremely controversial, polarizing figure — especially in the wrestling business. Whether you were a fan, a production person or one of "the boys," you either loved him or hated him. But it's important for me to mention, in the inimitable words of Vince McMahon no less, "*that* was yesterday."

Vinnie Ru is a changed man. I never thought I'd see the day I'd say that, but I do so today with absolute certainty. Through his faith, he has finally found the peace and happiness that has eluded him most of his adult life.

Also, in the interest of full disclosure, I should mention here that I am not a Christian. I personally don't believe in organized religion, which I feel is a whole different ball o' wax from spirituality. "You say heathen, I say secular humanist."[3] When Vince first told me about his awakening and rebirth, however, I couldn't be skeptical — there was a quality in his voice that I had never before heard from him, a clarity and a passion in his words that dispelled any doubt I might have had. I remember telling him how happy I was for him to have finally found that missing piece to his life's puzzle. It was a long, hard journey for Vince, but he had finally, honestly, found the peace he desperately needed. For that, I'm proud of him and I support him 100%.

And now, as promised, on to the heavy stuff. . . .

When I was in college, I was an English/Theatre double-major (a surefire double-threat to unemployment agencies across the country). At the time, I fell in love with a one-act play by Samuel Beckett called *Krapp's Last Tape*. In the piece, we spend all of our time with the titular (and only) character — a bitter, crusty 69-year-old man named Krapp.[4] In the play, we see him go about his existence as he has

---

3 To be (awkwardly) sung to the tune of "You Say Potato . . . "

4 Stop snickering, kids. It's the man's name.

every single day for the 50-plus years: he listens to journal-esque audio recordings he made in the past, when he was a younger and (presumably) more ignorant man. He takes great pleasure in scoffing at his past foolishness and naïveté as the tapes play, completely oblivious to the fact that his younger self is doing the exact same thing on the tapes themselves. Krapp (age 69) listens to a tape of Krapp (age 35) discussing how foolish he had been at age 19 — and, of course, Krapp–35 is aware of his past ignorance from (what else?) listening to tapes that he had made when he was 19. Krapp–69 offers a running commentary on Krapp–35's musings that suggests the cyclical nature of his existence, believing he has grown in wisdom, and unaware that his intolerance and negativity have been the only constants in his life, stranding him in a stagnant rut he can't escape — because he's unaware he's stuck in it.

What in the world does ANY of that have to do with Vince Russo and this book? Everything, my friends.

Forgiven began life as a very different book, written by a completely different person. His name was Vince Russo, but he's not the Vince Russo I know and love today. This book was originally entitled *Welcome to Bizarroland*, and it was written by an extremely bitter, angry and unhappy Vince Russo back in 2000 — whom I'll hereafter appropriately refer to as Vince–2000. The book was a tell-all diatribe in which no one Vince ever worked with was spared his barbs. It was vicious and it was ugly. It was a product of Vince–2000's perspective at the time.

In *Welcome to Bizarroland*, Vince looked back on the past events in his life with a jaundiced eye, and he had an extremely critical view of his naive perspective as he had embarked on his career in the WWF — we'll call *that* Vince Vince–'90s. As Vince–2000 looked back on the Vince–'90s, he did so with an admittedly arrogant perspective, as if to say, "If I only knew then what I know now." Just like Krapp.

Then, before *Bizarroland* was published, Vince–2000 had a revelation. In one fell swoop, Vince–2000 died and Vince–Forgiven was born.

This book, like *Krapp's Last Tape*, is a Chinese puzzle box of different perspectives. Vince–Forgiven took *Bizarroland* and tore it down to the foundations. Vince–Forgiven was no longer interested in attacking the people he had worked with for so many years. Vince–Forgiven had a new outlook on life, and he wanted it to show through in his work. He was tired of contributing negativity, and wanted to pass on what he had learned.

This book, therefore, is a product of Vince–Forgiven taking extended passages from *Bizarroland* (written by Vince–2000) and commenting upon them from his newly enlightened perspective. The insight he's gained in the relatively short time since being reborn is truly amazing, as you'll discover for yourself as you read on. You're in for a fascinating journey as you lose yourself in Vince–2000's tales of Vince–'90s progression from academic textbook salesman to his role as one of the most influential figures in the history of the wrestling business . . . only to find yourself snapped out of *Bizarroland* and back to reality by the honest, wise and insightful perspective of Vince–Forgiven.

Unlike Krapp–69, however, Vince–Forgiven *has* learned from his past. That's what gives this work the uplifting sense of closure that Beckett's masterpiece lacks.

I truly hope you enjoy the multiple perspectives of Vince looking back on Vince looking back on Vince. I'm incredibly proud of him for arriving at the place he is now, and I couldn't be happier for him.

There have been times when I looked up to Vince like the big brother I never had, and there were other times I wanted to put him through a freakin' wall. But after all the ups and downs we've been through, both together and apart, I like Vince Russo. That's *my* perspective. After you finish this book, I hope you'll share it.

— Ed Ferrara
Chicago, Illinois
April, 2005

Sometime in October, 2003...

Chapter 1

THE DAY I DIED

I hate Jeff.

All these years thinking that he was a "true" friend . . . who was I kidding? Deep down he was always a wrestler, never caring about anybody but himself. You think by now, after being beat up in this God-forsaken business for more than 10 years, I would have learned my lesson. But, no — for some sick, demented reason I continue to believe in people — continue to believe they are honest, sincere . . . what a schmuck.

Man, I loved the guy — from our days together in the World Wrestling Federation I thought Jeff Jarrett was the real thing — a true friend. I should have known there were no true friends in wrestling . . . only acquaintances. To think I went to bat for this guy — I put my job on the line for him. I fought JR, Bruce Prichard and Vince himself toe-to-toe when they saw nothing in him. And this is what I get, this is what it all comes down to.

What's going to happen to my friendship with his wife, Jill, a person who I care about dearly? And those adorable two kids — every year he would send me a Christmas card with Jocelyn and Jaclyn on it, and my hard heart would melt like a Hershey's kiss left in the car on a summer's day. Man, I love those kids.

How could he do this to me? How could he chose this guy over me — a guy who personally attempted to hurt me and my family over nothing more than money, greed and power. Friendship is more than that. It has to be!

This is my rock bottom. My heart, once fueled with love, is now hardened with hate. I never thought I would hate my best friend. Never, not Jeff, he was "different."

I don't know what else to do. I don't know where else to go. I can't believe for one minute that this is it. I've spent my entire adult life on a journey to be the best I can possibly be. I forfeit my entire life, my family, my values and my morals to be labeled the most successful sports entertainment writer in the history of the business . . . and this is what it comes down to. As I free-fall down the mountain, my heart is calloused with such pain, such hate, such ugliness. So this is what it's all about? This is the meaning of life? God creates you — and then the joke's on you.

Look at yourself. Look at what you've become. Your heart that was once filled with compassion and love is now fired by hate. For 42 years you have turned your back on me to get to this point in your life. I was always there — I was there from the moment you took your first breath. I was there to take care of you, to guide you, to protect you . . . to love you. Vince? Are you going to listen to me now?

I knew that voice. My entire life I had heard it; just didn't want to listen. Yes, I allowed it to guide me, but I would never completely give into it. I didn't need it. Subconsciously, I knew what it was, who it was and what it wanted. But I chose not to listen. Now God was no longer taking no for an answer.

The voice that once lay dormant in my heart was now screaming at the top of its lungs — God had seen and heard enough. At that moment, his spirit transcended from inside my body and blanketed me. I no longer had a choice — he was taking over whether I liked it or not.

Following that moment of divine intervention, I was placed in my '99 Jeep Wrangler and led to the local church, a place called North Metro that I had never been to before. Once inside the auditorium, I was directed by a bald-headed preacher, a six-foot-seven former University of Arkansas football player by the name of Mark Henry. That day, in front of a sold-out house, Mark Henry spoke directly to me. As I left the church that day it was clear: the old Vince was dead, and the new Vince had been born.

My entire being was now overflowing with love and forgiveness. My feelings of brotherhood towards my friend Jeff Jarrett were stronger than ever. For this was never about him, but rather, me. There wasn't an ounce of hate left in my body — only kindness, understanding and compassion. From there, God led me to his book, which I ate up on a daily basis. Right there, within those pages, was the blueprint to follow, and the very meaning of life.

Growing up, this was something you only heard, or read about, usually concerning those who were weak or desperate. But this wasn't *Reader's Digest* — it was my life, and it was all very real. Suddenly, gaining a life's supply of knowledge in a single moment, everything became crystal clear. I couldn't as much as throw half a used toothpick on the ground because I now fully understood — this was God's creation, this was God's world. I cried, then I cried some more. If only I had listened earlier.

At that moment all that had mattered to me was no longer important, and that which hadn't seemed important now meant the world. I have never looked back.

All the glory be to God.

Early October, 2004

Chapter 2

TRIBUTE TO OSCAR MADISON

"A good writer hates to write, but loves to have written."

I first heard that line in my early teens, stated by none other than Oscar Madison, portrayed by Jack Klugman, on the TV sitcom, *The Odd Couple*. The story goes something like this: Oscar had been paid money up front by a publisher to write a book pertaining to sports, but every time he sat down at his typewriter (yes, they used typewriters in those days), the blank page lay limp and lifeless before him, growing bigger and whiter with every dripping second.

You see, Oscar hated to write, as I think most writers do. There's just something about that blank page — the emptiness, the coldness, the intimidation. Top that with the pressure of a deadline and you have something that's quite unappealing. Yes, good writers hate to write. But my, oh my, that finished product — that masterpiece in which every word is carefully and methodically laid in just the right place and just the right order, that moment when the little numbers on the bottom of each page add up to another number that is now significant. The "finished work" — there is nothing like it.

But man, I hate to write — I always have. It's such a chore. As I mentioned earlier, there are few things in life that are more intimidating than an empty white page staring you right in the face, not saying a word. It's just that look. That empty stare begging you to dress its body with something . . . anything. So you sit . . . and you write. You turn on the TV . . . and you write. You have a cup of coffee . . . and you write. You check your E-mail . . . and you write. You spell-check . . . and you write. This agonizing process seems endless until you finally reach those two glorious words: THE END.

For six months, starting on January 10, 2000, I went through this agonizing journey. I sat at a computer in the back of my store, a CD Warehouse in Marietta, Georgia, and tortured myself through this process. Between customers I carefully plotted each word with the precision of a Hollywood plastic surgeon. A little cut here, a tiny tuck there, trim the fat in just the right place. Yeah, this was going to be my legacy. This was going to outsell King, Seuss, Stern, all of them — because this was my life in professional wrestling.

And, you should have seen it. I mean, it was *all* there — everything you ever wanted to read in those other wrestling books but wouldn't, simply because those wrestler/authors were under contract to Vince McMahon. The fact is, he was the one who got them the book deal in the first place. They certainly couldn't write anything to taint the good name of his company — even if they wanted to! But me? *I was free to say whatever I wanted about whomever I wanted.*

As the timeless cliché in wrestling goes — this one was going to be "no holds barred." I was dropping the dime on everybody. I had known everything they had ever done. I was going to be the younger brother who spent weeks collecting all the evidence on the older brother, until I had just enough to tell mom. Man, this was going to be bad. Heads weren't just going to roll — they were going to explode. And wrestlers who were husbands? As we say on Long Island, *fahgettaboutit!* They were in for the worst of it. Because no matter how bad I was at times, through it all I NEVER cheated on my wife. To me, this would be the ultimate disrespect to the mother of my children. Call it the Italian in me, but I've always had a massive problem with that.

Man, you should have read this thing. I clutched it to my chest, tighter, and with more love than I had ever held any of my own three kids. Yeah, this was my REAL baby! I mean, you just had to see the way it was crafted. It was sewn together with every expletive you had ever heard. A tapestry of curse word, after curse word, after curse word.

Have you ever heard an uncensored Colin Farrell interview? If you haven't experienced this in your lifetime it's a must. I recently saw him on the Independent Film Channel's *Table for Five,* a dinner-setting format where people in the biz openly talk about the biz. On this particular episode, there were a lot of heavy hitters. Farrell sat there breaking bread with the likes of Ben Affleck, Kevin Smith and Jennifer Garner, to name a few. Let's just say that the "color" spewing out of Farrell's mouth that day was so offensive that poor, innocent Ms. Garner was 13 going on 30 weeks before the movie ever hit the big screen! I mean, man, this was Jennifer Garner. Did Farrell forget she was at the table? I mean, do you expect me to believe he didn't have the discipline to edit himself at least until dessert?

In my line of business it's called shock value. You sandwich vile on top of vile, then force-feed it to the customers watching and listening. In my heyday, I was no different. My language was plain *filthy* — there's no adjective that describes it better. I swore at home, at work, in front of my kids, my wife and my parents, on the phone, on paper, in E-mails and most certainly — in front of the "boys" — the wrestlers. There, it was acceptable, because it was the only language we understood.

Looking back now, I really don't understand my logic. In my late 30s and early 40s, did I think it was cool to stain the air with my words? Was it hip? Cutting edge? What was my point? I mean, I openly shot out curse word after curse word while I was on the phone in front of my daughter . . . my baby girl. Was that cool? Was this what I wanted her growing up doing?

"Hey mom, !@#$% Barney's over. Will you change the !@#$% channel and put on !@#$% *Rugrats?*"

Getting back to the book — it was indeed, "colorful." Yup, in my hands I had the Holy Grail. You see, throughout my life I'd gone through phases of what I wanted to be when I grew up, as we all did. I'll lay it out in stages for you. As a child it was Batman; pre-teen, Tom Jones; young teen, Willie Mays; teen teen, Gene Simmons; young adult, an author. There was always something about wanting to write my own book. It just seemed like it would be a great accomplishment. A legacy, something I could leave behind for the grandkids. And, here it was, I'd done it! (Even though I wouldn't have allowed my own kids to read it.) My entire life — from watching Hulk Hogan as a kid to being sued by him as an adult — it was all right there, my entire 40-plus years in 300-plus pages! This was going to catapult me to the next level: Oprah, Ellen, Katie, Conan — they were going to stand in line to book me for their gabfests. I was Rocky Balboa, standing on the very top step of the Philadelphia Museum of Modern Art, screaming at the top of my lungs, "Yo, Adrian . . . I did it!"

The last thing I ever expected, not even in my wildest dreams, was that I'd spend the next few months reworking it.

Despite all the work, all the energy, all the love, it was back to the keyboard. However, even though the colorful language had to say bye-bye, replaced with the obligatory !@#$% the old manuscript has been kept basically intact, so you can see firsthand where the Old Vince was, and where the New Vince is. Throughout the book there are also various revelations (highlighted in another font), where the new Vince comments exclusively on the old Vince. What do I mean by this old Vince/new Vince thing? Isn't Vince Russo — Vince Russo?

Okay, here goes: the original book, in its raw form, was never going to be published, because I wasn't going to allow it. The reason being: what once made me gleam, now made me grimace; what once made me laugh, now made me cry; what once made me so proud, now made me ashamed.

That's what God will do to you.

The reworking of the original manuscript of *Forgiven* (originally titled *Welcome to Bizarroland*) is extremely symbolic. In one day, in one moment, God had wiped out an entire lifetime. With just one revelation he created an entirely new man. To this very second I am shocked by the things I do, the things I say, the things I write. This isn't me; it can't be. What happened to that other guy — the swearing, absentee father, unloving husband, work-driven "sweetheart" who used to live in this exact house, wear these exact clothes, sit at this very desk. That guy is dead — passed away. *Nah, nah . . . nah, nah, nah, nah . . . hey, hey, hey . . . goodbye.*

Once again, in trying to break it down to something simple, let me relate it to Hollywood. I know there was a *Stepford Wives*, but what about the Stepford husbands? I mean, I could write the thing, I'm already playing the part. On the outside — looks the same, acts the same, dresses the same. But on the inside, somebody else, different being, different temperament, different agenda, different personality, different heart. Only one problem, this isn't Stepford, this is Marietta, Georgia. And this is very real.

So how did this happen? After 42 years, how does one man become a totally new creature? How does Hyde turn to Jekyll? How does a fire-breathing dragon turn into the town's gentle mayor (my *H.R. Pufnstuf* reference for this book)? How does evil turn to good? How does darkness turn to light? To understand the end of a life, we'll have to go back and examine the beginning.

Originally written January 2002,
through July 2002

(Only the language has been changed to protect the innocent)

Chapter 3

WHY IS MY MOTHER BITING HER HAND?

I grew up on Long Island, New York . . . yadda, yadda, yadda. Who cares? Man, I've read so many books where the author gets into such trite details, in what appears to me to be no more than an effort to fill as many pages as humanly possible. I'm not going to torture you with that here. I'm thrilled you bought this book, so I'm going to give you the most misery for your money.

How come growing up we don't realize our families are dysfunctional? It's not until later in life when we watch *Dr. Phil*, or *Jerry Springer* for that matter, and say, "Hey, I know her . . . That's my mother!" But, before I can get to the Fruitinator (that's my nickname for my mother — a fruitcake who wore *Terminator*-style glasses for a short period because she thought she was going blind), I have to talk about the guy who created the Fruitinator, my grandfather, John Savarino.

As Italian as you can possibly get, my grandfather had a huge influence on me growing up, but not in a particularly good way. You see, even though it was the norm at that time, Granddad was a male chauvinistic oink. He had to be — he was Sicilian. With a pencil-thin moustache straight out of every gangster movie you ever saw, John J. was, no doubt, a man's man. If you're an old-school Italian and you're reading this, you know exactly what I'm talking about. The second my grandfather would walk in the door from work (he worked in the garment district in New York City), wearing his black fedora and carrying a worn *New York Daily News* under his arm, my grandmother, or "Nana," would be there to wait on him hand, foot, arm, toe . . . you get the picture. If his black coffee wasn't on the table at the exact moment he took his hat and coat off — there was going to be trouble. Man, this guy was my idol. After the black coffee came the wine, came the pasta, came the peaches with wine, and everybody was happy. The man was the boss and his wife took care of him — the rules were real simple for Granddad, it was unspoken Italian *law*. He was simply the king of his castle. This would have a huge influence on my adulthood. In many ways, I treated my wife Amy the same way. I was the boss, I took care of everything. As the great Ralph Kramden once said to his wife Alice, "I am the captain of this ship and you are nothing more than a lowly, third-class seaman."

Growing up, both Ralph Kramden and Archie Bunker were huge influences on me. The way they assumed the position of head of the household was nothing short of inspirational. In my teens I used to constantly tell my father, "If you were more like Ralph, or Archie, Mommy wouldn't treat you the way she does!" The art of writing a television show could be found right there in these two sitcoms. *The Honeymooners* and *All in the Family* were two of my early influences as far as comedy was concerned. Their dialogue, story lines and character development was ingenious. And, the acting wasn't too shabby either. Jackie Gleason's precision timing and Carroll O'Connor's priceless facial expressions were near perfection. These two legends were clearly ahead of their time.

Getting back to my granddad, while he secured his spot at the head of the table, my father, Jim Russo, usually found his comfort zone somewhere underneath it. Why? He may have been too scared to come out, afraid that the Fruitinator was lurking somewhere in the surrounding area, clutching a list of things for him to do.

It's just this simple — my mother dominated my father. I think the fact that my dad was five-eight and weighed 140 pounds soaking wet might have had something to do with it. Jim, as I playfully but respectfully called him, was petrified of the Fruitinator. And, what a nag — Mamma Mia! Jim do this, Jim do that — to this day, it's Jim do something . . . *anything!* Before remote controls, my mother wouldn't even get off the coach to change the channel — Jim had to do it! Man, this sad sack did everything — wash the floors, do the dishes, all "women's" work — it drove me nuts.

But the truth is, he just did it so he wouldn't have to hear her. No different than many husbands today. I mean, how many times do we do something just to get the wife off our back? But, regardless of his lack of chauvinism, I still greatly treasured my dad. He was such a hard worker, setting the standard for me as I got older. He worked for a government contractor that made parts for military equipment . . . I think. I remember him working overtime every night to provide for me, Fruity and my sister, and I never heard him complain about it — he just did it. Unfortunately, his hard work never got him very far. My dad was such a nice guy, people just took advantage of him. That's the nature of the beast. Vince McMahon always used to tell me, "Pal, it's the law of the jungle — eat, or be eaten!" Well, on more occasions than one my father was eaten alive. But he never cared — as long as he could play his softball on Sundays. Softball was his drug. A very religious man — even though it wouldn't rub off on me, no matter how many times he would drag me to church — my father, a grown man, would literally go to church in his softball uniform before his game on Sundays. To this day he doesn't miss a mass. But then again, is he really so religious, or is he just trying to get out of the house? Hmmm.

As much as I respected my father as a man, I swore to never grow up like him. Yes, I would adopt his work ethic, but no, I wasn't going to get walked on. He was just too good a man for that. A lot of my rebelliousness is a tribute to my father. I stood up for myself because on many occasions, he hadn't. But again — it all goes back to looking into that mirror. Today, at 73 years old, my father can proudly look into that glass and know that he didn't screw anybody. He was a proud man who worked hard — no shortcuts, no backstabbing. Today I can clearly understand that his heart was as pure as they come. They just don't make them like him anymore.

But, my mother. . . .

My mother, her real name is Theresa, made up for my father's apathy — she wouldn't take anything from anybody. She was so much like her old man, John J. If you crossed her you were done. My mother has held grudges that still go on to this day — and now she's over 70!

Now that's a real Italian. Screw me once — shame on you, screw me twice . . . *forget it — you'll never get the chance to screw me twice!* I am so much like my mom in that respect. I just hate being dicked around. My philosophy has always been that nobody should take anything from anybody — not even the boss. And I lived my life that way. I strongly felt that we were all in this together — no one person is better than the next. However, if there was such thing as a boss — the Fruitinator was clearly one of them.

While I was growing up, my mother didn't just wear the pants in the family, she wore the socks, the shoes, the Guinea-tee, the whole outfit! I never asked my father for anything, I always went to my mother. If I wanted money, permission, the car — she had sovereign authority. She was also the disciplinarian, she was the law of the house and she laid it down with vigor. While I was under his roof, I don't remember my father ever laying a hand on me — except that one time. . . .

●　　●　　●

Okay, once me and my friend Mike got my father a bit anguished. You see, Jim didn't have much, but he had his lawn — my father cherished his lawn, if you saw Danny Aiello in *29th Street* you know what I'm talking about. He'd cut it, rake it, trim it, thatch it, water it, watch it — it was his Garden of Eden. In other words: The Lawn Was Off-Limits! Well, kids being kids — we insisted on playing on his *Field of Dreams* on those occasions when he left it unguarded. On this particular day, soccer was our game of choice. So there was me and Mike kicking the soccer ball about on Jim's glorious carpet. Little did we know that Jim was crouched down in hiding on the other side of the backyard gate, just waiting to see if any trespassers would violate his oasis of green. Just as I yelled, "He shoots — he scores!" with a lion's roar Jim leapt from his crouch and came after us with his sterling-silver grass clippers.

Mike and I — we were outta there Road Runner style! We'd never seen Jim like this — the small, gentle, quiet man transformed into Leatherface right before our very eyes! In our haste to get away, we left behind the poor, innocent, black-and-white checkered ball. What a mistake! In a frenzy, Jim, unable to catch the younger, agile kids, got to the soccer ball instead. In Jason Voorhees fashion, Jim firmly put the innocent ball between his legs and with precision stabbed it repeatedly with the clippers. Not believing what we were seeing, Mike and I carefully wandered back into the scene. Jim looked back and gave us a look that was half Nicholson in *The Shining* and half Riff Raff in *Underdog*. Now, in all his glory, I looked my father in the eye and said innocently, "Dad . . . that's Mike's ball." All of a sudden there was another transformation — this time from the out-of-control Incredible Hulk to the quiet, meek and weak Bruce Banner. Not knowing what to do or say, I mean the soccer ball lay dead in front of him — Jim slumped his shoulders and did what he always did — apologized. He then went quietly back into the house, the grass clippers tucked gently between his legs.

•   •   •

Apart from that incident, Gentle Jim was such a laid back kinda guy. In many ways, he was a saint. To this day he has one of the biggest hearts I've ever seen. . . . Wait a minute, let me back up for a second. . . . Okay, he had a huge heart when it came to *kindness*, but he was the cheapest human being you ever met. Let me put it to you this way — Gentle Jim used to wash his car with kerosene, in order to save on the Turtle Wax. He was just so cheap — he never went into his pocket for anything. I remember him telling me the same story every Christmas from the time I was five until I was 25: "When I was little and we had no money, the only thing I got for Christmas was a cowboy suit — and I was happy." I remember thinking, year after year, "What does that have to do with my drum set, or my Nintendo, or my stereo?"

But the truth is my father really had no money to spend because my mother always took it from him. Jim would come home from work every Thursday and just hand his paycheck over to Terrible Terry (my mother's second pet name). She paid the bills, bought the groceries and basically spent the rest of it. My father actually used to have to keep a miniature, plastic piggy bank full of quarters in case of an emergency — and I'm not kidding. Yes, Rin-Tin Terry (yet another pet name) was the banker and the law. But if you're the law, you must mete out some form of discipline. How Terry kept me in line was unique. First, she would scream at the top of her lungs, then follow that up with idle threats and the famous, "I feel my blood pressure going up!" From there, my mother would do something that, I must admit, I never saw any of the other mothers do. She would place her hand — usually her right one — into her mouth and bite it as hard as she could.

She claimed it was an Italian thing — but I never saw anybody, or anything ever act in that manner before or since. Not even in cartoons had I seen such a bizarre ritual, you'd think that *Ren & Stimpy* might have tried it once — but, never. I mean, my mother would leave her own teeth marks on her own hand. Is that normal? I remember one time when me and my friend Richie Misbach got my mother so riled up that she went through the screaming, the blood-pressure bit, the hand-biting — and our sides were splitting with laughter. At that point, she grabbed a belt and viciously whipped Richie and I after she had trapped us between my bed and an adjacent wall. We were laughing so hard we didn't even feel the pain. But, that was just my mother — always a flair for the dramatic, forever with teeth marks in her hand.

Now I fully understand that the family was dysfunctional. Back then, you just lived with it — there were no counselors to go to. And, what proud Italian would go to a counselor anyway. No, it was much better to settle your differences by screaming from room to room and biting your own hands. Dr. Phil would have had a picnic with this unruly crew. Its only saving grace was the backbone that held the family together with spit, glue and farina pie — my grandmother, Anna Savarino.

Man, I loved Nana. An extremely religious woman (she even let Jehovah's Witnesses into the house), she was my everything. The kindest, sweetest, caring, gentlest woman you would ever know, she cushioned the chaos of the thunderous hailstorm. Just picture it — there was the Fruitinator biting her hand in the kitchen, my Grand-father demanding something in the dining room, my father hiding out, watching a game in the den — and my older sister probably somewhere on the phone talking to her six-foot-eight boyfriend otherwise known as the Goon (that's a story for another time). But nothing fazed Nana, she would maintain control as the rigatoni boiled and the homemade sauce simmered. She was Edith Bunker, Andy Griffith's Aunt Bee, Mother Teresa and your kindergarten teacher all rolled into one. She would affectionately call me her "doll baby onion pie," which for some strange reason meant the world to me. She was the family rock — the most strong-willed female I ever knew.

Without warning, my grandmother passed away from a heart attack when I was 18 years old; she was only in her 60s. The world as I knew it was never the same. The family as I knew it would also never be the same. I was raised on the ritual of going to my grandparents every Sunday for some form of macaroni (after Jim's Sunday morning doubleheader, of course). Though we yelled and screamed and my mother did some occasional hand-biting, that house on 21 Poplar Street in West Hempstead, New York, was filled with the warmest love I had ever known. That's the way it is in an Italian family. The yelling never superseded the love . . . never. But with the death of Nana came the death of tradition. Day by day, week by week, month by month, the family grew further apart. The glue jar was empty. Society and our culture were pulling us apart, and there was no farina pie at the end of the day to bring us back together. Years later, John J. would die alone in a nursing home. The stubborn, bull-headed Italian man never overcame the death of his wife. At the end of the day, Archie couldn't survive without Edith.

As my grandfather grew older and began to lose his senses, my mother kept telling me over and over again that I needed to go see him before he died. But I never could. This mountain of a man was my boyhood idol, and to see him weak and frail would have been too much even for me. When Granddad died I didn't attend the funeral — I couldn't. I didn't want to remember him that way. In his last days, my grandfather came to Jesus, after staying as far away as he possibly could for his entire life. Now I understand that he did this for one reason only — to assure himself that he would one day see his Anna again.

I'm going to point out certain instances in my life where, now that I've been saved by Jesus Christ, I can clearly see that God was present. Unfortunately, having been blind to his light at the time, I just couldn't see the grace he was desperately trying to extend.

The first instance took place at the time of the unexpected death of my grandmother. As I said here, for as long as I could remember, it was a ritual that every Sunday was spent visiting with my grandparents. The ratio of them coming to our house, compared to our going to theirs, was 25/75. They were the elders, so out of respect you just went there more often. As I got older, when my grandparents would visit I was usually off doing something else. With my teens came girls, cars, freedom and

Elvis Costello. It pains me to say this now, but I was beginning to outgrow them.

However, I can remember vividly that last weekend prior to Nana's passing. That Sunday, my grandparents showed up unexpectedly. On this occasion, for some reason, I can remember being especially happy to see them. At the same time, I was overcome with a feeling that I should stay home and spend some time with them. That Sunday I enjoyed the company of my grandparents and did little else. A few days later, my grandmother was dead; I would never see her on this earth again.

I now know it was God's voice that spoke to me that day. In his special way he was telling me what was to come that week, and his message blessed me with more time with my beloved Nana. Though at that time I didn't understand what I do now, and I wasn't ready to accept God into my life, I did realize one extremely important thing — that we should savor every minute, every second with the ones we love. You never know when God will take those whom you cherish the most. It is imperative to treat your loved ones like it's the last time you'll see them — every time you see them. Better yet, treat everybody that way. Everyone you come across in your everyday life, they are all God's children, and that's exactly how they should be treated. Just stop for one second and try to visualize what a world like that would be like; a world where we treated each other with love, dignity, respect, honor, forgiveness and grace.

Chapter 4

HANDSOME JIMMY
AND LUCIOUS JOHNNY

Now that I've established that those I shared my house with were a few partridges short of a family, it will seem inevitable that I would be forced to rely on some sort of vice to escape the everyday madness. Like a lot of kids, I chose television. From as far back as I can remember I was raised on, and by, the boob tube. Some of my fondest memories involve sitting on the couch with my dad and just becoming a part of Yogi Bear's world. Man, I loved that bear, but I have to admit, I was never a big fan of his sidekick, Boo Boo. Always whining, crying and complaining about something, always in that high-pitched, Fran Drescher voice, "But Yogi, what if Ranger Smith finds out?" Do you think that for one minute Yogi cared about Ranger Smith? Yogi owned Smith. It was all about getting that illusive pic-i-nic basket, by any means necessary. You've got to respect that. Even at the age of five I was taken with an animated mammal simply because he was sticking it to authority.

But then Yogi got soft.

Enter Cindy Bear. Southern twang, frilly umbrella — Jellystone Park would never be the same. And Yogi went gaga over her. Suddenly he was no longer chasing the basket, but like every other adolescent male — he was chasing the skirt! Why, Yogi, Why? He lost it all — the swagger, the confidence, the cocky manner — suddenly, he had those pesky little cartoon birds flying over his head everywhere he went, whistling self-consciously whenever Cindy strolled by. Yogi left me with no choice — the bear was out, and the Caped Crusader was in!

I said it when I was six, and I'll say it again in my 40s, the original *Batman* series was the greatest television show ever created, and the actor behind the cowl (as the Mad Hatter would refer to Batman's mask), Adam West, was a genius. In portraying the superhero, to use one of my favorite sayings, West just flat "got it." In the Russo vernacular, "get it" means wink-wink to the audience. During my WWF run in the late '90s, we aired a commercial during the Super Bowl with the tag line: "WWF . . . get it?" The message was designed to tell the audience, "Wrestling is fake; lighten up, have fun with it." This was the exact swagger and confidence with which Adam West portrayed Gotham's favorite crime fighter. The show was a classic example of the writing being solid, but the actor "getting it" to the point of making it off-the-charts entertaining. And this exact formula was what made Stone Cold Steve Austin, Mick Foley and the Rock the megastars they were. Writing like Shakespeare won't necessarily get you to where you want to go — it's all about how your actors play it out. That's why, in wrestling, some guys get over (become popular with the fans), and some guys don't. At the end of the day, they have to carry the ball, they have to deliver the written word. West delivered the word with dead-eye accuracy, much the same way the aim of his bat-a-rang would crack the devilish Egg Head.

•   •   •

"It Feels Like the First Time."

Ah, yes, that classic Foreigner song brings back memories. A boy of six just doesn't forget the first time he fell head-over-heels, gaga, in love. I attribute my loss of innocence to *Batman* as well. I know what you're thinking — no, his leotards weren't a turn-on. But I can't say the same thing about Julie Newmar's skin-tight catsuit. What male tot can ever forget the warm, tingly feeling they first experienced when Newmar pranced onto the TV screen. It was like the feeling I got when my dad took me to go see my favorite team, the San Francisco Giants, play the New York Mets at Shea Stadium — combined with a snow day at school, and topped with two full sleeves of Chips Ahoys chased with a tall, cold glass of milk.

Yes, this clearly had to be love. As corny as it is to put it this way — Newmar was the cat's meow. Even Batman got all silly over her. Up until that point I didn't think he even liked girls! After catching an episode which featured the feline, I wanted to grab my crayons and write all over my Batman coloring book, "Me & Catwoman," "Catwoman & me." This was pure, unadulterated puppy love. Julie Newmar, wherever you are, thank you for making me a man!

Over the years my imaginary love relationship with boob-tube beauties would continue. As a matter of fact, let's take a look at my Top-10 "Dream Fantasy Television All-Chick Weekend":

1. PAMELA EWING

The whole enchilada. Very sexy — showed just enough, but not too much. That little southern accent helped. Killer body.

2. LAURA PETRIE

Doesn't matter that she was in black-and-white. Back in that era television had *never* seen anything like Mary Tyler Moore. Just look at those reruns on Nickelodeon — Richie's mom was on fire! Those tight dresses, those skirts showing just enough leg for the time — I'm telling you — she was fine.

Now, maybe MTM didn't age gracefully, but even today, I'd take her over Rose Marie in her prime!

3. LEAH REMINI
As Doug's wife, Carrie, in *King of Queens*, Leah is every husband's fantasy. And, she's got that whole New Yawk thing going on to boot. Sexy, killer body — killer accent. Talks back a little too much for my taste, but as long as she knows when to keep her mouth shut, everything will be fine.

4. CHER
Now, I know Cher probably won't be on anybody's list, but back in her day she was it. First off, in the opening monologue with Sonny, Cher never wore — how should I say it — undergarments. If you were a young kid at the time, you went to bed thinking about that. Heck, as an adult I still go to bed thinking about that.

5. BARBI BENTON
I hate to admit it, but I sat through *Hee-Haw* every week just to watch Barbi Benton. Man, those cut-off Daisy Dukes were just something you never forgot. What didn't this woman have? She could be much higher on the list — but then again — she was on *Hee-Haw*.

6. YOUNG SALLY STRUTHERS
Sally Struthers — let me rephrase that — *young* Sally Struthers. Back in the early '70s there was nothing like Gloria Stivic on television. As a young kid, who didn't notice those short miniskirts, that tight stomach, those two, giant, monster . . . eyes? Wow, Archie's little girl was every little boy's dream — "Those Were the Days."

7. JEANNIE

Call me crazy, but I liked Jeannie (Barbara Eden) much better when she was in civilian clothes. That Harem outfit was okay, but it was those killer legs. The one thing I never understood about *I Dream of Jeannie* was why Major Nelson didn't just move into the bottle with Jeannie and never come out?

8. CHRISSY SNOW

You have to put Suzanne Sommers on this list — if you don't, something's wrong. However, the reason why she ranks only eighth is because the character was just too absent-minded for her own good. I don't think dumb blondes are as appealing to men as some women believe.

9. JAYNE KENNEDY

To me, I never noticed Jayne Kennedy for her body — she was just a natural beauty. And at the time, when I was about 12 or 13, J.K. exemplified that forbidden fruit . . . and we all know what I'm talking about. She was just downright dangerous.

10. CONNIE SELLECA

And you thought I didn't have any class. During her *Hotel* years, Connie was the most beautiful woman ever to hit the small screen. And, you always looked at her as a lady. You never wanted to do more than just hug her. When all was said and done, that was the kind of woman I really wanted . . . when I grew up, of course.

HONORABLE MENTIONS:

Susan Dey (Laurie Partridge), Valerie Bertinelli (Barbara Romano), The Golddiggers (Dean Martin's variety-show dancers) and Diana Rigg (Emma Peel, *The Avengers*).

●　　●　　●

After *Batman* ended its run, I was forced to hang up my terrycloth cape and mature to the age of nine. Though the Caped Crusader was highly respected, it was time to seek out a new, "real" role model. It wouldn't be difficult . . .

A microphone stood in a single spotlight, then a voice from above would say, "Ladies and Gentlemen . . . MR. TOM JONES!"

I'll say it, because I can now get away with it — I wanted to be Tom Jones. This man was the hippest thing since the Footsie (a toy from my youth — if you haven't experienced the Footsie, then you haven't lived). His moves, his mannerisms, ladies throwing underwear *everywhere!* The Fruitinator used to punish me by not letting me watch *This Is Tom Jones.* That may seem gay now, but at the time it was cruel and unusual punishment. I mean, the Welshman was just so cool — every gyration turned the women in the audience to goo. What power there must be in entertaining — thousands of screaming fans there just to see you. Growing up, that sensation always appealed to me. There was something about power I was intrigued with at an early age — not just any kind of power, but the power of entertainment. Which leads us to my original attraction to the World Wide Wrestling Federation (WWWF).

I remember that day as if it were yesterday. It was the early '70s, I was maybe 11 at the time, and I was watching our 13 inch, black-and-white, $69 Emerson television set in our family's guest room. There was no cable in my area yet, so we were only able to pick up a handful of stations. I was flipping through the UHF channels, when I came across something that I just couldn't take my eyes off — a grossly overweight man in a Hawaiian shirt, with a rainbow of rubber bands somehow attached to his walrus cheeks. As if that wasn't enough, this real-life cartoon character was standing adjacent to two flashy, flamboyant, long-haired, shade-wearing blondes. The trio was Captain Lou Albano, Handsome Jimmy and Luscious Johnny — a.k.a. the Valiant Brothers. Their charm and charisma reached out and pulled me inside the television set. There was just something so exciting about this. It was new, it was fresh and it was *entertainment.* I knew it the first time I laid eyes on it — these guys were actors and they were good. Now please, don't misread that last sentence — these guys no doubt were athletes, but they were, first and foremost, performers. The ring was their stage, and the fans their audience. The event was nothing more than a play, chock-full of compelling and titillating story lines. It was larger than life, and there was nothing else like it.

Over the years, I became a dedicated wrestling fan — not as a mark (somebody *obsessed* with the wrestling business — wrestlers get highly offended when others in the business refer to them like this), but as a fan. From the moment I saw Captain Lou and the Valiants, I recognized the wrestling business for what it truly was — sports entertainment. I mean, how could anybody possibly think this sideshow was *real?* The business was what it was, and I enjoyed it for being just that. Back in the day, two of my all-time favorites were Chief Jay Strongbow and the "Big Cat" Ernie Ladd. The Big Cat, he was just "it." Not only could he whoop any man, but his way with words was nothing short of brilliant. His best schtick came when he would refer to a very young Vince McMahon Jr. as "Mr. TV Announcer." When I got into the business years later, it was both an honor and a privilege to meet all my boyhood favorites. Not only did I get to break bread with the Valiants, Captain Lou and the "Big Cat" (who had the biggest hands I'd ever seen), but I actually got to work with Chief Jay during my early days in the WWF.

In the "What was I thinking?" category, when I was in the 7th grade, me and my friend Richie Misbach (the same kid the Fruitinator assaulted with a belt) actually used to tape up our thumbs and then load them up with pennies before we went to school. In a crowded hallway, we would then proceed to jam our thumbs into the throats of unsuspecting "opponents" in homage to our hero, Ernie Ladd. Man, was the Big Cat a great role model for a 13-year-old, or what?

Okay, I guess there was a little mark in me after all. . . .

Nah, I mean, I was simply a fan of the business. I attended a few live events a year and followed the product on the boob tube. To me, wrestling *was* one of the best forms of entertainment television had to offer.

Chapter 5

THE BEST
DAYS OF MY LIFE

At about the age of 18 I lost touch with the wrestling business. I went away to college at Indiana State University (Evansville campus), and began to concentrate more on losing my virginity. Yes I admit it, I entered college a virgin — not that there's anything wrong with that.

In my junior high school years, I dated the same girl throughout the 8th and 9th grades. This was the first time I was introduced to sex. Like any kid that age, I was curious about girls and was in quite a bit of a hurry to figure the mystery out. So experiments went on . . . then more experiments . . . and yet more . . . 'nuff said. The table was set, and after going through the soup, salad, appetizer and main course, the sweetness of the dessert tempted my very boyhood. But at that time, I also felt a "presence." There was just something there that stopped me from experiencing that tasty, but extremely dangerous Sarah Lee cake. I'm pretty sure that it had nothing to do with my upbringing, because neither of my parents ever mentioned the word *sex* to me. It was just never talked about. There were no birds or bees — you found out what you found out by watching HBO after the parents went to bed. So what was it? My conscience? Well, I don't believe in Jiminy Cricket either. No, there was something there that stopped me, something that made the potential negative consequences of the act crystal clear. Needless to say, it was the same "something" that told me to spend time with my grandmother just days before she died.

Looking back now, I know I was protected. I just wasn't sure who or what I was being protected by. With no guidance, and no education about sex, I could very easily have been a guest on *Maury*. I could have been the 16-year-old dad standing onstage and barking to the crowd, "You don't know me! You don't know me." But, that never happened. I never had sex. I was being protected from myself.

Thank you, God.

Within the first three months of college I lost my virginity. I was 19 years old. Believe it or not, I was "taken advantage of" by a blonde bombshell who had a lot more experience than I did. The truth is, I never even saw it coming. As a matter of fact, we were innocently playing tennis only a half-hour before the show began! Then, before I knew what even hit me, I was aced. The girl was going to have her way with me and there was nothing I was going to be able to do about it. And that's the way it went down. *Wham, Bam, Thank-you Sam.* When it was all said and done, and she said, "Goodnight, Irene" and left, I remember lying in my bed and thinking, "Is that it? Is that what the big deal was all about?" Obviously, it should have been a big deal to me — and it would have been, if I had been in love with the girl. But there was no love — just one, cheap moment of hot monkey love. Man, did I miss out. I know I almost sound like a girl here, but who cares? In this book you will learn everything about me — not just the highlights, but the lowlights as well. Losing my virginity to someone I never cared about was a lowlight. Nineteen years of purity was taken away forever by a single moment of lust. And, in the end, it just wasn't worth it.

I don't think I was ready for the female attention I received when I went to college. During my teen years on Long Island I had two girl-friends — *two*. The second I stepped into Evansville, Indiana, I was the "boy from New York City" every girl had to have. Just think about it — the same girls, living in the same town, with the same guys, for the last 18 years. I was Kevin Bacon's Ren in *Footloose*, I was the forbidden fruit they all wanted to gnaw on. But to be honest — I just wasn't that way. After my episode with the blonde bomber, I was intimate with just one other girl before meeting my wife in my second year.

So here's a first I promise you will never read in another ego-driven book where wrestling is involved — *I have been with only three girls in my entire life.* Looking back now, sex was never really important to me. If it was there, fine. If it wasn't, no big deal. I was never the hormone-driven animal on the prowl. Rather, I was always interested in the "relationship." That was just my makeup, the morals that were instilled in me.

As I began to mature as a person, I was driven away from the world of professional wrestling. When I reached my late teens and early 20s, the World Wrestling Federation, which I had grown up on, was removed from the menu and replaced with things of greater importance. Working my way through school (even though the Fruitinator will tell you she funded it all), I held down two jobs. As if that wasn't enough, I was also editor of the student newspaper, the public relations director of the Student Union Board and vice-president of my fraternity — Sigma Tau Gamma. I was the !@#$% in charge of the pledges. Man, we tortured those poor young kids. We even stooped to the level of making them walk around town smoking tampons. Oh, what it was like to be young. I had *zero* responsibilities, unaware that those "years of freedom" were actually molding me into the person I would someday become.

I learned a work ethic in college, something I would later base my entire life on. I literally worked my butt off — not in the classroom, but in the areas that actually meant something to me. Now, let me say this — in the hope that my kids don't read this book for many years to come — *anybody can get a college education.* I coasted through college. First off, I wasn't stupid enough to take classes that were difficult. That meant staying away from anything that had to do with numbers or the ozone layer — in other words, science and math. I mean, why would *anyone* take calculus? What are you going to do with calculus in the real world? At what point in our lives are we going to be forced to *add letters?* It's just not natural. Then there's the earth sciences. Does anybody really care how many layers of rock the earth consists of? Am I going to hack through them all at some point in time? Where am I going — to China?

I have to stop myself for a second — is there anyone out there who actually thought they could dig to China when they were kids? C'mon, raise your hands. I know I did. But getting back to earth sciences — forget it, man, take the easy classes. Try communications. Communications was a no-brainer for me. I mean, we all have to communicate, don't we? And how can anyone fail public speaking? You go up there in front of people and you speak — simple. Or what about interpersonal communication? Just watch *Oprah* or *Dr. Phil* and you'll pick it up.

All right, I've got to come clean about something here. I'm a Christian now, so I'm just going to bare my soul. During my high school and college days, I had a motto: When in doubt, *cheat!* When the going got tough, I cheated my way through both high school and college because I realized early on that very little of what I was learning would apply to my life. I mean, how many of you out there really know where, or what, the Mason-Dixon Line is? How many of you know who fought the war of 1812? How many of you used the knowledge gained in science lab when you cut opened that helpless, innocent frog? After earning my money in the entertainment field for the past 12 years, I know a frog's anatomy not only didn't help further my career, but the subject never even came up.

Now, as a responsible Christian I'm not advising you to cheat — I now understand how morally wrong it is. And to illustrate how God has changed my life, I recently took an on-line test in Seminary school that may have been the hardest exam I have ever taken. Now, if I had opened my book to help me with some of the answers there is no way, no how, my professor would have found out. I was in Marietta, Georgia, he was in Denver, Colorado — unless he was David Blaine, he wouldn't have had a clue. But, in this life — my new life — the thought never even crossed my mind. Why? Because God would have known, and at this point that's all that matters to me.

Getting back to my education — I am a bit concerned about what our kids are learning today, especially at the high-school level. I just wish the curriculum were more geared towards what those teenagers are going to need to know as young adults to survive and hold their own out in the real world. To this day, I don't understand why I was forced to struggle with algebra for three years. Solving mathematical equations has had no relevance to my adult life whatsoever. By the time a student reaches high school, they already know their likes and dislikes, their strengths and weaknesses. Why not let teenagers concentrate on those areas that are going to help them with the career path they decide to follow. And, not to mention — if I'd have learned as much about Jesus Christ in high school as I did about Napoleon Bonaparte, I might have saved myself 25 years of depression.

Getting back to the pride thing — I worked around the clock as editor of the student newspaper. Being the chief meant that the paper had my name stamped all over it. If it lacked anything, it was because of me. I took full responsibility and great pride in my work. I jumped in headfirst and gave my blood, sweat and tears. To me it was a challenge — if I succeeded I would have achieved a great accomplishment, but if I failed, *I* failed. But even back then I knew I wouldn't fail — I just wouldn't allow it. To me it was all about winning the challenge . . . every challenge. You see — this wasn't Intro to German — this was the real world.

Chapter 6

COLDCOCKED

Day and night I worked on the student paper. *The Shield* became my passion, my lifeline. In my mind I was Lou Grant; the head honcho calling all the shots. However, to my credit, I never got drunk with power — *never*. I respected those who wanted to help me; they didn't have to, rather they chose to. During that time, I really learned how to get people to work for you. It was all about motivation. You had to give them a reason to want to help you succeed. The people working for you — your employees — genuinely had to like and care about you. This is where those "Dr. Phil" interpersonal communication classes actually kicked in. People thrive on praise — all they want to be told is that they're doing a great job. Throughout my life, I never felt that I was better than anybody else. I realized that we were all in this together — you get out of this world exactly what you put into it, it's that simple. That was never taught to me by my dad, or the Fruitinator, but rather something that just seemed instilled in me.

(That's why most people in power tend to be [insert expletive here] — they never put anything into it — they simply take the shortcut.) These people are scared to death of being exposed, because as elementary as it is, what goes around comes around.

I've learned something in the past year of being a Christian. In my life A.S. (after saved), God's system of checks and balances is so prevalent that sometimes it's scary. It goes back to the "what goes around, comes around" thing. The principle is simple: you live your life as Jesus did, you take steps forward; you live your life in the flesh, you go backwards.

Trying to live my life in Jesus has been the most difficult thing I've ever had to do. And, I use the word "had" because in the big scheme of things, there is no other way. If you want to fulfill your life as God meant it to be the moment he created you, you must follow the example set by his son. Many people don't understand this, but one of the secondary reasons Jesus was sent to earth was to be the model for how we should go about living our everyday lives, each moment we exist on this earth. Go find the nearest bible and read your four gospels: Matthew, Mark, Luke and John. They serve as a blueprint for how we should act as human beings. It's all right there — love, understanding, forgiveness, compassion — every trait our Christ wore like a crown when he walked the face of this earth is all right there for us to inherit. And, to be blunt — God doesn't pull any punches, either. He clearly states it's either his way, or the highway. But he does give us the freedom to choose. The same freedom he gave to Adam and Eve from day one. It's what we do with that choice that determines everything. I know, that for the better part of 40 years when I was presented with that choice my answer was, "Thank you anyway, don't want any." And, I didn't get any either — no peace, no love, no hope, no patience, no understanding, no nothing — a big, fat, goose egg. Now, was that God's fault, or mine? He clearly gave me the instructions (the gospels) and I chose not to follow them.

Did you ever stop to think that when things aren't going well it may be because you are doing something you aren't supposed to be doing, and subconsciously you know it? For the past six months, I've been spending a lot of my time counseling some of the wrestlers about problems they are having both inside and outside the business. Whether those problems are job-related, relationship-related, or money-related, I find the same pattern over and over again — they're doing something in their lives they shouldn't, and know they shouldn't, be doing. From drugs to alcohol to adultery to not giving in to forgiveness, they are not living their lives according to God's will.

Put this theory to the test. The next time you are having a problem, stand in front of the mirror, take a long look at yourself and see if you can find that problem within — see if it may come back to something you are doing. We must all point the finger at ourselves, because none of us are perfect — we're human. So, the only thing we can do is to ask God for forgiveness of our sins, and try to live our lives every single day, minute and second as Jesus Christ lived his.

I also discovered something about myself during those *Shield* days — I thrived on controversy. I think it just came from getting real bored, real fast. I always needed something going on around me, something exciting, something I could sink my teeth into. Again, acting the role of Lou Grant, I soon found my real-life Watergate, the situation that would give me my 15 minutes of fame (even though I've had at least 15 more since then).

It all began my junior year at Indiana State. An avid basketball fan, I was following the season of our Screaming Eagles rather closely. My fraternity was a big supporter of the team, and a few of the players were even frat brothers. Over the course of the year, a strange pattern began to develop. Two of the best players on the team, Clarence James and Thurber Davis, were confined to the pine for the majority of the games. Nobody could understand why, but the players thought it was obvious — they were black, and the coach was white. Being the "journalist" I was, I loved a juicy scoop, but the fact remained that this could have been nothing more than a case of sour grapes from two players who weren't getting the playing time they thought they deserved. So, in trying to live up to the standards of the profession I was training for, I interviewed head coach Creighton Burns at length. Being a New Yorker, I didn't know how to beat around the bush, so I went right for the meat and potatoes. I told the coach that James and Davis were accusing him of being racist, and that they felt the color of their skin was the only reason they weren't playing. Without hesitation, Burns called the idea ludicrous. He informed me that his former college roommate was baseball Hall-of-Famer Rod Carew, who happened to be a black man, so how could he be labeled a racist? I must admit, Burns was rather convincing, perhaps as convincing as James and Davis. So, even though I wanted to break "the big one," I had nothing more than a case of he said/she said. That was until my Deep Throat came forward.

With the story all but dead, I was approached in the strictest of confidence by one of the white players on the team. The guy confirmed everything James and Davis had told me. He even went as far as to say that Coach Burns had told his white players to stay away from James and Davis. The player than added that if the coach ever found out that he had come to me with this information, his scholarship and college career would be over. What was a young journalist to do? Well, again, controversy being my middle name, I went with the story. Without revealing my source, the headline of the next issue of *The Shield* read, "Creighton Burns — Is the Final Curtain Falling?" Only 21 at the time, I had no understanding of the implications of my story. Living in the Northeast all my life, I had little idea of what the black/white issue was. But in the Midwest, I soon learned it was serious business.

Reliving for a moment my first real brush with racism, I'm immediately filled with hurt when I think of a person who, while working in World Championship Wrestling, publicly labeled me a racist simply to gain leverage in a lawsuit against the company. I have never spoken about this situation until now, but the accusations broke my heart. I was so hurt by the remarks, I simply didn't know what to say. There was no way I was going to defend myself, because the fact was, I wasn't a racist, and God knew that as well. This is what I'm talking about when I cite individuals looking to gain at any expense necessary. In time, people like this will be dealt with — not on my clock, not on their clock, but on God's Timex. My role in working with Christ is simply to forgive . . . and I have.

Let me clearly state that in my *Shield* article, I never at any time suggested that Coach Burns was a racist. That wasn't for me to decide. I simply presented the facts, both sides of the story, and let the readers decide for themselves. Call me naïve, but I really had no idea what I was getting myself into — to me it was *just* a story. Well, before I knew it, it was all over the local radio and newspapers — it was *huge* news for the small city of Evansville. People from all types of media were calling me, and I swear to you I had no idea what the big deal was . . . nor did I know that the story was going to get even bigger.

A few days after the story broke, three white basketball players from the team knocked on my apartment door. They said they wanted to talk about my article, so I asked them to step into a nearby laundry room off the hallway so that we wouldn't disrupt my roommates. Well, as soon as I set foot in the room, one of the players hauled off and coldcocked me — punched me square in the face. I never saw it coming. It was the first, last and only time in my life I have ever been hit. I think I went down, I honestly don't remember, but as soon as I gathered myself I dragged myself back to my apartment. There, my four fraternity brothers were waiting, and it was on! In the days that followed, the fraternity as a whole decided to boycott all the men's basketball games. It was getting really ugly, and eventually the Dean had to step in. In the end it all worked out, but I'll never forget the feeling — I loved every minute of it! It was such a rush. I don't think it had so much to do with being in the spotlight. It was the controversy that was exciting — it was unpredictable. Years later I would realize it was that one incident that forever instilled the "flair for the dramatic" in my very being.

Chapter 7

IT'S ALL ABOUT WINNING

As I stated early on, even though much of my original manuscript has remained intact — certain things had to be "revisited." God, my father, turned my life upside down, changed me at the very core of my soul. Looking back now, it saddens me to see the person that I was, and how I chose to live my life. I tell my kids this on a daily basis — if I knew then what I know now, my life would have been so much simpler. I didn't, but I do believe that I had to take that journey to my final ending . . . and his beginning. God was there from the first step, I just chose to ignore him. I wake up every morning thanking God for allowing me, after more than 40 years, to allow him to take over my life — mentally, physically, spiritually and emotionally. Every ounce of Vince Russo belongs to him.

Unfortunately, for you to fully understand that transition, I need to talk in detail about the old Vince.

For me, it had everything to do with winning and losing, and nothing to do with how you played the game. I've always wondered — who really believes it's how you play the game? I'll tell you who — losers. It was all about winning and nothing else mattered. The more you won, the stronger you became. The more you failed, the less you were. Sounds heartless? It was, and so was I. But at the time, I was being truthful.

I remember my father asking me, "Vin, don't you have any compassion in your heart?" Well, if I did, I certainly never let it out for air. To me, it was always about the "truth." Telling it, living it, no matter how much it may have hurt others.

I was clueless to the fact that at that point in my life, the real "truth" was light years away. My motto was, if you weren't man enough to tell the truth 100 percent of the time then you'd never be true to yourself. Whereas there might be some meat to that wisdom, I now understand that the truth, at that time, may have not been the truth at all, but rather the way I looked at the world. Back then I never looked at losing as a way of growing; today I do. I had to lose the battle, my battle, and face the reality of "I'm not" in order to understand and accept the fullness of the Lord's "I am." I also now understand that maybe a loss isn't a loss at all — but rather a gain. The truth is that sometimes things didn't turn out the way *we* planned because that wasn't *God's* plan. You see the difference?

I'm now certain that I was confusing truth with honesty at the time. Why? Because I saw "my opinion" as the truth. Today, I consider that ridiculous. When I stated, "If you aren't man enough to tell the truth 100 percent of the time . . ." I understand now that I should have said, "If you aren't honest with yourself 100 percent of the time. . . ." It was, and still is, important for me to look myself in the mirror regardless of what I might see. At the end of the day, you have to be able to live with yourself. There have been times in my life when I absolutely buried myself by being honest. But you know what? I can look in that mirror — I can look my children in the eye and know that I did the right thing.

Unfortunately, I can't say the same thing about a lot of individuals I encountered in the wrestling business. But I do understand that it's the nature of the beast. I'm not condoning it by any means — it's just the way the business was built. You see, from day one, the wrestling business was controlled by promoters who were interested in only one thing: making all the money. As a result, they never "hired" any of the wrestlers — providing them with health care, dental care, insurance, death benefits, that kind of thing. Instead, they gave them jobs as "independent contractors," which to me means you can work anyplace else — but the catch was, you never could. What the promoters created was a wrestler-eat-wrestler world. Everybody was in competition to get that illustrious "spot." So, with the "boys," it was always about doing whatever you had to do to keep your spot. That meant lying, cheating, stealing, hurting and lying some more. That's why the majority of the wrestlers I've known are sick with paranoia. They are always looking in the rear-view mirror to see who might be serving them up for lunch.

That's what the wrestling business was built on, and is still fueled by today. I've always said, "It's tough to be a regular guy and exist in the wrestling business." But I had to be honest for the sake of my own self-respect. If you don't respect yourself, you will respect no one. That's the one thing I can say for Vince McMahon — the guy never lied to me. He may have been insensitive at times, but he never lied. That's why I always had such great respect for him. He said things to me even when they hurt. Perhaps he would not be truthful 100 percent of the time for business reasons — dollars and cents. But I'm not taking about that — I'm talking about man-to-man, when it's all on the line, looking another human being in the eye and shooting straight. Any heat that I had, or have, with any of the boys (the wrestlers) today is for that one reason alone. I was always honest with them, and on occasion that was not always what they wanted to hear. But guess what? I can live with that. I'd rather somebody be hot with me over the truth, than over a lie.

Just for the record, back in the day, I didn't always practice what I preached. I didn't win all the time. The truth is, during my wrestling career I lost on several occasions. As a matter of fact, there were many times when I was done in by the politics of the business. But on every occasion, I knew exactly what was going on. All I had to do was glance over my shoulder and see the huddles in corners quickly breaking up. I got it — especially in World Championship Wrestling. But my mindset was that I was getting paid to do a job, so I was going to do the best job I could. I made it my policy to never get caught up in the politics, because I just wasn't interested. If politics were going to be my downfall, then it just wasn't meant to be in the first place. Again, with God now clearly running my life, I understand that he always looked after my best interests. It was in my best interest to leave my position with wcw just three months in, fully realizing that I could be breaching my lucrative contract. And everything turned out okay. I can look at my children and know that one day they will be able to appreciate that their old man stood tall and stuck to his God-given values regardless of the circumstances. In the end, when the last fan leaves the arena, all you're going to have is yourself. At that point, you're either going to be able to live with yourself . . . or not. It will all depend on how you chose to live your life — by your rules, or by God's.

I want to make one thing clear — when I talk about winning, I'm not talking about winning a game. In life, you play a lot of games. You're going to win some, and you're going to lose some — it's the law of averages. When I was 13, my team won the Little League World Series, when I was 14 we lost it — no big deal. What I'm talking about are the *big* battles, the ones that really make a difference in your life. The ones you can't afford to lose.

I won my first big battle when I was about 17 years old. It was on a battlefield that every guy knows — dating a girl who thinks she's better than you, and trying to humble her. Her name was L (I'll use the initial in an effort not to get sued for defamation of character — *again*), and from day one she took the position that I was just lucky to be going out with her. And you know what? At the time she was probably right. She was this high-maintenance, popular princess and

I was unsocial, introverted and couldn't be bothered. From the first day we met, everything was a head game. She'd call, she wouldn't call; she's nice, she's Witchiepoo (all right, my second reference to *H.R. Pufnstuf*). You know the routine — as guys, we all go through it at some point. Well, call me a glutton for punishment, but I got into the game. It became an intriguing battle of who's gonna zoom who first. Don't misunderstand me, I truly believed I was in love with L, but the fact was, I dug her because she was the female equivalent of me. So the game grew more intense with each date. Neither side was going to lose. This was the ultimate Batman-Superman showdown to end all feuds. And you know what? Looking back now, the whole situation was whacked. I mean, we really did care for each other, but the win was the most important thing for both sides.

Some time during the school year, L beat me to the punch — she broke up with me. I'll never forget it. I drove away from her house, my eyes leaking on the steering wheel of my '73 Camero as the words of Elvis Costello's "Allison" blared from my eight-track. I'll never forget L's cocky last words. Intending to hurt me, she said, "Vinnie, there will be a me and you — but there will never be a me *and* you." L was the first and last girl I ever cried over. But as heartbroken as I was, I realized that the game had just begun. In my mind there had to be a loser before there could be a winner, so for the months that followed I began to play a masterful game of chess. The spacing of the phone calls, the accidental meetings, the occasional cards — all carried out with precision timing. On one occasion I even tied a stray dog to her car, one of those shaggy canines, and left my calling card — a Gene Simmons trading card — attached to his collar, just to get L's attention.

Man, what was I thinking?

When I was a teenager, Gene Simmons of KISS was my god and savior. I bought my first KISS album, *Rock-n-Roll Over*, on my 16th birthday, and from that day forward my life would be forever changed.

Those teenage years I looked up to Simmons — I drew inspiration from him. Above my bed I had this poster of the "God of Thunder" shot, looking up from his platinum, dragon-boots. That particular photo was just so powerful, I looked at it every night, drawing strength, thinking there wasn't anything I couldn't do.

Again, here's something else I promise you will never read in any other ego-driven wrestling book: the first time I saw KISS, at Madison Square Garden in 1977 with my friend Brian Chykirda, I *cried*. You know, like when teenyboppers today go see Justin Timberlake. Yeah, I cried — I'm not afraid to admit it — that's how much Gene Simmons meant to me.

I remained loyal to Gene Simmons and KISS into adulthood, and even passed the tradition along to my own two boys. As a matter of fact, they were with me the night I got to meet "the Demon" himself. That's right — for as bad an experience as WCW was, one good thing came out of it. I had the opportunity to meet Gene Simmons — my boyhood dream became a reality.

A couple of years later, at the age of 42, the one and only true idol made himself known to me — that being Jesus Christ himself. Looking back at my boyhood idol, I was so far gone to the other team that it was scary. No, I don't believe Gene Simmons is a devil, devil-worshipper, or a "Knight In Satan's Service," but I do believe that it was dangerous for me, at such an impressionable age, to be looking up to someone whose values and beliefs were a bit tainted.

Over the years, Gene Simmons has made it abruptly clear to anyone who will listen that for him it's all about women and money. Hey — whatever floats your boat, but with Christ running my life, it is so clear to me that those two things mean zero.

I found out firsthand that money doesn't bring happiness. In my best year at WCW, I made $535,000 — and I was miserable every minute that I earned it. I've said it once, and I'll say it again, the only difference between me making $500,000 a year or $50,000 a year was the amount of DVDs I bought — *that's it!* And, let's face it, how many DVDs do we buy that we really don't need anyway? How many times do you have to watch *Rocky* before it gets old? Okay, maybe that's a bad example, substitute

Ernest Goes to Camp. All kidding aside, money does not make you happy. Part of being a Christian is understanding that "your" money isn't "your" money at all. It belongs to the one who created you — God. Without God you would have *nothing*. The treasures you have on earth are given to you by God, and they are given for one reason — for God to see how you manage them. How you manage your earthly gifts here will determine what gifts you will be given *when it matters* — in eternity. So, I'm not dissuading anybody from making as much as they want, I'm just advising you that your riches may be a test. Whether you pass or fail is totally up to you. But remember one thing: you exit this world the same way you entered — with nothing.

As far as women go — look, I had a pretty powerful spot in the wrestling business, and there were, and are, many a female looking to break in and willing to do anything for it. You do the math. Again, my question is: do the nasty and you achieve what? You have good stories to tell the rest of the band, or the locker room? Meanwhile, you've degraded your body — which isn't yours, by the way, it's God's temple — and you've violated another human being? Just tell me, what has been accomplished?

Thanks, but no thanks. I'm content being with the love of my life for more than 20 years, and enjoying the fruits of that relationship: Will, VJ, and Annie.

Finally, days before I was to leave for college, I won L back. She knew she couldn't live without me once I was a thousand miles away. L told me what a mistake she had made, and how she truly loved me. Without blinking, I looked L in the eye and said, "There is no way I'm going to be committed to you when I'm a thousand miles away. In other words *(here it comes),* There will be a me and you . . . but, there won't be a me *and* you." Man — what a rush. What an accomplishment. What a win. It just felt so good.

The point? At that moment, I had learned an extremely valuable lesson — you can get anything you want in this world as long as you work for it. Nothing is out of your reach. Not getting the girl, not meeting Gene Simmons, and not even working side by side with Vince McMahon.

Dear God,

It pains me deeply when I see the kind of person I was before I surrendered to you. To think that it was "I" who accomplished this, and "I" who accomplished that, makes me realize how lost I was without you.

Since you saved my life, I truly understand that everything that has happened to me in this life has been your will. The highs and the lows were all by your design. For more than 40 years I never saw the road I was walking, until you made it clear as a Colorado spring. Every circumstance, every instance, every experience, every step of the way was mapped out by you for one reason . . . it would lead me directly to the one who loves me the most.

Father, I thank you for saving my life, forgiving me my sins, never giving up on me, loving me unconditionally and, most of all, for your son, Jesus Christ. Today and every day I live my life to glorify yours.

— Vince

Chapter 8

THE BIGGEST
WIN OF MY LIFE

Following the "L Triumph," I had many other huge victories before I became associated with the World Wrestling Federation. The most impressive and significant, however, came when I won the hand of Evansville native Amy Gartner in marriage. Now, get this picture — here I am, Catholic, Italian and from New York. Ms. Gartner, on the other hand: religion, Baptist; nationality, Baptist; place of origin — Bible Belt. In other words, this had all the makings of a sitcom.

When I met Amy, I knew within a short period of time that she was the one for me. The truth is, the minute I set foot in Indiana I knew I would marry a girl from the Midwest. They were just so much more "human," so much nicer. The majority of Long Island girls were all about themselves: the hair, the make-up, which club they were going to. They were forever on a journey to "get themselves over" (a wrestling term we will get more into later), their popularity and status meant *everything*. The only way they knew was their way. In

Indiana it was different. I mean, the girls actually *cared* for you, just like your mother did. They cooked for you, coddled you, babied you and catered to you around the clock. I now realize, at the time I met Amy, maybe it was a combination of a mother thing (the fact that I'd left home at 19 and moved a thousand miles away didn't mean I was ready for the experience) and a male chauvinistic thing (the way my mother dominated my father) — but I'm neither ashamed or embarrassed to say I needed a woman who would take care of me. When I met Amy in my junior year at Indiana State, I knew she was that woman. I was already tired of the dating scene, and I just wanted one special person to come home to.

Recently, my son Will asked me, "Dad, how do you know when you're in love?" Even though I know that's the age-old question, I actually think I know the answer. I love my wife, Amy, because she was and is everything that I'm not. She filled the missing pieces to my puzzle and made me whole. Whereas I was strong, bull-headed, confident and driven, Amy was the complete opposite — vulnerable, fair, honest and fulfilled with life. Whoever coined the phrase "opposites attract" was dead on the money — Amy and I had NOTHING in common. In contrast, when you look at my relationship with L, she was everything I was. She wasn't my better half, as Amy is, because *she was me.* And you wonder why I believe in God? There is no way coincidence brought me to my perfect mate, living in Evansville, Indiana, of all places. Consider the road which led me to Amy in the first place. I had to graduate high school early, enroll in college, realize I wasn't ready for it, drop out of college, get a real job in the real world on a real assembly line where my father worked, realize I had to go back to school, run into a friend who I hadn't seen in over a year and let him talk me into going to college in Evansville, Indiana. That's fate, my friends. That's the Lord's plan.

If it hadn't been for Amy, I don't know if I would have ever been able to survive the "wrestling bubble" I had somehow landed in. Amy was my rock, my constant, my backbone. And today I thank God for providing such a gift.

From the first moments I spent with her, I could tell Amy was a saint, hands-down the nicest person I had ever met. I envisioned myself spending the rest of my life with her — there was just nobody more complementary to me. Unfortunately, I don't think Amy's mother felt the same way about the relationship as I did.

This would be the biggest battle of my life to date — the main event. In one corner, you had an Italian Catholic from New Yawk, while in the other corner stood a self-righteous General Baptist from Middle America, usa. There's no question, I was the underdog going into this one. I had everything stacked against me, including the home-field advantage. On paper, this appeared to be a war I couldn't possibly win . . . something I *thrived* on. In Alta Gartner's mind, I had no business dating her daughter. Yeah, I said "Alta." In the Midwest people have *unfamiliar* names like that. Amy's grandmother and aunt were named Ora and Ura, for crying out loud! Getting back to Alta, she didn't approve of me and I knew it. I was everything she did not want in a son-in-law. I took great exception to this. I treated Amy like gold and literally cherished the ground she walked on. But in my view, this made no difference to Alta. On more occasions than one, I tried to have civil conversations with Alta, trying to let her know how I truly felt about her daughter, but those words seem to fall on deaf ears. It seems that every conversation we had, Alta would turn to her Bible and start quoting from it — a ritual that rubbed me the wrong way. I never appreciated, and still don't, when people use the Bible to, in a sense, "scold you." If you are a non-Christian, the words aren't going to mean anything to you — *nothing*. This was exactly where I stood. Even though she felt she was doing the right thing at the time — in essence Alta was distancing herself from me.

Since becoming a Christian, life in general has become much clearer. If Alta sat down with me today and recited those same words, we would be in unison on each and every verse. But back then — write down these words — *I wasn't ready.*

In the past year, I've learned first-hand that you can't force Christianity on anybody. If they aren't ready to receive it, they won't. No matter how hard you preach, it will simply go in one ear and out the other, just like Alta's words did with me. To accept the words of God your heart has to be ready. The only one who can do that is God himself. God spent 42 years preparing me to understand his vision, but that vision was fully understood not on anyone else's time, but on his.

As much as I respect and appreciate my mother-in-law today, I feel she made a mistake in quoting the Bible to me at a time when I wasn't ready to understand. Today, as I spread God's word among the boys, I too am faced with that dilemma. You're not going to save anybody, and quite frankly it's not the job of Christians to even attempt to do so. All we can do is try to lead you to the Lord, or make you aware of him. If your heart is ready he will take it from there.

While I'm on the subject, I'd like to clarify one point. Even though I'm a Christian, I am not "religious." In being a Christian, I am simply saying that I'm a follower of Christ. I read his word, study the Bible, pray on it and attempt to walk this earth in the manner that he did. Religion to me means rules and regulations. You can do this, but you can't do that. Religion is man-made, while Christ is the *real* magilla. Remember, there is only one God. No religion is necessarily right or wrong — it's just an interpretation of God's word. That's why I was turned away from religion, and turned toward God — I just didn't realize it at the time. The difference between these two schools of thought is crucial. Don't let religion scare you. Rather allow God, himself, to enlighten you.

Despite the religious differences between Alta and myself, the truth was I loved Amy for who she was, not what she was, I just wish that her mother had understood that. But the harder Alta made it for me, the more determined I became. I wasn't going to lose Amy, regardless of the circumstances.

So the struggle continued. Alta would pull Amy one way, while I yanked her in the other. It went back and forth this way for awhile, until Alta gave me the motivation I needed. I'll never forget it — one day during one of our "Coming to Jesus" conversations, Alta looked me square in the eye and said, "I just don't see your point, Vin. When you graduate college you're going to go back to New York anyway."

Without hesitation, I replied, "How do you know that? How do you know I won't marry your daughter and take her with me?"

Alta laughed confidently and said, "Oh, I doubt that."

Without even realizing it, Alta had lit me up like WWF pyro. That one response gave me all the incentive I needed. From that point on I knew I wasn't going to lose, I wouldn't allow it. How dare she! Did she have any idea who she was dealing with? I was from NEW YAWK!

From that point on I was on a quest. I knew that I was going to have to eat it for a while, being that I was on Alta's turf, but at the end of the game, after graduation, Amy was coming home to Yankee Stadium. Once that diploma was in my hands and I was out of "Evanspatch," victory would be mine!

In my mind I knew exactly how it would play out. Alta was no longer a threat. I kept my cards close to the vest without revealing my hand. But I knew that when the final card was played, I would be raking in the entire pot. As graduation grew near, I knew I had to pop the question to Amy. Regardless of what her mother thought, I was truly in love with her. I just couldn't see waiting to get married. That would have meant me just seeing Amy on holidays until we were ready. No way — I was ready now. Like everything else in my life up to that point, I was going all the way with this. So one night, in a Chinese restaurant, I proposed. She accepted, and we set a date: September 10, 1983. Now the pressure was on. I was graduating college in May and getting married in September. I had to get a job and prove to Alta that I could support her daughter. In the meantime, I knew Alta would be working on Amy, trying to change her mind, while I looked for employment in New York.

Just to set the record straight, so there's no heat, no misunderstanding, let me publicly state to the world that, today, I wholeheartedly love my mother-in-law. Why? Because not only did I grow up, I now also have a little angel of my own. Her name is Annie.

In my early twenties, I couldn't understand Alta's point of view and I didn't *want to*. But, as they say, God works in mysterious ways. With the unconditional love I have for Annie, I can only imagine, 10 years from now, her bringing home a 20-year-old Vince Russo. At that age, I was a rebel, and Alta saw right through me — as any good mother would. Vince Russo was ready to take over the world and go through anybody to get there — including her! That's all Alta was trying to do — protect her daughter.

To her credit, Alta had enough love for her daughter to let Amy go, and find out for herself. I think in her God-loving spirit, Alta may have also believed that this kid from New York really *did* love her daughter. Today, Alta can know she did the right thing by allowing her daughter to grow up, even though it might not necessarily have followed her time frame. That's love, and that's why, after being married to her daughter for 21 years, I now feel proud that I didn't let Alta down.

You know, I always used to tell people that my mother-in-law and I had nothing to talk about. We lived in different worlds, with different morals, different values and different ideas. For the first time, a little while ago, Alta and I sat down and opened up a bit to each other. This time, what was different from all the other times was that we had God in common. It took me 21 years to see where Alta was coming from, and as I listened to her words of wisdom, I could only say to myself, "What was I thinking?" But then again, I also realize that I wasn't ready. At that point in my life it wasn't all about God — it was all about me. After a 21-year journey, on a very dark and desolate highway, my heart changed. God was now first in my life and Vince Russo was bringing up the rear.

As I sit here thinking about my marriage to Amy, I actually can't understand how it's possible. For 20 years I just wasn't there — not just physically, but spiritually, mentally and emotionally. I can remember Amy's infamous battle cry, "We don't communicate!" My response was, "I don't want to communicate — I want to watch the game." So we didn't communicate — we were just kind of there. Looking back, I just didn't know how to be a husband, and once the kids were born, I didn't know how to be a father. I was so young. I didn't know who I was, or who I was supposed to be. I now know for a fact that God was always there —

always. There is just no other reason why this woman would have stayed with me. God gave me the greatest gift of love in Amy, and he gave her to me for a reason. For 20 years, Amy tried to lead me to God, but I wouldn't listen. There were just too many other things that were more important to me. I don't know how, but Amy never quit and never stopped believing.

So here we are today — communicating — with the topic of discussion usually being God. To make you really understand how profound that statement is — I'm going to reprint a paragraph from the original manuscript which I wrote two years ago, so you can experience, first-hand the psyche of the old Vince. The exact paragraph — word for word:

Can you believe when Amy gets hot at me she says, "We have nothing in common?" How many guys have heard this line over and over again? I say this — we have nothing in common, so what? Do I expect Amy to be a San Francisco Giants fan? Do I expect her to watch girls show Howard Stern their boobs every night on E? Do I expect her to stay up until 3 a.m. with me in hopes of catching Shannon Tweed naked on Cinemax? These are the things guys do — they're guy !@#$ things. I mean, think about things women like: Oprah and that goof she has on her show — Dr. Phil — Martha Stewart, the !@#$ Lifetime Channel. Please! Any guys who have things in common with their wives aren't guys. They're . . . well . . . they're "women!"

Now, you're going to read that and tell me God doesn't exist. I actually thought that was funny when I wrote it — now I see it as one of the saddest things I've ever read.

By the way — today, I never miss *Dr. Phil.*

Chapter 9

EVERYTHING YOU EVER
WANTED TO KNOW ABOUT COLLEGE
PROFESSORS BUT WERE AFRAID TO ASK

I graduated from Indiana State in May and went back to New York on a full-time job hunt. I made *New York's Job Bank* my bible, and was determined to get a position in publishing. I didn't know what I wanted to do in publishing, but I did know I didn't want to write every day, as in journalism. For some reason — I guess my age — it never dawned on me that journalism didn't necessarily mean writing for a newspaper. I could have written for a magazine, perhaps a column a month. But what did I know? I was only 22.

In a matter of months, after literally sending out hundreds of cover letters and resumés, I finally bagged a job interview with CBS Publishing. Of course, all I looked at was the "CBS" — who *really* cared that it was their publishing division? It was CBS, and as far as I was concerned, I was in television.

What a dope.

I tap-danced my way into the job, getting it on the strength of the boss's assistant thinking I was hot. So, what do you do as a sales representative for CBS Publishing? Get this — I had every college in the Long Island–Queens–Brooklyn–Staten Island area, and my job was to sell the professors the textbooks that they were going to use for class. Do you get that? No, I mean — *do you fully understand?* My job was to call on college professors in all disciplines and sell them books in areas I knew *nothing* about. I'm talking calculus, chemistry, art, abnormal psychology — every subject known to scholars. I didn't have a clue, nor did I want one. You want to talk about arrogance — meet the college professor! What a pompous bunch of "authorities" they were, and I do mean all of them. But hey, I had an expense account, a company car and was making a whopping $14,500 a year — *plus* a bonus if I met my quota. The question was, how was I going to meet my quota when I didn't have a clue what I was doing? The answer was easy. Do what I did best in high school — cheat.

When you get placed in a situation you have no business being in, you just need to survive. That was my strategy, because praying was something little kids did before they went to bed. Again, Vince McMahon's law of the jungle — "Eat, or be eaten." Was I going to allow some holier-than-thou, glasses-at-the-end-of-your-pointy-nose professor beat me? No way! In my mind, not only was I better than them, I was smarter. There was a way around it, I just knew it — all I had to do was figure it out. Enter Howard Weiner.

A red-headed, spectacled, hip Jewish salesman, Howard could sell you both the Empire State Building and the Brooklyn Bridge in a two-for-one deal. This guy was far and away the best I have ever seen, and that says a lot, considering I've worked with wrestlers for 12 years. Howard was as smooth as the belly of a pup, he was the "true" game — he knew how to play it, how to talk it and how to make money, *big money,* from it. Being a street-smart kid from the Island, I hit it off big-time with Howard. As a matter of fact, we got along so well, he decided to take me under his wing. Howard became my mentor years before *Seinfeld* made it cool. And, in taking the responsibility, Howard taught me not only how to play the game — but how to master it. There was a definite shortcut to this business, a shortcut that would make my job easier — and my wallet fatter.

At that time, I felt as if all college professors had something in common — they all appeared to be bitter. I also felt that every college professor thought they were worth more than they were actually making. Many felt the job was beneath them, as most seemed to either want to be world-renowned authors or Pulitzer Prize winners. Very few I sat down with seemed to actually care about their students — and I broke bread with hundreds. It just appeared as if they wanted to get their tenure, then get out. Do you really think they cared about the textbook they were going to use for class? First off, what really is the difference between calculus books — when you get past all the X's and O's, calculus is calculus. College professors could teach from any book — they were all quite similar — so the question was, what book were they going to choose, and more importantly, *why?*

I've got to be honest with you — as quick as I was on my feet at the time, I don't know if I would ever have picked up on this if it weren't for Howard. In my most corrupt nightmares, I just would have never thought of it. I mean, we're talking about some big-time colleges here — Queens College, St. John's, Stony Brook, Brooklyn College — this was the world of higher education, it couldn't be "dirty." But it was; it was pigsty filthy. It was all about money, and how much of it you could put in the professor's pocket. And, it was as simple as no blood, no foul.

In the textbook business, there's a term called "desk copies." If a professor chose to use your company's book in his class, he would require a few desk copies from you — one for the office, a back-up for home and perhaps an extra one just in case. You starting to get the picture? The "extra one" was the key. Many times those few extras would equal a case of 24, or even 48. Now then, what would a professor do with 48 extra desk copies, you ask? Let me do the math for you: 48 books at $40 a pop at the college bookstore equals $1,920. Multiply that by two semesters, perhaps a summer course or two, and you're looking at $5,000 extra income per year for that professor. You get the picture — *free cash!* You grease my palm, I grease yours. I was blown away by the lack of integrity of the professors. Howard had been making a killing using this system for years. Year after year, he was the number one salesman, and it seemed that everybody knew but me. The office knew what was going on — there was no doubt about it. But once again — no blood, no foul.

My first two years as a sales rep I successfully made my quota, and then some. With the Weiner Principle, it was fairly easy. Was it a shortcut? Yeah, it was, but the way I rationalized it was there weren't any victims. I didn't screw anybody, and I didn't take anybody's job. I just did what I had to do to make a living. Did I regret it? How could I? All the sales reps from all the publishing companies were doing it. If I didn't play the game I would have been chewed up and spit out — again, it was survival of the fittest. In many ways I had no choice. But I didn't like it; it was flat-out wrong. College kids whose parents were paying beaucoup bucks to send them to school had no idea how corrupt many of these professors were. To this day, it is one of the best-kept secrets in faculty lounges across college campuses in America. In time I knew I had to get out of the business. My conscience was just weighing too heavily on me.

It's just amazing to read the above passage. Today, there is just no way I would be able to be a part of that. These days, every morning when I wake up I make myself accountable for everything I do — from throwing a piece of paper on the floor, to yelling at my kids, to not greeting somebody with a warm hello. To live in Jesus you must be ready, willing and able to align yourself with him 100 percent — no exceptions.

If you fail to forgive somebody, not gonna happen. If you cheat on your income tax, forget it. If you cut someone off in traffic, take two steps back. Living your life in Christ is the *ultimate* commitment. Yes, it's difficult — perhaps the hardest game I've ever played. But just look at what your playing for. Not money, a car, a plasma TV, or any other unnecessary luxury that's going to break down after a few years of wear and tear. But rather the greatest gift you can ever be offered — the gift of eternal life; the gift of spending every minute of every day with the one who loves you the most. You're playing for God's gift. Take all your chips and push them into the center of the table — in your entire life there will never be a hand more worthy than this . . . not even close.

Chapter 10

WHAT IS HAPPENING TO ME?

As I began my career with CBS Publishing in the summer of '83, Amy was tying up loose ends at home in Evansville in preparation for our wedding day. I knew Alta would do everything possible to make Amy have second thoughts, but to Amy's credit she withstood the pressure. Our wedding date was set for September 10, and I wasn't going to let anything stand between my love for her and the altar. But inside, I was never more scared in my life. I was 22 years old, what did I really know? Things were moving faster than a Randy Johnson fastball. Between my new job and the build-up to the marriage, I was beginning to lose it — literally. Just days before my wedding during my flight to Evansville — it all hit me at once. That two-hour flight would change my life for the next four years.

I remember it as if it were 10 minutes ago. I was flying back to Evansville to see the bride-to-be, and I was overcome with a feeling that the plane was going to crash. Suddenly I was in somebody else's body, living someone else's life. It was surreal. This was a dream. This wedding just wasn't going to happen — it couldn't. As we (my grandfather, John J., took the journey with me) glided over the Midwest, I calmly waited for the plane to nosedive into farmer Green Jean's harvest. I wasn't at all nervous — this was just my fate. Something drastic had to happen — there was no way that this wedding was going to take place. But the crash never came. . . . At least not right away.

It's hard to put into words. Looking back, it was as if I were watching this whole scenario from above. Mentally, physically, emotionally, I just wasn't there. I had absolutely zero control. It wasn't a case of cold feet, because if it had been, I would have just pulled the plug. From the bottom of my heart, I wanted to marry Amy — I wanted to spend the rest of my life with her. But I was scared out of my mind. I remember asking everyone if I was doing the right thing, and they all said *yes*. Of course they did, they'd bought plane tickets and gifts. I guess that's also what they thought I wanted to hear. But inside I was begging somebody to tell me otherwise. I was begging somebody to stop the madness.

Reality? Nothing was going to stop it. I was in church, my friends were all in tuxes, even my fraternity brothers (Beans, Flouder — they were all there), and this marriage thing was going down. I remember, about one minute before showtime, pulling out the old Chevy Chase line from *Vacation*, saying, "This is crazy, this is crazy," but it fell on deaf ears. My friends laughed like I was kidding. If they'd only known what was going on inside . . . but nobody did, not even those closest to me. On the other hand, how could they have known? I was always the most together one of the bunch, the most level-headed, the most responsible. I began to ask myself, "Who is this guy standing here, because it sure isn't Vince Russo." Man, I was in a bad movie. I was pleading for somebody to yell "Cut" and get me out of there.

Cue the organist.

It was a full house. The boy from New York City had packed them in. All these people, and not one with any idea what I was going through, including Amy. I tried to keep my composure, because the last thing I wanted to do was embarrass myself in front of everyone — remember, pride was always a big deal to me. This thing wasn't going to end up on *America's Funniest Home Videos*. No, I was going to get through it, without any help from Amy, my parents or my friends.

As I stood there saying my vows, my voice was cracking like a child's. I remember the crowd being touched by this — if only they knew what I was going through mentally and emotionally. If only I had a clue that the worst days were yet to come. Somehow, some way, I made it through the ceremony, but from that day forward I was a different person. It would be four years before the old Vince Russo would return.

In reading those last few paragraphs, it's now as clear as ever to me that at a time when I needed God the most I never even asked for his help. I never attempted to talk to him — not even once. I think my reasons were twofold: first, I was too proud — I didn't need anybody's help, I could do it on my own. Second, I was ashamed and embarrassed because I didn't even know him. There wasn't even an informal relationship — no lunch, no walks, not even a hello. He was a stranger.

Or so I thought.

Chapter 11

DEATH ON TWO LEGS

Whereas my college years were perhaps the best years of my life, the four years immediately following my marriage were no doubt my worst. To this day I don't think anybody realized how serious my situation was. For the first time in my life I understood why people committed suicide. Think about that. Was I suicidal? Maybe not, but I wasn't far off. It's hard to explain. It brings back memories I'd rather forget. I just felt like I was trapped inside some kind of a shell. I could see, hear, taste and smell, but I couldn't feel. The real me was screaming to get out, but I was a prisoner, chained in this awful place. There were many times I truly believed I was going crazy. I was scared to death that I was just never going to be the same person again — that I was going to feel this way for the rest of my life. I became a stranger to Amy, my family and whatever friends I had left. I visited my family doctor frequently, but all he could do was prescribe these little blue pills that were making me crazier than I already was. I even spoke to God, asking him, over and over again, "Why are you doing this to me?" But there was no answer.

I couldn't understand at that time that God owed me no answer, no explanation. I had never spoken to him before, unless it was to ask him to assist in a Giants' win. I had no relationship with him — I didn't even know him, my own father. Why should he have answered my prayers when I hadn't been there for him for 22 years? Was he going to help a guy who never even thanked him? Not even once? That's a misconception many people have — that if we pray to God, he will answer those prayers. Unfortunately, it is not that simple. He will answer if it's his will to do so. God isn't going to bless us — any of us — if we don't deserve his grace.

If we live our lives, in our world, our way — then obviously we are telling God we don't need his help, just like I did. However, once we make that leap of faith, once we make that commitment — once we pack our bags and move from our world to his, we will be blessed with his gifts and promises for the rest of eternity.

Again, I had to rely on myself to get through. The problem was that the end of the tunnel offered no light. I was crawling through the dark depths of hell without as much as a penlight. It was my worst nightmare. I had no idea what was going on. Perhaps I had just taken on too much in my life over a brief three-month period. I'd started a new job, bought a co-op and gotten married. Remember, I was only 22. I had gone from no responsibilities to carrying the weight of the world on my shoulders. The truth was, I was just too young to handle the situation.

Looking back, there is no question I was suffering through a deep depression — one fueled by horrific panic attacks. Every morning I would wake up, shower, shave, blow-dry my hair and get dressed. Before I would even leave the house — less than a half-hour after I showered — I would be sweating through my clothing. From there, I would drive to a college campus to do a job I despised. The driving part really sticks out. I don't even know how I got to my destination. My mind was just a haze. Many times I would go into the men's bathroom and just talk myself through the day. When I would sit down and talk to a professor I'd be sweating, unable to catch my breath. I knew the easy way out would have been to just stay home. I was a sales rep — nobody knew where I was. But I was petrified to make that choice, not because I cared about the job, but because I realized that if I began to stay home I might end up confined to my room forever. Every day I would force myself out the door, and every day would be worse than the last. But I needed to push myself. I understood that nobody was going to get me out of this but myself.

My situation put a tremendous amount of strain on my young marriage. Amy and I were becoming strangers. Suddenly she was alone and a thousand miles away from home. All she talked about was going back to Evansville to be with her family — needless to say, that wasn't helping my situation. The fact was, she was driving me deeper into the void. I have no idea how our marriage stayed together. At the time we just had no business being married.

For four years, I lived my life that way. After a while I didn't even want to drive because I was afraid something terrible would happen to me. You've got to understand — *I wasn't there.* I had no control; this was just happening to me. Up to this point, my whole life had been based on control. I was always in control of every situation. Now I had control of nothing . . . I was an infant. Deep down, I knew that it was simply a case of mind over matter. I had to beat it. I couldn't live the rest of my life like that. I wouldn't go to a shrink, because that would have just confirmed that I was losing my mind, so I had to reach out from within. I had to pull myself off Elm Street.

In August of '86, something happened that saved my life: Amy got the news that she was pregnant. In nine months there was going to be a child in this world who would bear my name. I was going to be a father. This was the motivation I needed to pull myself together. Amy and I were going to bring a child into this world, who was going to be depending on me. I couldn't fail this kid. My child's father couldn't be bound in a strait-jacket. Over the next nine months, I literally "fixed" myself. I became more alert, and caught myself every time I began to fall back. By the time my son, William James Russo, was born on May 1, 1987, I was more or less back to normal.

Man, I cried like a baby when Will was born. When the doctor did the old snatch-'n-scoop from out of the canal and onto Amy's stomach — I just lost it. This was my kid . . . my son. Your whole life just can't prepare you for that moment. In an instant, everything changes. What mattered before meant nothing now. It was immediately all about that kid blanketed in goo. After four years of playing the lead in the worst horror movie I'd ever seen — this was far and away the greatest single moment in my life. And at that very instant I realized more than ever how much I loved Amy. I'll tell you one thing though — childbirth, I could never do it. Though I'm a male chauvinist, I give women all the credit in the world for having babies. Being a practicing hypochondriac all my life, I say, "Thanks, but no thanks."

Looking back, that whole day was a miracle from God. A life gave me life — it's just that simple. Though I didn't realize it at the time, I now know that God was right there. As Will was pulled from Amy's womb, I was pulled from my eternal hell — there's no other explanation. Unfortunately, I still wasn't getting it. I still didn't understand. As clear as it is to me today, my pride blinded me back then.

It was all about me. I pulled myself out. I made myself better. I *fixed* me. I, I, I.

Man, did I waste a lot of time.

Getting back to childbirth, I would just to like to say something to all those who have children. When the bills stack up, when your job stinks, when you're fighting with your wife, just go back to that day . . . the day, or days, when you saw a child — your child — come into this world. It took me a long time to understand that, second to God, nothing in this world matters more than those kids. Money, success, your job — when you're old and retired you're going to reflect back and realize that even though that's where all your energy went — none of that meant a thing.

It just wasn't important. But guess what? It'll be too late and there'll be nothing you can do about it. "Cats in the Cradle." Trust me — don't wait another minute — do something about it. *Today!*

In putting an end to this chapter in my life, I also want to say, to any teenager or young adult out there who may be reading this book, if you ever experience any of the symptoms I talk about, please don't handle the situation like me. Obviously, in that period of my life I needed both God and professional help, but I was just too proud and stubborn to seek out either. I was in the wrong place — and faith and a qualified professional could have saved me a lot sooner. Today, I also realize I was not alone. I recently read the autobiography of Donny Osmond, who had no doubt visited the same place I had. It's common, but when it happens to you, do yourself a favor and address it immediately.

Chapter 12

THE COMEBACK

1987 was no doubt my comeback year. Aside from Will (he was named after former San Francisco Giant Will Clark, though to this day Amy thinks we named him after her dad — a great man in his own right) being born, I realized a lifelong dream — I opened my own business. No more publishing, no more colleges, no more crooked professors. I was now going to do something I truly wanted to do — work for myself. As I stated earlier, you get out of a situation what you put into it — as long as you are the one controlling the situation. From this point forward there was going to be no "outside interference" slowing me down, no bosses telling me what to do and how to do it. I was going to control my own destiny. I was going to be the chief.

While peddling textbooks for CBS, I got a weekend gig at a store called Video Breakthrough. A fine, trendsetting establishment, "VB" was a video superstore before video superstores existed. They had the latest in video technology, along with thousands of movies for sale and rental. The store was founded and built by two high school teachers chasing the same dream I was. They designed, crafted and built the place from the foundation up. When construction was complete, it was a movie wonderland. And they both took such pride in it — it was their "baby." Working as a sales consultant at Video Breakthrough, I treated the company as if it were my own. My bosses treated me with respect, and in turn, I pushed hard to help make their dream become a reality. The role was right up my alley, too. I was a big-time movie buff. To this very day I can quote every line from *Saturday Night Fever* and *Rocky*. I've always loved the movies and television. To me it was the perfect escape. And as a writer, I feasted on good dialogue. In my opinion, the words always made the movie.

Movies played a big role in my life as I grew up, and perhaps one of my best childhood memories was of my father taking me to the drive-in to watch a 10-hour Ape-athon.

I was a huge *Planet of the Apes* mark, and when I was about 12, my father took me to see all five pictures in succession — from the original, all the way through to *Battle*. The monkeyfest began at about 8 p.m. and ended somewhere near 5 a.m. Jim was out by the second one, *Beneath the Planet of the Apes* (it was also the worst). But I'm proud to say that I made it through all five. I'll never forget my father doing that for me — those are the things that count. He didn't know Cornelius from Curious George, but at the time, he knew it meant everything to his son.

With the birth of Will, things really began to turn around. And, shortly after his arrival, I bought Video Breakthrough. Well, I didn't *actually* buy it — my parents refinanced their house to help me mortgage it. I think we paid about $200,000 for the store, half cash/half note. I promised my parents that the business would pay them back — and it did, but only for about four years. At one point, business was so booming we opened a second location. There were no superstores at the time — we were it. Our stores were hip, the customers loved us and we all worked out butts off . . . except, of course, the Fruitinator.

First of all, Fruitsy hated the customers. Why? Because, in general, she hates everybody. To get out of working, she would start an argument with me five minutes into every day, then throw her hands up and say, "That's it!" Then she'd grab her pocketbook and go home. Every single day this happened. I opened up the store at 10 a.m. and closed at 10 p.m. — I was there *every* minute. That came to 84 hours a week, but I didn't even care. I dove in head-first and never even came up for air. Unfortunately, Amy was raising Will by herself. What was I supposed to do? Finally, I had everything I wanted. My days of working for somebody else were over. I controlled my own destiny, and I was going to be big-time successful. . . .

I should have seen Blockbuster coming.

We were making money hand over fist; I was literally stuffing it into safety-deposit boxes. It was coming so fast, we just didn't know what to do with it. We were all working so hard — me, my father and my partner/boyhood pal, Jimmy Monsees. And we took great pride in our business. Will the Thrill's Video (we changed the name) was a huge success. I smelled early retirement, baby, until somebody ripped the wind from our "sales." About a mile down the road from our original location, the construction of a building began. It looked like an ordinary building to me, until the sign went up — "Coming soon: Blockbuster Video." They had done their homework. They knew we were the only game in town, and they knew we were a success. Immediately, my parents panicked. My father had just taken early retirement, and now he was screwed. I did everything I could to calm the troops, but the writing was splattered all over the proverbial wall. We just didn't have the money to compete with them. We'd buy 10 copies of a new release to rent, they'd buy 50. And all our "loyal" customers who we had kissed up to for well over four years — forget it. People aren't loyal. If they could get *Dirty Dancing* from Blockbuster the first day it came out, they were headed to the blue and yellow. Well, at least we had our second location, and that was a goldmine.

They soon figured that out as well.

That's right — across the street from our new store, Blockbuster

Video opened up another of their own. We were dead in the water. Eighty-four hours a week became 100 — it didn't matter. The fat lady hadn't just sung — she'd given a whole concert, with two encores to boot! On principle alone we hung in there for about a year — but the end was inevitable.

Chapter 13

NOW WHAT?

I couldn't believe my bad luck. It had taken me four years to get my life back on track, and now this. Amy should have divorced me. Since we had been married I spent *zero* time with her. I was always obsessed with work, my success, the challenge — and for what? I had no clue what I was going to do, but I knew I had to do something. Will the Thrill's receipts were down to about $100 a day. The customers were gone. It was *The Omega Man*, and I was Charlton Heston. Everybody abandoned us. I needed to find a new line of work, but I had no idea what that was. The last thing I wanted was to go to work for someone again. What can I say? Corporate America and I mix like Jerry and the rest of the castaways from *Survivor 2*. I'm a free spirit — I just can't handle rules and regulations.

Enter John Arezzi.

One day while working in the video store, a man in his late 20s walked into my nightmare. He introduced himself as John Arezzi and told me that he had a wrestling talk show on a local Long Island radio station. Arezzi had heard of Will the Thrill's through some listeners who had come to my store on occasions when I had done promotions involving wrestlers. Over the years, we had WWF superstars Jake "the Snake" Roberts, Demolition and Brutus "the Barber" Beefcake. Literally thousands of fans would show up when we had wrestling promotions, with lines wrapping around the entire strip mall. I remember the first one we did with Jake. About an hour before he showed up, I went outside to look at the crowd. Well, it was more like a mob. I remember thinking, "What did I do?" I was so concerned that I called in the police to help maintain order. What a promotion — but at Will the Thrill's, that was the way we did things. We decorated the entire store like a snake pit, with running water fountains, hanging moss and everything. What a bunch of marks we were and, to his credit, John Arezzi knew it. John's show, "The Pro Wrestling Spotlight," was struggling and John needed help. He asked me if I would be interested in advertising on the show. Fully realizing that John might be nothing more than a shyster smelling the money of a mark, I decided to get in on the game anyway, because I saw an opportunity. I needed a new profession, and I saw John as my ticket into the world of professional wrestling. Sure, on the surface he seemed a bit shady, but he also seemed to have all the right connections. With my business savvy and his black book, I could make this thing work. Exactly where I was going with it I had no idea, but I had to go somewhere, because Will the Thrill's was hanging on by its short hairs.

So, I was on to my next chapter. Little did I know at the time that it would be a chapter I would continue to write for more than a decade.

Chapter 14

MY DINNER WITH JOHN

I began doing business with John Arezzi in late November, 1991. And what a venture it was. I paid for a good chunk of John's show every week. Amy thought I was out of my mind. My video stores were going out of business, and here I was handing money over to a stranger so he could play on the radio every Sunday morning. But John was just business — he had a love and a passion for wrestling, and he was focused on success. But again — why did Amy stay with me? I never fully realized what I put her through until I started actually getting it down on paper! It was always the Ralph Kramden get-rich-quick scheme. Everything was the next big thing. Man, were my priorities out to lunch. It was always about me, me, me — with Amy having little or no say in the matter.

From a business standpoint I thought Arezzi's show had a lot of potential. While there was room for it to grow on a production level, John was very passionate about wrestling. Like me, he grew up with it, and that love never left him. I also felt the show could grow as far as our audience was concerned. It was on a local radio station with a weak signal, drawing the same audience and the same callers week after week. We definitely needed to expand if it was going to become profitable. So I did some research, and contacted other radio stations in the New York City area that were selling airtime. Within a few weeks, we struck a deal with WEVD in the heart of New York City. With 50,000 watts of power behind us, we were now ready to make some noise. We kept the show on Sundays, but we moved it to 11 p.m., a time slot where more listeners would have their ears to the radio. Now reaching the entire tristate area (New York, New Jersey and Pennsylvania), our show grew dramatically — as did its price tag. The hour on WEVD cost us roughly $1,500 per week. My video store alone was not going to carry that, so we — mainly I — had to come up with other income to pay for everything.

Doing what I did best, I went back to writing. John and I began to publish a biweekly newsletter, *The Pro Wrestling Spotlight*. Within a month, business was beginning to pick up. We took in more than 500 subscriptions, but remember, it cost us money to have the newsletter laid-out, typeset, printed and mailed. In other words, a good portion of the dough to stay on the radio was still coming out of the pocket of the dying Will the Thrill's Video. I've got to tell you, I was busting my butt to make this thing work. I even hit the pavement in search of sponsors. But I didn't feel John was putting in the same effort I was. I felt he was using me for the money; but then again, I also saw the situation as an opportunity, so I just dealt with it. I took the venture seriously — as a matter of fact, seriously enough to actually get into the ring.

Chapter 15

MY LIFE AS A GRAPPLER

You've got to understand something about me. When I get into something, I go *all* the way. I wanted to learn every aspect of the wrestling business. Yeah, I was a fan of the product. But what went on inside — behind closed doors — in the locker room? I wanted to know the complete ins and outs of the game. Understand — *I never wanted to be a wrestler* — I simply wanted to get an education, to be a student of the game. All I needed was a teacher.

My quest for sponsors for the "Pro Wrestling Spotlight" brought me to Brooklyn, New York, the famous home of Gleason's Gym. Gleason's was located directly under the Brooklyn Bridge — you couldn't get any more raw than this. This place was the real deal. If you wanted to learn how to box, you went to Gleason's. Man, it was straight out of *Rocky*. There was nothing glamorous about this joint at all — it was basically held together by blood, sweat, tears and a lot of spit. But it was a slice of life — Brooklyn at its finest.

Located in the back of Gleason's was a ring a tad bigger than all the others. Sitting next to a small office, it was Johnny Rodz's wrestling ring. Now, if you're a New Yawker, you know who Johnny Rodz is. During his prime, Rodz was a wrestling legend. Sure, he was a perennial jobber (a guy who loses matches for a living), but he was the best at what he did. Plus, there was always that "unpredictable" label. On any given night, whether it was a high school gym, or Madison Square Garden, Rodz could beat you. Even if he lost 100 straight matches, you would always remember that one win. One of my favorite things about Johnny Rodz was the fact that he had character. And he was a tough son of a gun. Deep down, inside, you knew that if the wrestling business was a shoot (real), Johnny Rodz would have won a lot more than he lost. In his 50s then, Johnny could still go. Every day, in the back of Gleason's, he would bounce around green (inexperienced) hopefuls looking to make a name for themselves in the wrestling business.

The old barter system — not only is it what America was built on, it's what enabled me to learn the fundamentals of professional wrestling. In exchange for free advertising on the "Pro Wrestling Spotlight," Johnny Rodz agreed to train me in the ring. Now, keep in mind, at the time I was less than 200 pounds, so rather than take the grappler course, I opted for managerial training. I just wanted to learn the bare essentials, how to bump (fall) without hurting myself. I didn't want to learn a thing from the top rope; my purpose was to get a better understanding of the business, not to break my neck. For approximately three months I drove to Gleason's Gym from Will the Thrill's Video two or three times a week. It was a good two-hour ride. And guess what? Amy thought I was nuts. But I knew what I was doing. I had a plan, and this was part of it. I was on to my next venture, and I had to learn everything there was to know about it.

At Gleason's I would just take flat back (the traditional wrestling "bump," where you hit the canvas flat on your back), after flat back, after flat back. My back ached, and still does to this day. But, not only was I determined, but I also wanted to earn respect. Once you're in it, you realize the wrestling business is built on respect. As the old saying goes — you have to pay your dues.

Old Vince, new Vince: neither one ever really understood the concept of having to pay your dues. Is having to "pay dues" legit, or is it a question of somebody feeling that somebody else has to go through what they went through to get where they are? I'll tell you right now: *it's bogus, and I question the relevance of the theory.* "He hasn't paid his, or her, dues," is something you hear every day in the wrestling business. The phrase is often used simply for one reason — as a way to keep others down.

Somehow we feel that when someone says somebody else hasn't paid his dues, we need to agree. It's just something we've accepted in our society.

Give me a break! The bottom line is, if God has given you God-given talents, you go directly to the head of the class. Did LeBron James pay dues? Did Michael Jordan pay dues? Did Britney Spears, for that matter, pay dues? No, these people were talented, so they went to the front of the line. Now, on the other hand, if somebody isn't good enough, yes, they need more seasoning, they need more practice, more experience. But to help them grow, we need to be honest with them.

So my advice is this: if you ever get into the wrestling business and you know in your heart that you're ready, and you suspect somebody is trying to keep you down by saying, you haven't paid your dues, tell them very politely, "Thanks, but no thanks. I'll find another 'club' to join."

I was paying my dues because I just wasn't good enough. But I couldn't pay them quickly enough for my taste. And not only was I gaining respect, I was also shoveling it out. Man, being in that ring every day — it was an eye-opener. These guys worked so hard. They all shared the same dream, and they were all determined to see it through. They put their bodies through hell, never realizing that a serious injury could end a career before it even started. I take that back — maybe they all realized it, but didn't care. I had never experienced a work ethic like that before. And every one of these guys deserved to make it — unfortunately only one or two would.

A few guys who did make it to the big-time came out of Gleason's, most of them getting their start with Extreme Championship Wrestling (ECW). Standouts such as Taz and Tommy Dreamer were both trained by the Unpredictable One, as were a couple of blue-chippers who came out of my class, Devon Dudley and Big Vito.

Big Vito, a.k.a. Vito LoGrasso, was in my opinion the cream of the crop. To date, he hasn't quite had the success of the others, but in time, hopefully he will. Vito was, and still is, one of the hardest work-ing guys in the wrestling business. The guy would go through a brick wall for you, whether he was getting paid $50 for the match, or $500. He oozed pride and he worked every match as if it were his first . . . and last. I immediately gravitated towards him. I felt his passion. I've always admired someone who works that hard, that's why I've never been a fan of guys who get into the dance through the back door, via politics — knowing somebody. I truly felt a responsibility to help Vito make it, but at the time, who was I? Nothing more than a going-out-of-business video-store owner who was desperately trying to make it himself. But regardless, Vito and I did share something spe-cial in common — we were both following a dream. And that's what the wrestling business is built on, dreams. Every guy breaking into the business wants to be the next Stone Cold Steve Austin (even though there'll never be another). The majority never make it. Many fail not from lack of talent, but from lack of perseverance. Believe me, it's a long, hard road — it just doesn't happen overnight. Vito was past 35 when he actually made it in the business, and I give him all the credit in the world for that. He might never have got into the big-time if it wasn't for me giving him his break at World Championship Wrestling (WCW), but that had nothing to do with his heart, desire, work ethic and drive, it was just politics. In the end, Vito LoGrasso made it because Vito LoGrasso *deserved* to make it.

With three months of training under my belt, I was ready to per-form in front of a crowd. Johnny Rodz was promoting a spot show somewhere in a small town in New Jersey, and he booked me on the card. My first official role was to manage the number one monster heel (bad guy) in the territory: Skull Von Krush, a.k.a. Vito LoGrasso. I was thrilled to get the opportunity to manage Skull. To this day, I wouldn't have shared this experience with anybody else. Skull — Vito — was what the business was all about. I was both proud and honored to stand in his corner.

Chapter 16

VICIOUS VINCENT ROCKS

Oh, yeah, I had the costume made, the whole nine yards. And yes, Amy thought I was nuts. But Vicious Vincent was ready to dominate the wrestling world. I was larger than life — in my own mind, of course. Black satin jacket with red, yellow and orange flames firing from the bottom, black spandex shirt, matching pants, fringe everywhere and a fluorescent orange baseball bat — what a gimmick. But don't kid yourself — I was taking this real seriously. If nothing else, I couldn't embarrass Skull — he worked too hard and took pride in every match. And why shouldn't I have taken it seriously? Especially being that tonight his — our — opponent would be the crafty, ring veteran Cousin Luke — yeah, the cousin of the WWF's Hillbilly Jim and Uncle Elmer.

All right, so it wasn't Madison Square Garden, but it didn't matter. The truth was, it was a high school gymnasium and there were probably about 50 people there. But believe me, I was as nervous as if we were truly on the corner of 34th and 7th. Just the idea of performing in front of a live crowd was enough. The fact that many of them were missing teeth didn't matter — they were breathing, I think. But despite all the excitement, I was here to learn. I wanted to experience life on the other side of the curtain: the brotherhood between the boys, the unity of the locker room, how this all came together. And that night I was a student. I sat back, I watched, I listened and I learned. It was fascinating just to hear the boys go over their matches with each other, how every move was completely choreographed — rehearsed many times. The jargon they used — a language only they could understand. The respect, the code, the honor among the boys was something I would never find again like this at higher levels. It shed a new light on the business for me. This was their 9 to 5, they were blue-collar workers with blue-collar attitudes busting their blue-collar butts for every blue-collar penny they made. And believe me, at this level it wasn't much. The pay scale for the talent who performed on the card that night was somewhere between $50 and $200. Nobody was going to get rich — not at this level — they were simply there to pay their dues. Unfortunately, that's what many of them wind up doing for their entire careers. To this day, there are territories all across the country where aspiring sports entertainers drive three, four hours to make a show, only to earn $100. That's either dedication . . . or stupidity.

Though in the end many fall short of their dreams and aspirations, they view it all as time well spent. The experience is an investment in their futures and in themselves. The experience was also life-changing for me. Never before, in any field that I had been associated with, had I witnessed such a display of hope, honor, love and dedication. It's what this world of sports entertainment was supposed to be about. Unfortunately, once you reach a certain level, it doesn't resemble anything like this, mainly because on this level politics just do not exist, because no one is making money — not the promoter, not the boys, *no one*. Looking back, there is no doubt that the innocence of the wrestling business is what attracted me to it. I cared about the people I worked with. It was *The Shield* all over again, the work ethic was second to none, and I knew then — in some capacity — it had my name written all over it.

So now the stage was set for the managerial debut of Vicious Vincent. Prior to the match, Skull, myself and Cousin Luke had gone over it numerous times in the locker room. My big spot would come once Skull was holding Cousin Luke up against the ring ropes facing the crowd. Being the dastardly manager I was, I would pop up on the ring apron with my orange baseball bat and nail Cousin Luke, which in turn would allow Skull to score the pinfall. Of course, Cousin Luke would duck the bat, causing me to nail the bald German by accident. This would allow Luke — the good guy — to get the 1-2-3 on the bad guy, Skull. Yeah, I was just starting to learn about "babyfaces" and "heels," but I hadn't made it even that far yet. At this point, all I was worried about was not screwing up — not making them look bad. These guys were professionals and I was honored they would even allow me in the same ring. Whether there were 20 fans or 20 thousand, it never mattered, the work ethic was the same: *Spaldings to the wall!* Man, I wasn't going to screw them up. I couldn't. Remember, back in those days I wrote the book on pride!

Ding, ding — it was on!

The match went according to plan. There was Skull holding Cousin Luke against the ropes for me, and here I came! Without missing a beat, Luke ducked my swing and *bang!* — baseball bat right across Skull's head. Realizing what I had done, I hopped off the ring apron as a helpless Skull lay flat on his back in the middle of the squared circle. After Luke got the pin he came after me. Wait a minute — this wasn't in the script! Luke grabbed me by the throat outside the ring and I just went with it. Growing up, I had seen Captain Lou in this predicament over a million times. I begged my butt off, I sold it as if I were grasping for my very last breath, good enough to convince Cousin Luke to let me go. I then remember telling Cousin Luke it wasn't me who hit him with the bat, but rather Skull. Typical '70s rasslin' — the heel sells his own guy down the river — this was about as good as it got. But wait . . . it wasn't over, not quite yet. After Cousin Luke left the ring area I went into the squared circle to check on Skull.

Remember, this was all improvised now — I'm strictly going on what I had seen on the boob tube for so many years. In an effort to bring Skull to, I slapped him in the face a couple of times. Once he gathered himself he asked me what had happened, and I explained to him that Cousin Luke had hit him with a baseball bat. Man, what a lying, filthy heel I was! Unfortunately, Skull was smarter than that. He got up and started to push me around. I tried to beg him off as well, but this time it didn't work. I remember Skull whipping me into the ring ropes and saying, "clothesline." I was getting an education right there on "calling it in the ring" (when two wrestlers actually call the spots of the match — on the spot — as the match is happening). As I sprang off the held-together-by-black-electrical-tape ropes, Skull came off and nailed me with a clothesline. I went down like a kid picking an unclaimed dollar off the floor. Not wanting any further damage done to me (rather, my character) I picked myself up and beelined it to the locker room.

Following the match, both Skull and Cousin Luke congratulated me. To this day, Vito will swear to you that I really "potatoed" him (hit him for real) with that baseball bat. However, despite the controversy, I realized two things that night. First, that that was my last professional match. I had no interest in becoming a wrestler, manager or competing in the ring in any way, shape or form. I'd be lying if I told you it wasn't a trip to be out there, but I've lived my life by one law — when you try to be something you're not that's when you fail. I wasn't a wrestler and I wasn't going to try to be one. But the second thing I learned was a very different story. By the time the locker room had cleared out, I realized that this might be my calling. I really related to the boys — I had such great respect for them, and I felt that I just wanted to work *for* them. I didn't know in what capacity yet, but I just wanted to lend myself to their cause. Again, I think it all went back to the work ethic. When I see somebody work that hard, I just want to roll up my sleeves and jump in there, to help them accomplish their goals. I want to help them make it. I just thrive on challenge — what can I say?

With the in-ring experience now under my belt, it was time to get serious. I knew that sports entertainment was the field I wanted to be in, I just didn't know in what capacity. Was it radio, magazine writing, or perhaps a position more monumental than that. I had no idea what lay ahead for Vicious Vincent, but I was soon to find out.

Chapter 17

STEROIDS —
HOW THEY CHANGED MY LIFE FOREVER

Between WEVD and our biweekly newsletter, John and I were on a roll. Whereas my money and drive were helping to create a following, his controversial opinions were creating a stir — one that would eventually lead to our split.

To this day, there is no question in my mind that John Arezzi loved the wrestling business. I never questioned his dedication, but I did question his approach. If I was the pot, John was the kettle, and like me, John was always looking for that one story, that one angle which, from a journalistic viewpoint, he could revel in and make his own — much like my Creighton Burns story in college. John seemed to thrive on controversy and, I guess you could say, on the spotlight as well. Still, that's not much different from this author. What I didn't understand was why John Arezzi wanted to be the guy to take down the mighty Vince McMahon. To this day I still don't really get it. It either had to be a sincere gesture of righteousness, or a severe case of ego — your guess is as good as mine.

Part of me was skeptical about John wanting to "do the right thing." Early on in our relationship, I began to hear stories about how many people John had allegedly attempted to con before me. The unsuspecting souls he allegedly owed money to on Long Island read like a list of Elizabeth Taylor husbands. But, again, this was based on rumor and hearsay. But *if* it was true, I could be the next name on the list. I was determined to be smarter than that. If John was going to use me for my money, then I was going to use him to get my foot in the door of sports entertainment. Though I had a plan, it wasn't going to be easy. Our philosophies were completely at odds. We were both trying to get to the same place, but John was looking to take a shortcut — a shortcut that would inevitably have been the downfall of us both.

The reason why I never quite understood John's determination to take down Vince McMahon was because, in my opinion, without Vince, there would have been no wrestling, no sports entertainment business. But if Vince was indeed guilty of foul play involving steroids, as John suggested, should he have paid the consequences regardless of his position? *Sure, but remember, you're innocent until proven guilty.* The bottom line was, without Vince there would be no us — *do the math!* Add to that the fact I was a huge fan of Vince — he'd given me years and years of enjoyment growing up — why would I want to lead a witch hunt to bring him down? At the time it seemed ludicrous, but it was John's M.O. No doubt we had a problem on our hands. I wanted to do a fan-friendly wrestling radio show that would complement the World Wrestling Federation, while John wanted to do a *60 Minutes* exposé-type thing that would clearly smear the business.

At the time that the partnership between John and me formed, Vince McMahon was being indicted on steroid-trafficking charges by the federal government. The feds claimed Vince was illegally distributing steroids to his wrestlers. Of course, those charges opened up the floodgates for the mass media. Everybody from Phil Donahue to Geraldo Rivera jumped on the bandwagon. What started as a steroid scandal soon became a three-ring circus, as individuals came out of the woodwork accusing Vince McMahon of rape and a series of other outlandish charges that would later turn out to be false. One of my favorites was a story concerning Vince and a television announcer showering together, which made Vince a blatant homosexual. *Please!* You have no idea how a light dust of *Enquirer*-style gossip can snowball into a deadly avalanche with the help of the media unless you've experienced it yourself. And, John was in the middle of all of it, constantly feeding all his "insider" dirt and gossip to a *New York Post* reporter by the name of Phil Mushnick. From there, Mushnick would print all of John's info in a paper read daily by millions. Wow! — this was my first experience with journalism outside of college. This wasn't the kind of integrity Mr. Vance talked about in class, but then again, this was the real world. The situation seemed to be getting out of control and because of my relationship with John, I found myself smack in the middle of it. The lid was about to be blown off this story — it was just a matter of when, and where.

The breakdown was going to occur sooner rather than later. In the winter of 1992, John booked a show based on McMahon's legal problems, steroids and all the other controversy that the media was in a frenzy over. Actually, it wasn't going to be a "show," but rather a Barnum and Bailey spectacular, with John as ringmaster. His mission was to put anyone who would join in his crusade to take down Vince McMahon and the World Wrestling Federation on air, while having no one on the other side to defend the accused. Again, I had to ask myself, over and over again — *why?* Why would you want to crucify the man who'd made your career possible? Without Vince McMahon, there would be no John Arezzi. But you know what? I was just as much to blame as he was. I let it happen . . . I even paid for the show! But believe me, I wasn't proud of it. I guess at the time, for selfish reasons, I felt like I had no choice. I mean, I was banking on Arezzi to get me into the business. It would have done me no good to sever our relationship that early on.

But still, that's a poor excuse. I should have killed the idea from the get-go, packed up the big top and silenced the clowns.

The "Crucify Vince" panel was set to do the *Phil Donahue Show* on Monday, so we had the distinct honor of having them on our radio show the night before. In the studio was newsletter writer Dave Meltzer, and former wrestlers Barry O and Superstar Billy Graham. Joining the show via Ma Bell was "living legend" Bruno Sammartino and Lord Littlebrook, a midget with a beef. John appeared to be in his element. This was his *60 Minutes* and he was Morley Safer. John thrived on this controversy; this is what it was all about to him. Me? I'd be lying if I told you it wasn't exciting. I was a part of something that was about to mushroom into the biggest story the wrestling business had ever known, perhaps ever will. But I was nowhere near sold on the idea that Vince was guilty. Unlike Phil and Geraldo, who seemed to be dying to roll over (more Geraldo than Phil), I had to be *convinced* that Vince was guilty.

McMahon's accusers had a field day. From Vince raping a female referee in the back of his limo, to Pat Patterson violating ring boys, the tall tales and allegations flew like gossip in a nail salon chock-full of yentas. They talked about sexually abusing midgets, a WWF referee with a foot fetish — everything imaginable. This show made the *National Enquirer* look like the *New York Times,* but in his mind, John had earned the Pulitzer Prize that night. Immediately following the show, he called Phil Mushnick and delivered the goods. Arezzi was Mushnick's "Deep Throat," and you knew it all would be in the *New York Post* the next morning — and it was.

For those of you out there who aren't familiar with the business, the "real" news of professional wrestling is distributed to hardcore fans through a somewhat underground channel called the "newsletter." The boys in the business refer to it as the "dirt sheet."

Again, two years ago, when I first wrote this book, this was the part where I lambasted every person who ever had anything to do with the writing of a wrestling newsletter. However, today, after being shown the light by my father, I see things differently.

Based on experience, there is just something about being a journalist. . . . I know in my case anyway, reporting the "straight news" just wasn't where it was at. Every writer thrives on controversy — the danger of the story, if you will. And, in the end, I really don't think it's about how many people will read it, but about beating everybody to the punch in dishing the dirt. From a professional standpoint, I really don't have a problem with this — under one condition — you at least back up your story with *reliable* sources. If you do your homework, legitimately, I'm cool with that. That being said, here is my problem with wrestling newsletters.

When something goes down, the newsletter writers very rarely seem to go to the source. Why? To be honest with you, I'm not quite sure. It would have been like me writing the Creighton Burns story in college without ever talking to Creighton Burns. Now, the reason I say this is because over the past 12 years, there has been much written about me — much of it deeply hurtful. However, over that 12-year span, during which literally hundreds, maybe even thousands, of stories have been written about me, I personally have been contacted only once or twice. So, the truth is, the people writing the stories are getting them second-hand. And who are the second-hand sources? Well, there are a few. First there are those inside the business who have an axe to grind with me (which was the REAL reason for me being labeled a racist). But then there are also those who want to stay in good favor with the newsletter writer, to ensure that they don't have anything negative written about *them*. This has always been my problem with the newsletters. Yes, the writers have to make a living, and I support that, but if you're going to write about somebody — especially if it's going to be negative — at least show a bit of integrity and try to get the other side of the story.

My second pet peeve with newsletters is that many times they present their opinion as fact. "Opinion" and "fact" are two very different things. "Vince Russo is an imbecile," and, "In my opinion, Vince Russo is an imbecile" are two very different things. Many times you confuse the reader when you state your opinion as fact. I greatly disagree with this practice. If something is a fact, back it up with facts; if you don't have facts — preferably first-hand — then it's simply your opinion. Just state that, and I'll never have a problem with a story.

The Crucify Vince Tour continued the next day on the *Phil Donahue Show,* the only difference being that the smut was presented in more of a PG version. John had asked me to go to *Donahue* with him, but I wanted no part of it. After the fiasco the previous night, I had seen and heard enough. In that studio there was such ill-feelings toward Vince McMahon, it was impossible for him to get a fair shake. On top of that, there wasn't a single soul representing the other side. I claim full responsibility for that. I should have assured that the mock trial was going to be fair. But I didn't — there was no one there to defend him, no one there to tell Vince's side of the story — and it was wrong. Seeing John on the *Donahue* panel that day distanced me more from him. I could barely even watch. Is this what he had worked his whole life for? Five minutes of fame? Watching John, I knew our little business venture was over. This whole thing was wrong; this wasn't what I wanted to get into the business for. I wanted to give something back to the industry that had given me so much while I was growing up. The last thing I wanted to do was screw it over. First of all, I didn't believe the story; secondly, if Vince was truly innocent — what was the point?

While I'm thinking about it, you know what used to drive me nuts about John? He used to wear these shaded glasses, and you could never look into his eyes. I'm not talking about the kind that lighten up when you go indoors — these were *permanently shaded!* John looked like a "shady" character to begin with, but not being able to look in his eyes made matters even worse. And, that's the way he came across on the *Donahue Show.* Here was a guy with questionable sources, spinning tales about Vince McMahon through black-shaded glasses. Are you going to buy a life insurance policy from this guy?

The day after his "Hollywood minute," John came to the video store to give me the lowdown. He told me everything had gone great, except for Superstar Billy Graham getting some heat with the rest of the panel. Apparently Graham came "off-script," so to speak. You see, the Superstar was on the panel to jab the steroid finger at McMahon, but apparently when the conversation turned to the sexual abuse and harassment of WWF ring boys, Graham became an authority on that subject, too. In my view, it came across like Graham was talking out of school — because he was. The fact was, he knew nothing about that part of the scandal; he was simply adding fuel to the fire. But part of the panel's agenda was about twisting the facts. It was all about saying whatever you had to say to bring Vince down.

I'll never forget that during that week, the WWF announced that Vince McMahon was going to hold a steroid symposium to lay out the new steroid testing policy he was going to mandate. Vince invited everybody to the symposium except John Arezzi . . . I don't know, must have been the glasses. My point is that he even invited Phil Mushnick and Dave Meltzer (writer for the *Wrestling Observer Newsletter*). I know for a fact he invited Meltzer, because that week on the phone Dave told me himself he had an "open invitation" to attend the symposium, but he'd graciously declined. He told me that whatever Vince did or said would be nothing more than blatant lies to cover up his guilt. Man, did I have a problem with this! Here's *the* wrestling authority declining to attend a major press conference that was part of perhaps the biggest story in the history of the business! Again, I'm sure Dave had his reasons, but I just questioned his choice. Did the press conference not matter? Or had everyone on the other side already made up their minds?

But wait, from there it got even better.

That Sunday night, when he opened the "Pro Wrestling Spotlight," John was on an adrenaline high. The Vince story was all over the media, and John and his underground had had a lot to do with it. They were talking to anybody who would listen and give them print. It seemed John would stop at nothing, as he soon proved within the first five minutes of the show. John immediately went into the news of the announcement of the WWF Steroid Symposium that would take place later that week. In his opening monologue, John stated, and I quote, "Not one person from the wrestling media was invited to attend." John's point was that Vince could work (lie to) the mainstream media, because they didn't have a clue as to what was going on, but he couldn't work the wrestling media, which is why they weren't invited. If this had been true, John would have had a point. But the fact is he flat-out lied, live, on the air. Meltzer had told me himself that he'd been invited; he was just declining to go. John knew that, but in stating that *no one* from the wrestling media had been invited, he gave our listening audience the idea that perhaps Vince McMahon did have something to hide. When those words came out of John's mouth I was livid. McMahon's guilt or innocence was one thing, but to spin a web of lies in order to swing the pendulum to guilty was a crock.

The strain in our relationship was growing by the minute, the tension so thick, you couldn't even carve it with the amazing Ginsu. Something had to give — it was just a matter of when and how. During the week John and I kept our distance from each other — he stayed home with his mother, while I was nickel-and-diming my customers to death at Will the Thrill's Video. Business was slow, to the point of being ridiculous. I knew I had to make my transition into professional wrestling sooner rather than later, but with John as my partner, I realized the whole plan could cave in at any moment. Whether I was ready or not, it was time for me to break away from John and give the wrestling business a go on my own. If I'd continued to follow his lead, I'd have been finished before I even started.

Without John's knowledge, I contacted the WWF Headquarters, located in Stamford, Connecticut, in the hope of getting into the steroid symposium which was now just a few days away. More easily than expected, I was able to get through to the head of their public relations department, Steve Planamenta. Oddly enough, John had known Planamenta before either of them got into wrestling, but any personal connection they may have once had, had since been brutally squashed by John's determination to take down Planamenta's boss — Vince McMahon. In his early 30s, Planamenta appeared to be your typical wrestling geek — balding, heavy black horn-rimmed glasses, the whole shebang. But the one thing I always respected about him was the fact that he *was* a huge wrestling fan and he wasn't afraid to admit it. Even though he was sitting in the Taj Mahal of professional wrestling, the palace they call "Titan Tower," Steve Planamenta was one of us. During my five phone minutes with him, I had to give the selling job of a lifetime. First and foremost, I had to separate myself from John, which wasn't an easy thing to do. The bottom line was I had guilt by association written all over me. Planamenta went on and on about how John had lied about this, and how John had lied about that, and whenever he gave me the chance to get a word in edgewise all I could say was, "I'm not John!" I begged Planamenta not to judge me based on John's actions. All I'd wanted to do was present the facts to our listeners — minus the spin — and let them decide for themselves. I didn't want to read about the WWF Steroid Symposium courtesy of Phil Mushnick in the *New York Post* the following morning — I wanted the facts first-hand! I wanted to be as responsible as I could be to both the WWF and our listeners. After giving Planamenta the pitch of a lifetime, I hung up the phone with him saying, "Let me get back to you." That told me that Planamenta had to get the okay from somebody above him. That somebody had to be either his boss, Basil DeVito, or *the* boss — Vince McMahon.

For the next hour I paced the back office of my video store like Wile E. Coyote awaiting the appearance of Road Runner. Don't forget, to me this was a vital piece of the puzzle. To reach the next step of my master plan, I had to be invited to that symposium. I had to gain some kind of credibility with Steve Planamenta. It wasn't about kissing his butt, or kissing the butt of the WWF, it was about taking a non-jaded, journalistic approach. I wasn't going to be anybody's judge or jury. First of all, I didn't know what the truth was; I was trying to find out just like everybody else. Oh yeah, and one more thing — don't think for one minute that a chance to meet Vince McMahon wasn't lodged in the back of my mind.

To me, meeting Vince McMahon was about reality — not a dream. That's the way I always perceived it. If I was to succeed in the wrestling business in the capacity I envisioned, Vince McMahon was going to be involved one way or another. Otherwise I was going to be nothing more than an employee working a job. But you see, looking back now, I can fully understand that my encounter with Vince wasn't my doing. In the first draft of this book I took full credit for the chance meeting. I made it happen — me. Now think about that. How many people are there who want to get into wrestling actually get the opportunity to meet Vince McMahon? What are the odds of a guy running a video store getting the opportunity to not only meet, but to later have a tremendous impact on somebody he had admired from a distance since he was a teenager? It just doesn't happen to everyone — but, it happened to me. Luck? Coincidence? Or divine intervention?

Having been born again, I truly believe that our plan was laid out for us from the minute we poked our heads out of our mothers' wombs. You have to remember — if you believe in God, then you believe he created us. If he created us — it was for a reason. In reading the Bible you will find that the reason God created us was to glorify his name and his kingdom. In other words, I've gone from a crazy mother, to being a KISS fanatic, to a controversial student journalist in Evansville, to meeting my soulmate, to deep depression, to crooked professors, to being a father, to owning a video store, two video stores, Vicious Vincent's World of Wrestling, Vince McMahon, the Rock-'n'-Sock Connection, to surviving a tragedy, to being in the middle of a screw job in Canada, a taste of hell (WCW), post-concussion syndrome, being sued, opening my own business — again, to a two-year turbulent relationship with a friend, leaving TNA/Total Non-Stop Action, coming back to TNA, leaving TNA, coming back to TNA, to glorifying God's name right here in this book.

That's where every story is supposed to lead, every single one. If it doesn't — it's by your choice, not God's. God gives us the freedom to choose. To put it bluntly, we can chose life or death. I chose life in the name of my Lord, Jesus Christ.

As God led me to my calling — without me even realizing it at the time — I came across many make-it-or-break-it situations. When you reach that point, you've got to be willing to go for it and trust the outcome either way. If it's God's will, you will pass the test — if it's not, you won't. But remember, if it doesn't turn out your way, you didn't fail — it just wasn't part of God's plan for you. When everything was on the line for me in wrestling, God put me into the situation fully loaded, with everything in my favor, but you must still have absolute faith in his lead.

God gave me the self-confidence in every instance to succeed. It was just meant to be. God gave me the power to believe in myself in those situations because that was his will. That's what a lot of the guys in the wrestling business have a hard time understanding today. Many of them don't make it as wrestlers simply because they weren't meant to be wrestlers. If it were up to me I'd be pitching for the Giants right now. But it's not up to us — it's up to God. He created us for a reason — one purpose — to glorify his name. When and how we get to that point is different for each of us. If we have complete faith we will reach, then walk, the path he paved. If we don't, it's because we decided to take a different turn on his road. We tried to force something that God just didn't have in the cards. Please, take it from experience, don't attempt to force anything — hand your life over to God today and he will take you to where you need, and want, to go.

It's funny, but while I was on my quest, when the video store was quiet — which was most of the time — I was inspired to read a book that somebody gave me by Napoleon Hill. It was called *Think and Grow Rich*. The book contained a story, from the early 1900s, about a nobody named Edwin C. Barnes, who envisioned himself working side-by-side with Thomas Edison. Barnes had a dream, as we all do, and with hard work, persistence and most importantly, confidence, he saw it through. Remember, Barnes envisioned working *with* Edison — not *for* him. Well, as I read that book sitting in my dead video store, in my mind I was Barnes and Vince was Edison. I didn't know Vince McMahon from Adam, but I'd made up my mind that, when all was said and done, I was going to be working *with* him.

But obviously, before I could work with him, I had to meet him.

I know, my story is beginning to sound like a fairy tale, but believe me, at the time it was far from it. So much was at stake. If I didn't reach my ultimate goal, I didn't know what I was going to do. I had no plan B. This was it — the whole kit and caboodle. And keep in mind I had a family. It wasn't just about me anymore. I had a wife and a son at home who were depending on me.

After what seemed like a decade the phone rang — it was Planamenta. "Vince would love to have you attend the symposium," Steve said. That was it. At that point, I knew I was on my way.

Now all I had to do was break the news to John.

Chapter 18

MEETING VINCE

During our conversation, Steve Planamenta made it clear that John was not welcome at the symposium. I had an open invitation, but only if I came alone. Personally, I didn't have a problem with this. John had been so blatantly negative towards the WWF that I couldn't blame Planamenta for not extending the olive branch. John dug his own grave. Getting into the wrestling business was John's dream, but I've got to tell you, his approach was questionable. Now, I'm not saying that if Vince McMahon was guilty we should have kissed his ass or covered for him — not at all. All I'm saying is that the jury was still out. John and the wrestling smarts (wrestling fans who think they know more than they do, and perhaps take the business a bit too seriously) had turned this into a witch hunt. Vince already had a noose tied around his neck; all they had to do was drop the floor beneath him. There was just no other side of the story being told. Whether it was Vince McMahon or Joe Blow from Bensonhurst, not only was it unfair, it wasn't right. In my opinion, whether he was telling the truth or not, Vince had the right to be heard. That's why I wanted to attend the symposium. I wasn't a seasoned journalist by any stretch of the imagination, but I was at least trying to show some integrity. That's why I accepted Planamenta's invitation and was going without John.

Needless to say, when I broke the news to Arezzi he wasn't a happy camper. As strange as this may sound, he couldn't understand why Planamenta would invite me and not him. To be honest, if I had been in Vince's shoes it would have been difficult for me to reach out my hand in a gesture of peace to John. I wasn't naïve — I totally understood that my being invited might have been a way for Planamenta to divide and conquer — get the mark away from Arezzi and we've got 'em. I wasn't stupid, I knew both what John was thinking, as well as the WWF. Though John was upset, he was going to have to live with it — I was going. So, on March 24, 1992, I drove to the Lake Ronkonkoma Station and boarded the Long Island Railroad en route to the Plaza Hotel in New York City.

I'm not sure why, but I was extremely nervous walking into the Plaza. In hindsight, I think the reason was twofold. First, I felt as if I was jumping right into the eye of the storm. Forget storm, this was Kansas and there was a tornado brewing. "Auntie Em — Lock up the dog!" But, unlike the so-called wrestling experts — my colleagues at the time — I was the only one looking for the facts. I was distancing myself further and further from them, solely because I was trying to do the right thing. Who was I to slant this story? Did I see Vince McMahon pressure his wrestlers into taking steroids? Had I seen *any* wrestler inject himself with growth hormones? Did I see Pat Patterson come on to midgets? No — I wasn't witness to any of this. There were so many allegations, and so few facts. The whole controversy was really getting serious, and the wrestling media was getting in deeper, loving every minute of it, thriving on the mainstream media attention.

A second reason to be nervous was that I knew I was going to the Plaza Hotel to meet Vince McMahon. I didn't know exactly how I was going to swing this, but I knew that it was going to happen. Remember *Think and Grow Rich*. If I was to make a go of the wrestling business, this was my make or break opportunity. In life, these were the situations you needed to take full advantage of. Times like these are few and far between, so when they present themselves — grab them. I realized that my chance of having a one-on-one with Vince that day was a million-to-one shot, but in my mind that didn't matter. It was going to happen, I knew it in my heart . . . and it did.

The steroid symposium went off without a hitch. The WWF put on a very professional presentation, headed by McMahon and Dr. Mario DiPasquale, a licensed physician from Ontario, Canada. Dr. DiPasquale specialized in sports medicine and was hand-picked by Vince to set up and see through a drug testing program that McMahon himself would enforce. Was it a dog-and-pony show? Sure it was, but you had to give Vince and the WWF the benefit of the doubt. Vince admitted on various occasions that there was indeed a steroid problem in the WWF and that he was going to take responsibility for solving it. You had no reason to believe or not believe him, you just had to wait and see how it played out. I was there mainly to gather the facts for our listeners and readers, not to sway them in either direction. To ensure that I wouldn't misquote anything that was said, I recorded the entire symposium on audiotape — a decision that would later pay huge dividends.

Oh, and just a *small* side note: that day, Steve Planamenta personally introduced me to Vince McMahon. Looking back now, 10 years later, it's hysterical. I can remember how nervous I was. My mouth transformed into a giant cotton swab — it must have made for some interesting breath. I'm not going to kid you, I could barely talk to the guy. The one thing that stood out the most was his presence. From that first day, I could just feel Vince's power. Everything and everybody changed the moment he walked into that room. By this point in my life, I've met many celebrities, but none of them carried themselves with the presence of Vince McMahon, not even my boyhood idol, Gene Simmons.

Chapter 19

MY SHOWDOWN
WITH PHIL MUSHNICK

The day following the steroid symposium, it was business as usual at Will the Thrill's Video, or so I thought. I arrived at work at around 10 a.m., ready to put in another 12-hour day. The routine was the same — coffee from the bakery and the *New York Post* from the stationery store. I never really liked the guy who owned the stationery store. I think it was because he had a really bad wig. That, plus the fact that his wife was cheap. Man that gal would nickel-and-dime you to death. If you were a penny short, you weren't getting the PayDay bar. So anyway, I'm sitting behind the counter of my store digesting the sports section of the newspaper, when I come across Phil Mushnick's column. I'd only gotten through a sentence or two before I couldn't believe what I was reading.

Remember I told you earlier that Phil Mushnick was personally invited by Vince McMahon to attend the WWF steroid symposium, but for whatever reason, he passed? Well, here he was less than 24 hours later, in all his glory, reporting on the event as if he were front and center! I couldn't believe it! This guy calls himself a journalist? And now millions of people in New York were reading this as if Mushnick's words were fact, not having a clue that the writer hadn't even been in attendance. I was furious. How could Mushnick get away with this; he flat out "Johnny Cochraned" McMahon's words, twisting them around in an effort to get *his* story across.

I immediately went to my jacket and pulled out the hand-held tape recorder I used to record the symposium a day earlier. Play, rewind, play, rewind. Everything Vince said, Mushnick had taken out of context. I finally saw — first-hand — how the media does it. I was embarrassed and ashamed at the same time. I had spent four years of my life studying to be a journalist, and now reality was smacking me across the face. It had nothing to do with knowledge, or education, all you had to do was bend the truth just a little to get your point across. Be, as they say, sensational. And, this was no small-scale operation — this was the *New York Post!*

I felt I needed to do something, but what? Who was I? People were going to believe me over Phil Mushnick? I had to call somebody, and John Arezzi was my only choice. So I called John and lambasted him.

"How can you align yourself with a piece of !@#$% like Mushnick?" I screamed. "Did you read his column today? It was all !@#$%, every last word, and I have the tape to prove it!"

John's response? There wasn't one. And even if he'd had a song to sing — my ears were set on mute. The story was now clear and I had the facts to back it up. A major smear campaign was in full-throttle, and showed no signs of letting up until Vince McMahon and the WWF were out of business. Man, was I furious at John! I can't recall how the conversation ended, but knowing me and my Italian temper, I'm sure I hung up. As the hours passed, I just became more and more steamed while I waited on customers. Little did I know at the time that things were just beginning to simmer.

It was well into the afternoon when the smoke began to dissipate in my head. I had to put this behind me. Dwelling on it would only have made matters worse. All right, so I had made a bad decision. Partnering with Arezzi didn't turn out to be a Lucas-produced, Spielberg-directed project. So it was more like *Hell's Gate* — so what? It was over.

And then Arezzi walked in. The gall! The spaldings on this guy! How dare he walk into my store, my place of business. What nerve, smoky-glass lenses and all.

"Are you !@#$% kidding me, or what?" I asked.

"Vince, we have to talk," John said.

I knew what he wanted to talk about. I was dangerous to him and Mushnick now. Knowing what I knew, I could singlehandedly derail their whole plan. If only I'd known how. That was the problem — I just didn't know where to go with this.

"Look, just let me make one phone call and you'll understand all this," said Arezzi.

Who is he going to call, I thought — his mother? But, you know what? I had to find out. This was the old watching-a-car-wreck theory — I didn't want John near my phone, but on the other hand, I had to find out what he was up to.

"Use the phone," I said. "Who are you going to call?"

"Just let me use it and you'll find out," he said as he walked around to my side of the counter, picked up the phone, and dialed.

"Hello. Yeah, hi, it's me. Hold on — he's right here." Arezzi then handed me the phone and said, "Somebody wants to talk to you."

I took the phone cautiously.

"Hello."

"Yeah, I hear you have a problem with me," growled the voice on the other end.

"Who is this?" I asked.

"Phil Mushnick," the voice answered.

Believe me, there was no hesitation on my part.

"Yeah, I've got a problem with you — YOU'RE A !@#$% LIAR!" I screamed.

Silence on the other end.

"I read your !@#$ column today — it's all !@#$. You know it and I know it! I was there. I taped every word McMahon said. You twisted around every quote to make him look like a liar, and you, some kind of righteous hero. You're full of !@#$, you piece of garbage!"

I don't even remember Mushnick's comeback. I know he had one, but whatever it was it landed on Helen Keller ears. Within minutes, I'd hung up on him. I turned and faced Arezzi, John was as white as Casper . . . I didn't need to say anything. Arezzi gathered his stuff from the office and left. I knew that it would be the last time I ever saw him.

The following day, Bob Raissman, a sports writer from the *New York Daily News*, called me to get my side of the steroid symposium story, and to find out what had happened with Phil Mushnick. I explained everything, from Mushnick's tainted story, to my audiotape with Vince's real comments, to my phone conversation with Father Goose, yadda, yadda, yadda.

The following day, Raissman wrote a story in the *Daily News* outlining how Vince McMahon had "bought me out." Yeah, Bobby, Vince McMahon is going to pay off Vince "Nobody" Russo in an effort to help clear his name. Yeah, and the *National Enquirer* really *does* have pictures of the alien that crashed in New Jersey. I would later find out that Mushnick and Raissman were good friends, with *The Post* getting an assist from *The News*. Journalism at its best.

Chapter 20

GOING IT ON MY OWN

Looking back now, the situation was a joke. My plan was to use John Arezzi's resources in order to establish myself in the wrestling business. But John's connections did *zero* for me. The truth is, I made the biggest connection on my own — Steve Planamenta at the World Wrestling Federation, and he was my next call.

I was compelled to call Planamenta to confirm that there was indeed a smear campaign in place, a well-oiled machine led by both Arezzi and Mushnick. I wasn't looking for anything — I just had to let someone know. I got Planamenta on the phone, filled him in on the last 24 hours — my thoughts concerning the symposium, Arezzi's reaction to it and my phone call with Mushnick. Relaying that information on to Planamenta made me feel much better. Planamenta thanked me for the call, but just before hanging up he asked, "What about the radio show?"

Good question. In my fury I'd forgotten all about the show.

Obviously, John and I weren't going to do it together anymore, but John couldn't afford to do it on his own and quite frankly I didn't know whether I still wanted to do it. But remember, Will the Thrill's was dying a slow death — I had to find another profession, and fast.

"The show? Quite frankly I hadn't even thought about it," I said to Planamenta.

"Well, look Vince, sit tight and I'll call you right back — I have an idea."

I hung up the phone, stumped. What could Planamenta possibly be talking about? I was both confused and excited. I was desperately looking for a break, and maybe this would be it!

Within minutes, Planamenta called back.

"Vince, I just spoke to my boss Basil DeVito and he suggested that you go on with the 'Pro Wrestling Spotlight' on your own — and we'll pay for it."

Wow! Talk about a break — this was the big daddy!

"What?" I answered.

"Do the show on your own — the wwf will pick up the tab," he confirmed. "Go ahead — call the radio station before Arezzi beats you to the punch. Call me back after you talk to them."

Planamenta then hung up.

I stood in the office of my video store trying to believe what I had just heard. Nothing, and I mean *nothing* in life is this easy. There had to be a hitch, and I had to sit down for a few minutes to figure out what it was. Again, thinking with my head and not my heart, Steve Planamenta wasn't just being Kris Kringle. He wasn't just handing over the keys to the North Pole unless there was something in it for the wwf. And, there was — the opportunity to finally rid themselves of a thorn in their side by the name of John Arezzi. Now, don't get me wrong, at his level John didn't make much noise. But he made enough, and if the wwf could rid themselves of an enemy — then off with his head. The truth was Steve Planamenta didn't care about Vince Russo, he was only using him. So they pay for the show this week — then what? Do I get cut off? I mean, who am I to the World

Wrestling Federation? I'll tell you who: just another mark trying to get into the business. This was strictly business, folks, and the business world is ruthless. It doesn't care about you or your family, it only cares about its gain. I was a pawn in Planamenta's game and I knew it. But what was my alternative?

Knowing the facts, I still had no choice, so I called the radio station and prepared to let the chips fall where they may. Unfortunately, they fell smack on the ground, because Arezzi had already beaten me to the punch. While I was talking to Planamenta, John was weaving his web of innocence to WEVD. Of course, John painted a much different picture, making me out to look like the bad guy while painting himself as the righteous hero trying to take down the corrupt business owner. I couldn't talk sense into the station manager. If John was good at anything — it was working people. The unknowing station manager bought his entire story hook, line and sinker and I was back at square one.

But remember, when you're back at square one, there's only one place to turn — within yourself.

Any wrestling fan who knows my history knows where I went from here. But, tell me, isn't there something amazing here? The situation Planamenta presented was my golden opportunity to get into the World Wrestling Federation. He'd laid the yellow brick road right before my feet. But it didn't happen. A huge opportunity was shut down with a resounding thud. Nine times out of ten, this would have been the end of the road . . . but not for me.

As the fairy tale continued, it took a detour and I found myself employed by the WWF after all. Think about how many times that happens. Think about how many people get not one, but two opportunities. When something is not meant to be, that simply doesn't happen. By my example, it is Saran Wrap clear that God himself had planned this for me. It was decided before I even had any say in it. That's why you can never force God's hand. You can't push for circumstances that you want, because it simply isn't up to you. It's up to God, and it happens on his clock. All you can do is pray that he shows you the road that was intended for you.

VINCE RUSSO

• • •

Last night was the Academy Awards, and I sit here first thing in the
morning at my store, behind my computer and *totally* disgusted.
Man, at my age I'm starting to feel like that grumpy old man Dana
Carvey used to portray on *Saturday Night Live*.

Somebody's got to *drag* Halle Berry out on the carpet for the
!@#$% speech she gave last night. Why the !@#$% does everybody
have to play that race card? Her bumbling babble was utter nonsense.
Does Halle seriously think that for the past 74 years the Academy
made the conscious decision to suppress the black woman from winning a little gold statute with a bald head? What African-American
actresses were overlooked for three quarters of a century because of
the color of their skin? Are you kidding me?

The only reason there may be a race issue today is because of people like her, with that kind of ridiculous mindset. If you deserve the
award — even if you are a !@#$% Umpa Lumpa, you're going to bag
it. Whoopi won it ten years back for her work in *Ghost*, what was that
all about? Oh — I get it — it was for "Supporting" Actress, not the
leading lady. Blow it out your !@#$%!!!

How often is a white player the MVP in the National Basketball
Association? What's the difference? Are all the sports writers around
the world prejudiced toward whites?

Just shut the !@#$% up and accept your meaningless trophy. Go
cry to Oprah — she'll put you on her show for an entire week. You
didn't hear Denzel get up on his soap box. No — the guy won because
he was the best actor this year, period.

I swear, I will *never* go see another Halle Berry movie! That is,
unless she decides to take her shirt off again.

Sorry about that last line, written by the old Vince. Again, I just wanted
to show you how far I've come. Whereas I still have rather strong convic-
tions about those who play the race card, I now have a whole different
view on award shows. *I hate them.*

If you want a red carpet, first-row glimpse at the "me, me, me" syndrome, just tune into any award show. Winner after winner after winner, you will experience more "I's" than an optometrist! It just boggles the mind to see how many Hollywood "superstars" think they did it all themselves. It was all them, no help, they just appeared here one day on earth, much like Arnold did in *The Terminator*. Just showed up in the middle of nowhere, naked and with nothing, and achieved "all this."

First of all, what is "all this" anyway? I would have to assume that "all this" refers to money. Money to spend on exotic trips, bathtubs made of gold, four Hummers, four garages to house those Hummers, guest cottages for guests who will never come, beds big enough to get lost in, gowns you'll wear once, shoes you'll never wear, caps so your teeth will glow and tucks so there'll be no tummy. You think I sound envious? Are you kidding me? I have "all that" and more — God is running my life.

Man, money is so overrated. We are driven by Wall Street's media campaigns, telling us we need this, we need that — now. Think about it — what do we really need to get by? Everything that God promised us he will provide to us anyway — food, shelter and clothing. If that's all we really need, and God promised to provide those things for us if we believe in him — then what are we stressing out over? Friends, if you take anything from this book, please believe that it's not money you should pursue. Money will never bring you what God will — never. I had money and it meant nothing — I now have God, and it means everything.

But getting back to the "I" Principle, why is it that people who win awards can thank people they barely know — but yet never thank the guy who really made it all possible? Why is the focus always on themselves, rather than God?

Chapter 21

RE-ENTER VICIOUS VINCENT

Usually I had a game plan; a well-thought-out game plan. I'd look at where I was, and decide where I wanted to go. Then I devised a strategy that would get me from point A to point B and put that strategy in motion. It was no different than winning Amy over. I had a plan and I saw it through. Back then, I felt that the most common cause of failure was not seeing your vision through.

When the going gets tough 90 percent of the population quit. That was the easy way out. I thought that was also the difference between making $50,000 a year or $500,000 a year — nothing more — nothing less. "All people are created equal" — that's a fact, so my question was, how do you stand out from the pack? Answer: brains and spaldings. I never felt, and still don't feel, like there's a need to kiss anybody's butt, because that will only get you so far. There will come a day when you will be judged. When you must stand alone, naked, and let your true self be seen. That is when those who take shortcuts are *done*.

I wasn't changing the course, kids. I had made a decision to get into the wrestling business, and guess what? — I was getting into the wrestling business, and I was doing it *my* way. When in doubt, I always went back to the basics. Strip away everything swirling around in your head and go back to square one. When I was first introduced to professional wrestling, I fell in love with one thing — the entertainment. It was a circus, and I wanted to be part of the big top, front and center. It wasn't about the politics, the Arezzis or the Mushnicks — it was all about the entertainment. So, if I was drawn to the entertainment, then entertainment would draw others. Provide entertainment, and they will come. Well, I knew of one guy who I thought was pretty entertaining, and his name was Vicious Vincent. Outspoken, brash, opinionated, he just didn't care what he said. I guess you could call him my alter ego. Vicious would say what everybody else wished they could say — but just didn't have the spaldings to say. Was he wrong at times? You bet he was, but that didn't matter. Vicious Vincent could become the Howard Stern of professional wrestling.

I've got to stop everything to give props to the genius, Howard Stern. I started listening to Howard back in 1983, when he was on WNBC in New York. I was only 22 years old, and as you read earlier, at a real tough point in my life. If I was inspired by anybody, it was Howard. The guy just didn't give a !@#$%. If he felt it, he said it. If it meant getting fired — so be it. He stood up for what he believed in. He knew what would work when others didn't have a clue. He stuck to his guns and never compromised himself. And, look at him today. His movie, *Private Parts,* should be an inspiration to us all. He represents the ultimate "!@#$ you!"

My wife despises me for allowing my kids to watch Howard Stern on the E channel, but I don't give a !@#$%. She doesn't get it. My kids should grow up with half the integrity Stern has, not to mention half the creativity.

Two years later, I can now clearly see that I was much like my "idol." Whether it was schtick or not, is not the point — the fact is, neither one of us were doing the right thing. We knew it — and we paid for it.

In my case, I almost lost my sanity. I let myself fall into such an abyss of depression that at times I didn't know whether to laugh or cry — and I often did both at the same time. Howard, on the other hand, not only lost his voice in many of his markets, he lost perhaps the thing most dear to him . . . his family. After resisting the pitfalls of radio and temptation for many years — Howard finally gave into his demons by divorcing Allison, his loyal better half and mother of his three children.

If you go against God's word there is just no winning. At times you may feel like you're on top of your game — but when the ninth inning rolls around you'll be shut out. Shut out of the only light that can save your life — the Lord Jesus Christ.

I had the name in a matter of minutes — "Vicious Vincent's World of Wrestling," a wrestling/variety radio show that would represent the way Vince Russo wanted to portray the wrestling business. No politics, no personal attacks, just pure entertainment. I would fund the show myself, and it would be the next step in my quest to work for the wwf, side-by-side with the master himself, Vince McMahon. In search of a home for the show, I contacted Arezzi's former station, where he and I began, wgbb out of West Babylon, New York. I signed a deal with the station manager, agreeing to pay somewhere in the neighborhood of $1,000 a week for a two-hour block on Friday nights. Even though my video stores were dying at the time, I would find a way to squeeze out enough cash to support my show. Amy again thought I was nuts. We couldn't pay our own bills because I wasn't even paying myself, but I would somehow find $1,000 dollars a week for a radio show? She just didn't understand. "Vicious Vincent's" was going to get me from point A to point B. I never doubted myself. I had a plan, I had a dream and I was going for it.

But the show would not succeed on Vicious Vincent alone. No, I needed to put my supporting cast in place. If I was going to be the Howard Stern of wrestling, then I needed my Robin Quivers. I looked no further than my childhood friend and business partner, Jim

Monsees. At the time, Jimmy didn't know squat about wrestling, but that was okay, I would carry him. I just needed a body next to mine to bounce things off.

To this day, Jimmy Monsees remains one of my best friends. Even though he is doing life in wwf prison — I put him in there myself about five years ago — and we don't talk as much as we should, I'll never forget what he had to offer as a friend. And, that's my point. In life, good friends are few and far between, so *value* them. Man, in the wrestling business I have taken a beating. You think people are your friends, but the minute you're on the outside looking in, as Apollo Creed said, "They drop you like a bad habit." It has happened to me over and over again. But true friends are there for life — no matter what. Jimmy would put himself on the line for me, whether I was Vince McMahon's right-hand man or a television salesman. It was never what I could do for him, it was always what he could do for me. I'll never forget that. I'll be there for him and the few good friends I have until the day I die.

My best friend in the world is a half-Italian, half-Puerto Rican guy by the name of Jeff Iorio. I've known Jeff now for, shoot, close to 30 years. Jeff is the kind of friend that I could see only once every 10 years, and it would be as if I'd seen him only yesterday. Think about how many friendships you have like that. That's what life is all about.

With friends, there are no boundaries.

You see, if Vicious Vincent was going to be a gimmick, or character, then Jimmy had to become one as well — thus, the birth of the "Mat Rat." Now only a "real" friend would ask a grown man to wear sunglasses and a top hat and talk like Minnie Mouse. But then again, only a real friend would do it. As the Mat Rat, Jimmy's job was to act like a complete fool and be the brunt of every joke I hurled his way. And he did it flawlessly. His character was so over-the-top that even I had a problem not cracking up on air. He was so good, I don't even think he realized it. The fact was, Mat Rat made the show. The kids loved him and the girls adored him — which was always the case with Jimmy in real life anyway.

"Vicious Vincent's World of Wrestling" — what a blast. The best time I ever had in the wrestling business. Skull Von Krush, a.k.a. Vito LoGrasso, was brought into the mix, making the show an absolute asylum. Skull was, and still is, a natural comic. He thrives on breaking you up, and on many occasions he had me losing it live. It got to the point that I couldn't even look at him without busting a gut. There's no question that we were on a roll, growing an audience at every turn in the road. The kids loved us; to them we were celebrities. Occasionally we would do our show live from an indoor batting cage called Whitey Ford's, and the tikes would show up in droves. We even organized monthly bus trips to WWF events for our fans — and get this, we even got paid to appear at a bar mitzvah.

There was no doubt that we were starting to make a name for ourselves. Using my Steve Planamenta contact, I was also able to occasionally get WWF stars on the show. When the WWF would come to our backyard, the Nassau Coliseum, we would do our show live in a dining hall prior to the event. There, about a thousand fans would be in attendance as we grilled WWF superstars right in front of their very eyes. Early on, I even had the privilege to interview Ric Flair. It was everything that I wanted a sports entertainment show to be. In time, we had syndicated the show — ourselves — into seven different markets around the country. No question we were well on our way. There was just one small problem, I was flat broke!

At this point — Will the Thrill's Video was dead, closed for business. What a shame. We were no doubt ahead of our time. To this day my dad, now in his 70s, won't even set foot in a Blockbuster. Screw them and their blue-and-khaki uniforms. Corporate America is heartless — plain and simple.

Chapter 22

YA WANT THE 3, OR THE 5?

So now what do I do? Oh — I forgot to tell you we had another kid along the way. That's right, a son named VJ. He entered the world blue because my wife needed two shots of Demerol to spit him out, but he's fine now — just a little whacked. Even though I cried like an infant when he popped out as well, I was almost too busy to notice. Here I was with a wife, *two* kids, a mortgage and no scratch. I had to concentrate on my goal, I had to make this thing happen at all costs — unfortunately, including what it cost my own family. While Will the Thrill's Video was on life support, I picked up a part-time job at an appliance store called P.C. Richards and Sons, the "Appliance Giant" of Long Island. Was I proud? No, I was embarrassed. At the time, I felt the job was so beneath me that I had to crawl on all fours just to get in the front door. But you know what? You do what you've got to do — especially when a family is depending on you. When Will the Thrill's finally closed its doors, I began working full-time at the Appliance Giant.

The more I write, the more comes back to me. I have to laugh when I remember a story passed on to me by a WWF employee, who shall remain nameless, concerning an open forum Vince held with his employees at Titan Tower, days after I left.

First off, let me say that the occasional "Open Forum with the Chairman of the Board" conferences were started at my suggestion, when I told Vince he had to address the troops as to why he was walking around the offices with a black eye — a story I'll get into later. But anyway, days after I left the company, and my name was all over the internet, Vince held one of his open sessions. An employee who was new to the company naïvely asked Vince, "Who is this Vince Russo I keep reading about on the internet?"

Without missing a beat, Vince said, "Vince Russo was a television salesman I gave an opportunity to."

Yeah, Vince was Walt Disney — he did it all by giving me the "opportunity," and I did nothing — typical Vince propaganda. Even after I had gone, he couldn't give credit where credit was due. He was the genius, and I was just some guy selling toasters.

Man, you have a way of just never forgetting stuff like that.

Perhaps my biggest pet peeve is the failure to just give credit where it is due. This wasn't just Vince, we all seem to have this flaw. Why is it so difficult for us to tip our hats to somebody rather than take all the credit ourselves? What is it about giving your brother a pat on the back that we're so afraid of? "Vicious Vincent's" would never have been successful without Jimmy, I would have never been successful without Amy, the WWF would not have been successful without every single person busting their butts onstage and behind the scenes. Why can't we just admit that?

I have to admit, when my credibility was attacked — as it still sometimes is — I became defensive; "I did it, I did it, I did it." Fortunately, when the grace of God filled my soul, it was no longer about me, it was about everybody else. I learned to give thanks and praise to everybody around me. That's the difference, being a Christian — everything about you changes. You just see the world differently.

At P.C. Richards, again and again I was the Salesman of the Month. Nobody could touch me. I sold extended three-and five-year warranties as easy as you'd sell Wimpy hamburgers. It just came easy to me. The rest of the salesmen despised me, but the truth was I just worked harder than they did. My first year at P.C. I brought down about $43,000, but it still wasn't enough. After paying all the bills and putting food on the table, there was just no scratch left to pay for a radio show.

The end was near for Vicious Vincent. I was on life-support, sucking on the last breath of air. But I wasn't going to let it happen — I couldn't. I had a plan, remember? Every night I would remind Amy of that plan. She still thought I was nuts and maybe for that reason alone I couldn't fail. Call it pride, call it whatever you want, but I knew that I had to see this thing through. But how? What was I going to do — pull a *Dog Day Afternoon* and rob a bank? No, I had to be practical. So I went back to basics.

Again, I was at that point in my life where you just roll the dice and you go for broke. But to get into the game you have to be willing to lose it all. Seven I win — snake eyes I lose. But, before you roll — you need to have confidence.

At this point, nine out of ten people would have written a letter to Vince McMahon. Give me a break! Do you think Vince McMahon actually reads his mail? Especially a letter addressed to him from someone he didn't know? Yeah, I had met him at the steroids symposium, but I would have had to have been out of my mind to believe that he would have remembered me. The truth was, Vince McMahon didn't know Vince Russo from Knucklehead Smith (if you don't know who Knucklehead Smith is you've *really* missed out on life). No, I had to come up with a more sensible alternative. Then it hit me . . . Linda McMahon. How many people, or marks, do you actually think had written to LINDA McMahon looking for a job? She *had to* read her mail. As the vice-president of Titan Sports at the time, many referred to her as the "business brains" behind the empire. Whereas Vince was running the show on the stage, Linda was directing traffic behind the scenes. It was a longshot, but what did I have to lose? I sat down and penned Linda a heartfelt letter. I told her of my trials and tribulations in the wrestling business; my dreams, goals and aspirations; and that I was literally hanging on by my last Washington (dollar bill). If my next step wasn't to work with the wwf , then there would be no step at all. I'd be a crippled wannabe, peddling Sylvanias at the Long Island Appliance Giant.

Chapter 23

THE PHONE CALL
HEARD 'ROUND THE WORLD

After a few more weeks, I was ready to pull the plug on "Vicious Vincent's." The financial burden became overwhelming. In my mind I tried to justify it. I had tried — done everything that I could — it just wasn't happening.

Ring-a-ling!

It was a weekday, sometime in March of '92. I remember being at the kitchen sink doing the dishes.

Why I was washing the dishes I'll never know. Real men shouldn't do housework. It's not in our nature. How many times did you see Archie Bunker with a vacuum cleaner in his hands? Be a man's man, for cryin' out loud!

Let's face it — that's what we all get married for. We all want to be taken care of, waited upon and loved. If you don't agree then you're either full of !@#$ or gay. Men do men's work; women do women's work — *period!* So why in God's name was I doing dishes?

Man, what was I thinking? I'm embarrassed by some of the things I wrote for the original draft of this book — but they need to remain as examples of how God changed my life. It's ironic that I used the phrase "in God's name." Nothing I did back then was in God's name — *nothing*. It was all in my name. I was my lord; I was my savior. And look where it got me.

"Hello, is this Vince Russo?"

"Yes," I replied.

"Hi, my name is Liz DeFabio; I'm Linda McMahon's assistant."

Here it was — the *Queen Mary!*

"Linda McMahon would like to speak with you."

What can I say? My strategy had worked like a charm. I had Linda McMahon on the phone. This was my opportunity — I sold like a salesman one percent short of his commission with only 30 minutes left in the month. I sold, sold, sold and sold some more. I barely let Linda get a word in edgewise, but from what I can remember, she mentioned to me that they were looking for freelance writers for the *World Wrestling Federation Magazine,* and that someone would be getting in touch with me shortly after WrestleMania IX, that weekend. Man, I had done it — I had freaking done it! My foot was in the door. That's all I needed: just a little crack.

After hanging up the phone I was on a Cheech and Chong high. Again, I had taken that chance. I had taken my spaldings in my hand and taken that next step. I was on my way, it really didn't matter where. All I knew was that I had been given the opportunity I needed to stay alive.

Just take one second and count how many "I's" appear in the previous paragraph. I did this, I did that — now "I" know exactly what was wrong with my life!

I took credit for *everything* back then. It was all about me, and how wonderful I was. How sad. How many of us go about our everyday lives doing the same thing, giving ourselves credit for everything we've done, everything we have. It's not just those actors and actresses I talked about earlier — it's all of us. Then we wonder why we go through the hardships in life. God is never going to answer any of our prayers as long as we put ourselves before him. But, the truth is, we need to come to our end in order to find his beginning.

Whether or not we want to admit it, God is responsible for everything we have. We've achieved or "earned" nothing without him. Once we come to that realization — and thank him for all he's done — then and only then will he bless us with the rewards that really matter in life.

True to her word, I was contacted the following week by the editor of the WWF *Magazine*, Ed Ricciuti. Since he called me at home and I was at work, I had to return his call from the Appliance Giant. I'll never forget it: when I called him back the guy answered the phone Dean Martin–bombed — seven sheets to the wind. I could barely understand him, but I didn't care. An Italian editor juiced up on a little vino — that was okay in my book! Ed immediately took a liking to me and me to him. It may have had something to do with the fact both our last names ended in a vowel.

Man, it means so much to me to be 100 percent Italian. I'm so proud of my heritage, and no matter who or what you are — there's nothing like Italians. We stick together, we look out for each other, that's just in our nature. In our eyes, Italians can do no wrong — it's always "them other guys." I think my pride comes from my late grandfather. I truly believe John Savarino's influence helped shape me into the person I am today. He was such a proud man — a "man" in every sense of the word. Stubborn, stuck in his ways, strong-willed, strong-minded, everything Vince Russo is.

As I said earlier, as the years passed and my grandfather grew older, I did everything in my power to avoid seeing him. I just couldn't picture Granddad as this fragile, old man. It would have busted my heart to see him like that. He always represented this strong individual to me, a man who was in every sense a man. Then one day, he died. After surviving numerous heart attacks and outliving my grandmother, he passed on. He was never the same after she died.

I miss my grandparents so much.

Looking back today, everything takes on a whole new meaning. My grandparents were together for over 50 years, and my grandmother went to church religiously at least once or twice a week. On the other hand, my grandfather never went to a single mass.

When Nana suddenly passed away, out of nowhere, my grandfather began to read the Bible every night. Before God embraced me, I never even gave it a second thought. Today . . . today I understand.

My grandfather loved my grandmother so much that he wanted to be assured he'd see her again — as stubborn as he was, he realized there was only one way to do that — and that was through God. You want to talk about miracles? Vince Russo accepting Jesus Christ as his lord and savior is nothing compared to John J. Savarino opening his heart to God. My grandfather was the strongest-willed man that I have ever known — but when Nana passed away, even he knew that he had come to the end of his life. Even he reached a point where he realized he could no longer go it alone.

A few months ago, my mother gave me the bible that my grandfather bought and read out of after Nana passed. The emotion, the love I feel every time I open that book is overwhelming. I can feel the presence of my grandfather, praying to God that one day he would see his precious Anna once again.

So here I am, TV salesman by day, Vince Russo, freelance WWF writer by night. Ricciuti started me at $150 a story, doing an average of two stories a month. Man, was the World Wrestling Federation a different animal at that point. It was still in that '80s phase of bigger-than-life cartoon characters, only by the '90s, you were already starting to see signs that it just wasn't going to work anymore. I remember doing my first piece on Bryan Clarke, who went by the name of Adam Bomb at that point. "Adam Bomb"? I don't know if the gimmick was a bigger joke now or then. But, I was still just happy to have my foot in the door. Whatever Ricciuti asked me to write, I wrote. To this day, that story on Clarke hangs in a frame in my office. That was more than a decade ago. Man, what a piece of fictional horse-poop. It's so hard for me to read today. But in my mind, at the time, it was nothing short of Hemingway.

After writing for a couple of months, Ed was sky high on me. Only problem was I didn't know if it was him or the whiskey talking. But I'm pretty sure it was him. For what it was — my written word was good. Man, I used to hound Ed every week for stories, much the same way I hounded the Fruitinator for a Yogi Bear lunchbox when I was going into kindergarten. "What next, what next?" I would ask. Then one day, after writing volumes of *Aesop's Fables*, Ed said, "How about interviewing Shawn Michaels, live and in person, for the next issue of the WWF magazine?" I've got to sit here and chuckle now. What a big deal that was to me at the time. It meant everything. My passion to get where I wanted had priority over everything. Amy, Will and VJ came a distant second. What a horse's ass I was.

Chapter 24

MY CATERING WITH SHAWN

My meeting with Shawn Michaels was to take place backstage at the Poughkeepsie Civic Center prior to *Monday Night Raw*. At that point, *Raw* was still in its infancy, and Vince was looking for his niche on the USA Network. Shawn was more or less in the same boat. For most of his career he had teamed with Marty Jannetty in the Midnight Rockers, a tag team that had moved from the old AWA to the WWF and was well ahead of its time. Due to some personal issues Marty was dealing with, Shawn was left to go solo. This was his first shot at making it on his own. A lot of people don't realize this about Shawn, but like many of us, he too grew up a wrestling fan. Since his teens he knew what he wanted to do and he followed that dream regardless of any discouragement thrown his way. Shawn was always considered a longshot, because back in the day Vince McMahon was in love with monsters (there are those who say he still is) — the six-foot-eight, 350 pound, genetic freaks. Shawn was under six feet, and less than 200 pounds soaking wet on days he ate potato chips and Scooter Pies. (Man, if you don't know what a Scooter Pie is, I feel your pain!) Physically, his chances weren't good. But wow, did he have heart.

●　　●　　●

Before I begin my assessment of certain WWF superstars, let me first say that the views expressed throughout this book are simply my opinion. These are my personal views, based on the time I spent with the individuals I'm talking about. It is neither fact nor fiction — simply my impressions.

Now then, about Shawn. . . . I've always felt a special bond with Shawn Michaels, maybe because it all really started with him that day in Poughkeepsie.

Shawn and I had a love/hate relationship from the beginning. My impression? He was probably a bit spoiled growing up, as many of us were. Shawn had a close-knit relationship with his parents — especially his mother. Mrs. Hickenbottom cherished the ground Shawn walked on, and he in turn treated her like a queen. Whenever I saw Shawn around his parents, he treated them both with the utmost respect and for that I applaud him, loudly. However, as an adult, if Shawn Michaels didn't get his way, he was difficult to deal with at times. And when he wasn't happy with something, he let you know. On more occasions than one I witnessed Shawn standing up to Vince — with Vince completely backing down. Now whether it was a case of Vince just not wanting to deal with him, I don't know, but nine out of ten times Shawn got his way with the boss. I never saw anybody else confront Vince the way Shawn did — *ever*. You've got to admit, the guy had a pair of brass spaldings on him. Deep down, I guess that's what I admired the most about him — he wasn't afraid to say anything to anybody. As a matter of fact, he was the only wrestler to ever physically threaten me — a story I'll get into later.

During Shawn's run as WWF Champion, I wrote many of his in-ring promos (the monologues he would cut) and almost every one of his pre-tapes (a taped promo that would be used at a later time) in which he would hawk tickets to the next "show nearest you." Now, don't misunderstand me, it wasn't that Shawn wasn't capable of writing his own schtick, because he was. It was just that Shawn wasn't capable of coming up with the verbiage Vince wanted him to say. At the time, Vince wanted Shawn to be this sappy, make-you-want-to-puke babyface — the total opposite of who he was. Shawn was a rebel inside and outside the ring — but Vince wanted him to be George Clooney. I had to write such vanilla promos for Shawn — we both questioned it, but Vince was the boss. No offense intended, but at the time, Vince seemed so far out of date it wasn't even funny. Eighties wrestling just wasn't working. All the old rules were breaking down day-by-day.

Rocky times would come between Shawn and Vince over the idea of him dropping the WWF title to Stone Cold Steve Austin at Wrestle-Mania XIV. At that time, Austin had become the golden boy, and Shawn felt as if Vince was just kicking him to the curb. Shawn became real bitter, real fast. And I can't say that I blame him. Vince did, and still does have a tendency to go from project to project. Well, weeks before the WrestleMania match, Shawn wouldn't even speak to McMahon. And of course, Vince didn't want to deal with the Heart-break Kid either. I was made the go-between for a few weeks. Man, it got stone cold ugly! Not only was Shawn threatening not to drop the strap to Austin at WrestleMania, but he told me, and I quote, "Tell Vince the belt will be at home on my mantle if he wants it." Then, about a week from the Granddaddy of Them All, Shawn cut a scathing promo on the boss on *Raw* that I will never forget. Every word was unscripted, with Shawn basically telling Vince — in front of a national audience — how he truly felt about him. But in the end, Shawn, being a professional, laid down for Austin in the middle of the ring at Mania.

Personally, though others have had their problems with Michaels, I really admired him. While he may have been difficult to deal with at times, I must say this: for starters, no question, Shawn was the best in-ring performer I had ever seen. Night after night he put his body on the line, not caring about the consequences. Unfortunately that would catch up with him later, as a severe back injury, along with some personal demons, would fatally stifle his career. Yeah, personal demons — something else we will get into later, because Shawn wasn't the only victim of his environment.

Looking back, Shawn Michaels may have been the first true sports entertainer. The guy had it all — the wrestling ability, the look, the jive — he just dripped charisma.

Currently, Shawn is once again back in the WWE fold. Only this time, something is very different — Shawn is a born-again Christian and a devout follower of Jesus Christ. I can't begin to tell you how happy I am for him. Following much different paths, both Shawn and I had many heartaches in the business. On two different levels, we were both becoming something that we were not. There is no question that we both could have been headed for disaster, and then the guiding light was cast upon us; the light that led us out of our physical, emotional and mental darkness and changed both our lives forever.

Where was I? Oh yeah, Poughkeepsie.

I couldn't say, "Screw Ricciuti," because to this day I love the guy. He actually gave me my break in the business. The guy could easily have been intimidated by me and buried me with Linda McMahon. I mean, that's the way things often work in the business. But not Ed; he did the opposite. The man put me over like a father selling his son to the little-league coach. But on this day, I said, "Screw Ricciuti!" The bald man threw me to the wolves! Here I am, a mark, greener than Herman Munster, and I'm just going to walk backstage into their world because I have a backstage pass glued to my chest? Was I nervous? I was staining my drawers! But I had to get the story. I learned that in Journalism 101 — get the story at any expense.

So I walk into the back like I'm somebody, chest puffed out, the whole deal. What? Was I trying to be like one of the boys? I probably was, but regardless — *I was in*. Aside from the backstage area of the

Poughkeepsie Civic Center being a dive, to this day I'll never forget the first thing I saw — the babyfaces, playing cards with the heels. Of course I knew wrestling was fake, but to see it with your own two eyes — what a trip the first time around. I remember the babyface was Hacksaw Jim Duggan, a legend at the time. And there he was playing poker with a no-good heel! They were all there, from Yokozuna to Doink the Clown. Like a bolt of lightning it struck me — I was in Bizarroland! This was straight out of a Saturday morning cartoon. Grown men dressed up in Halloween costumes, all eating together like one big happy family. For a second I was a 12-year-old kid again. The excitement of the moment began to drain the nervousness out of me — that is, until someone grabbed me by the arm.

"Who the !@#$% are you?" asked this Crocodile Dundee–sounding gentleman.

Wait a minute — that was no gentlemen — that was Tony Gerea, former WWF superstar! I grew up on Tony Gerea and his tag team partner, the Happy Hawaiian, Dean Ho! Now the guy was yelling at me! What an honor!

"I'm Vince Russo," I answered back. "I'm a freelance writer for the WWF *Magazine*. I'm here to interview Shawn Michaels."

"Wait a minute, I'll get him," said Tony.

Now forget the excitement, it was back to extreme nervousness. In a few minutes I was going to be face-to-face with the Heartbreak Kid himself. At this point, all I could think about was Vicious Vincent — the master plan to get my foot in the door. All those times my own wife had doubted me, never understanding my vision, my dream. I was on the inside — I was on my way.

The interview with Shawn went exceptionally well. I don't know, once he was sitting there right in front of me I just felt totally comfortable. The reality had sunk in, and at that point I was just doing my job. Maybe I just felt like I belonged in this world. Maybe it was because it was a land of misfits, a subculture of human beings who didn't subscribe to everyday, normal life. My whole life I had felt that way, I had felt different — like there was just something else out there for me. Was this it? Was the world of sports entertainment my Mecca?

Following that memorable night in Poughkeepsie, it was back to the real world at the Appliance Giant. Without breaking a sweat, I continued to exceed the other salesmen by leaps and bounds. I was now a man on a mission, clearly seeing the road ahead of me. This job was merely a bridge to my future.

Seeing the light at the end of the tunnel is what continues to get me through life, day by day. You've got to have a game plan. You've got to know where you're going and envision yourself there. There have been so many times in my life where I was close to falling into a deep depression because of what I was doing at the time. Come on, even if you hate me, you've got to admit that I'm better than a TV salesman. But I had to do it. I had to suck it up to get to that next place. I always kept myself positive. I kept reminding myself why I was doing this. Again — you've just got to have the utmost confidence in yourself. It's mind over matter, plain and simple. Right now, I'm in a place I don't particularly want to be in, but again, it's a stepping stone, something I need to do right now. Tomorrow? That's a whole other book.

Seeing the light at the end of the tunnel is what continues to get me through life, day by day. . . .

I wrote that two years ago, and just looking closely at those words, it's evident what I was experiencing not only at that time, but since I graduated college.

Before I was saved, my life was a chase. I was always going after the next thing because I was never satisfied. No matter what I did, no matter what I accomplished, there was this constant void that remained empty, hungry. Just look at my life, where I've brought you thus far — it was always on to the next thing, the next thing, the next thing. It was the amazing race, and the destination was unknown. I was that gerbil we've all seen running around on a steel wheel, always finishing where I started. I was in constant search of something. I thought it was a lot of things: fame, money, success. However each and every time a hurdle was jumped, I still felt the same.

The only one who could change that, was my savior and friend. In Jesus I found peace, contentment, *full* satisfaction. The looking stopped and the living began. Unless you've experienced it, it's hard to understand. But it's real. Read my words. Look at me then, and look at me now. You're not looking at the same person.

That was the purpose of this book, and I thank God that he blessed me by letting me write it over two years ago, only to comment on it in a new light. It was his way of showing you what he does to a life once he is allowed to take over.

I am a walking, talking, living, breathing testament.

Day by day, my motivation remained that next call from Ed, that next assignment. I must have told the guy a 100 times over how I wanted to work full-time for the Federation. At the time there was just nothing available, so I continued to freelance. I can remember those Saturday afternoons like they were yesterday. I'd be doing a monster day at the Appliance Giant, 9 a.m. to 10 p.m., but when the wwf came on all the tvs at noon — I would stop, look and know I would be there someday. Little did I know it would be sooner rather than later.

Chapter 25

RICCIUTI OUSTED!

It was like any other normal day at the Appliance Giant — *brutal* — when I was paged with a phone call. It was Ed. I was always so pumped up to hear from him, as his voice always reminded me of why I was hawking CD players at this lowly place.

"Vince . . . Vince fired me. I'm no longer editor of the magazine."

My first reaction was shock. I mean, how do you fire a guy like Ed Ricciuti? The guy was, and still is, one of the best on the planet, a true gentleman who always looks out for everyone else before himself. I just didn't get it. Ed was such a likeable guy . . . how do you fire him?

"Vince . . . you should apply for my job."

"WHAT?"

I had only been freelancing for some eight months. I never expected this to happen — not this quickly. I wasn't even over the fact that Ed had been fired. But there he was, thinking about me before he'd even made it to the unemployment line. I've got to tell you, people like Ed

Ricciuti are few and far between, especially in the wrestling business. Again, I'm sure part of it went back to that Italian thing — we always look out for each other. But in writing this book, I've realized that if it weren't for Ed I would *never* have had the opportunity to achieve what I did in the WWF. Ed was my mentor, and I will never forget what he did for me.

So here it was — my shot. It had taken me well over two years to finally get the break I'd been looking for. There was no doubt that the table was now set — all I needed to do was serve up the White Castles!

For those of you who don't know what they are, you've again been cheated. I first discovered the Castle some time in the late '60s or early '70s, during the routine Sunday trips to my grandparents' house.

Now keep in mind, White Castle was supposed to be a white, shiny, sparkling, bright, gleaming eating establishment. But inside, it was filthier than my son VJ's room. I mean an eatery — filthy, dirty? But that was the beauty of the place — nobody cared about the appearance. Man, it was all about those "Castles." A little square piece of brown meat smothered with onions, plopped with a pickle, drowned in ketchup and then neatly, *neatly* placed in a little bun exactly the size of the miniature burger. Unbelievable. There was nothing like them, and still isn't. "Krystals?" Are you kidding me? Nothing but a weak imitation.

Perhaps the best thing about White Castle was the belly-churning, onion-breath stinking *agita* (an Italian term for when food repeats on you). Oh, the *agita*. You would be burping up those bad boys for weeks — and they'd be tasting better every time.

The next day, I formally applied for the job of editor of the *World Wrestling Federation Magazine*. The person that would be doing the hiring was a British gentleman by the name of Tom Emanuel. Emanuel headed up the publications department, and had been doing so for several years. Tom had an excellent relationship with Linda McMahon, who by now *had* to know the name Vince Russo. So I did the resumé, got an audience with Emanuel, and literally once again sold like an MCI solicitor. Then I waited, waited, waited and waited some more. Man, that time was painful. Let's face it — I was either in or out. If I wasn't good enough to be the editor, then where was I going? What? Was I going to freelance for the next five years? No way — this was it, in or out.

Several weeks passed, during which I tortured myself mentally and emotionally. Man, I hate that part about getting a job. I guess that's why I hate working for people in general. Enough of the waiting game — was I in or not? Somebody tell me please!

Finally, Emanuel did. With that one phone call my entire life would change forever. With the words, "You've got the job," the Appliance Giant was dead, and Vince Russo was welcomed into Titan Tower. What part of that don't you understand? *Titan Tower!* The same Titan Tower where, only a few short months earlier, sometime in the middle of the night, the Mat Rat and I had delivered a demo tape to a security guard at the front door looking like two of the biggest marks you've ever seen! Captured on this cheap, plastic VHS tape were all our hopes and dreams of getting into the glorious "Fed." (I later found out only Howard Finkel, the WWF ring announcer, saw that tape.) Titan Tower — Mecca. The dream had come true. I'm not going to lie to you; when I hung up with Emanuel, I cried. They weren't tears of joy, but rather tears of relief. I knew at that time that it was a make-it-or-break-it situation, and to be honest with you — there was no plan B. There was never a plan B with me. The way I looked at it at the time, you only need a plan B if you forsee plan A failing. My mindset was: don't let it fail; see it through until it plays out just like you visualized. For me it was always about following the dream, no matter how difficult the journey became. See it, believe it, live it. My only problem was I never imagined, years later, that dream would become my worst nightmare.

When I was on my quest to get a job with the WWF — I referred to it as "my" dream. It was "my" dream, and "I" was going to make it happen. Nobody else was going to have any say about it. It was what I wanted.

How many of us live this way? How many of us decide that we're going to be what we want to be, and that's just the way it's going to be. If that's the case, then why didn't I play baseball for the San Francisco Giants during my prime? It's not because I didn't want to, but rather because I didn't have the gift. I think they call it the God-given gift. Sinatra had the God-given gift to sing; Groucho Marx had the God-given gift to make people laugh; Tiger Woods has the God-given gift to golf. The truth is, we all have a gift. We just need to go with our strengths (they're our strengths for a reason), pray and then God will unravel his plan for how we are to use those gifts to glorify *his* kingdom.

But keep one thing in mind — we aren't going to dictate to God what our role is going to be. If we do, then we are attempting to please ourselves, and that's not what God intended. As I stated earlier, that's why some guys never make it in wrestling. It's not necessarily that they weren't good enough — but perhaps it was not God's plan for them to be wrestlers. If they do become wrestlers because it was "their" desire and "their" dream, how many of them walk away miserable, years later, simply because they didn't listen, and didn't follow God's plan?

Given the current state of the WWE, many ask me why I don't go back to Vince. "Imagine the money you could make." Well, the answer is simple — that's not in God's plan. Writing wrestling was my God-given gift. God's plan is right here, right now, in me glorifying his name through these words.

God — you are everything. Without you I am nothing. Lead and I will follow. I am here for one reason — to carry out your plan.

Chapter 26

WELCOME TO TITAN TOWER

To those who say Vince Russo never paid his dues: digest this. Okay, so I was going to the big time — Titan Tower, located in beautiful Stamford, Connecticut. One small problem — I lived in beautiful Holbrook, Long Island. Yeah, I was going to move, but you don't sell your condo in a day. So, every morning the journey would begin: the Long Island Expressway, over the Throgs Neck Bridge, to 95, to Stamford, Connecticut. The journey was five hours a day — in traffic — door to door. I can still remember my first day on the job. When my trek was over at about 9 o'clock at night, I pulled into the parking lot of my condo complex thinking: "What have you done? Was it all worth this?" For that first week I was second-guessing myself every minute of the day, but things worked themselves out, and I finally sold my condo and relocated my family to Stamford.

Fortunately, the adjustment wasn't difficult, as Stamford was a lot like Long Island. But until we were able to find an affordable house,

Amy, myself, Will, VJ and Cagney, my mixed mutt, all had to contend with each other in a one-room apartment the company was putting us up in. Man that was insanely ridiculous! But again, we managed until we found that affordable house. I say affordable, because I was hired at $60,000 a year. I know that's not much, but at the time it was a fortune to me! I had never seen that kind of coin before. But in Connecticut, what you got for the dollar was limited. Put it this way — the Flintstones had a bigger house. Still, I was happy — that is until I was immediately reminded of Corporate America.

Man, I almost forgot what it was like working in Corporate America. I mean, there's nothing worse than wearing a suit and tie to work every day, especially when you're working for a wrestling company. Give me a break!

Another big pet peeve? Why do guys wear suits and ties to work? Who agreed to this unexplained ritual? Why must society always dictate everything we do or say? Why are grown men expected to follow this outdated dress code? Nobody wears a suit and tie hanging around the house. No — we wear loose clothing, preferably sweats — so we can be comfortable. So, why would we want to be *uncomfortable* eight hours a day, five days a week? A tight collar around your neck is the equivalent of wearing pants that are too tight. It's so uncomfortable, how can guys do it everyday? How do Pat Riley and Phil Jackson coach basketball games while rompin' and stompin' up and down the sidelines in Gucci suits? To me, it's one of the mysteries of life. When I went to Titan, I played the game of "Dress Up Ken" from March of '94 until December 31, 1994. My New Year's resolution was to *never* wear a shirt and tie to work again — and I never have.

Ironically enough, over a period of time, everybody followed my lead and left their shirts and ties at home. That is, of course, with the exception of those trying desperately to get ahead.

While I'm on the subject, when I was first hired by the WWF there was also an unwritten law that you weren't allowed to have facial hair. For whatever reason, Vince *hated* facial hair. Is that a questionable position, or what? I mean look what the beard did for Lincoln, or how about Lennon, in his early Yoko era. One guy freed slaves, while the other gave peace a chance. Were they bad guys because they skipped the Track II every morning?

I started at Titan literally weeks before WrestleMania X. So as you can imagine, it was a thrill to actually attend the Granddaddy of Them All as an employee, especially since it was being held in my own backyard — Madison Square Garden. My two fondest memories of that grand event were Linda McMahon telling me to "lose my gum" at the fan festival, and having the privilege of personally telling Owen Hart immediately following the spectacle what a great match he'd had against his brother Bret.

I can go on and on about Owen Hart, and later I will, but I'll stick to the story for now. WrestleMania X was the first time Owen and Bret worked a match of such magnitude together in the federation. In my opinion — they not only tore the house down — they ripped the plants from the garden. On a personal level, the match meant so much to the brothers. I don't know if I've ever met any two individuals with more pride than Bret and Owen Hart. It was just in their bloodlines. The Harts were a wrestling family, and even when they were boys, their father, Stu Hart, a wrestling legend in his own right, always expected a lot. Now don't misunderstand me, Stu was no Great Santini — the boys *wanted* to make him proud, and they always did. The business meant everything to Bret and Owen. Never, and I mean *never*, would these two guys just go through the motions. Every time out, they performed as if it was their last match — and you know what? The fans knew it, and respected them for it. There is just so much to say about these two men.

To this day, WrestleMania X really stands out, for several reasons. Of course the first is that it was my first major event as part of the Titan family. But the second? Little did I know that from that early high, everything would come crashing down around me. My Mecca would soon turn out to be a knife-wielding ghetto in the South Bronx.

Chapter 27

WORLD WRESTLING
FEDERATION MAGAZINE

So now I've got the office, the suit and tie, and I'm the editor of *World Wrestling Federation Magazine.* In those first few weeks, I was simply getting my feet wet. Let's face facts — what had I ever been the editor of, aside from my college newspaper, *The Shield?* It was a joke that I was even given the position. What kind of experience did I have? I'd watched wrestling as a kid? I'd hosted a radio show? I freelanced an article on Adam Bomb? Yeah, you're right — I had no business being there . . . but I was. So to educate myself, quickly, I buddied-up to the assistant editor, Louie Gianfriddo.

The last paragraph was written two years ago — at a time when Jesus Christ and myself were strangers at best. What's ironic now are my own words . . . "I had no business being there . . . but, I was." Wow, those words are sautéed in divine truth. I had no business being there . . . but I was. So who placed me there? And why?

I am so blessed to have the privilege of having my own words to reflect on from before I was saved. For those of you who think Russo is nuts, just look at the then and the now.

"I had no business being there . . . but I was."

Somebody had a reason for my being there — somebody I wouldn't personally meet until some 10 years later.

About six or seven years my junior, to know Louie was to love him. Talk about a Guinea! This guy was Capone, DeNiro, Stallone, Gandolfini, Pesci and Sinatra all rolled into one. Louie G. wrote the book on Guinea! The accent, the dress, the attitude, the little Guinea moustache — the cheeks swollen all the way out to Queens because his face was so overloaded with dip. I'm talking the real deal here. I swear to you, this kid had to be running numbers by day. And he was just so fascinated with gangsters. He knew every gangster, their nicknames, who ratted on who, who rubbed out who — he not only wrote the book on goodfellas, in his mind he lived it. *Fahgettaboutit!*

I immediately took a liking to this kid — again it was the loyalty thing. Louie was more loyal than a kennel full of basset hounds. If anyone messed with me, they messed with Louie. And believe me, this was an asset. Even though he was five-foot-nothing, Louie could deadlift more than 500 pounds. The guy was an amateur bodybuilder who won many a contest in his day.

Louie always compared the wrestling business to the mafia. "Are you on the inside, or the outside?" was his philosophy. "Cause if you're on the outside, it's no good. They'll never accept you as one of theirs." Well, no doubt I was on the outside, until Louie brought me in. He taught me the rules of "the road." In those early days, I traveled with Louie as much as possible, wanting to learn all about the life of the boys. The fact was, Louie was one of the best teachers I ever had. Louie taught me what the wrestling business was all about.

After hangin' and bangin' with Louie for a few weeks, I got a good sense of this new world. Behind the curtain was a society within itself. The laws were their own, and the rules of the real world just didn't exist. Being back in the civilized world right now, it's hard to explain. I felt like Alice in Wonderland. The morals were different, the values were different and the language was different. The jargon used when two guys are going over a match . . . I don't care how long you get hooked on phonics — you just weren't going to understand it. And *trust?* You can throw trust down a New York City street sewer. In this world, nobody trusts anybody. If you're not paranoid and constantly looking over your shoulder, you will get zoomed, and zoomed hard. No matter what anybody else tells you — it's a cutthroat business, a sports-entertainer-eat-sports-entertainer world. Like I said earlier, there are no morals — none. If you're the spouse of a sports entertainer and you're reading this book, I'm sorry. The chances are high that your husband or wife is cheating on you. As a matter of fact — just bet the house on it! It's the nature of the beast, kids — life on the road, living out of a suitcase, yadda yadda yadda.

The self-contained subculture of the business is what fascinated me. I'd always made an effort to look at things from the outside-in. It was mind-blowing, and the part of the business that still intrigues me the most. You'd have to have lived it to truly understand. So many of these guys couldn't exist in the "real" world. For many of them, wrestling is all they have ever known. They've spent more time in a locker room than they have in their own homes — and the wrestling world becomes their norm. But it never was for me. I hated life on the road. Every minute of the day I thought about Amy, Annie, Will and VJ. I always wanted to be back home with them. Each night after the show, when everybody would go down to the hotel bar, I just went up to my room to count down the hours before I would once again be home. That's why I've said it so many times — you couldn't be a normal guy and exist in this business. The boys loved life on the road. The camaraderie, the alcohol, the women, the pills, it was their way of life. For many, it's what they lived for. For me, it was the hardest part of the job.

While Louie was educating me in the business, Tom Emanuel was teaching me the ropes of publishing. Tom was open to new ideas concerning the magazine and I had about a million of them. With Tom's approval, I incorporated many new features into the mag, many which are still around today. Cliff 'em all, Vince Russo did leave his mark on the rag. During that time I also had to go over to the TV facility once a week and sit through voice-overs (when the announcers put their dialogue over an event that had already been taped). It was all part of the education, but man that was tough. Sometimes you'd sit there for five, six hours at a pop while the announcers would voice-over the same match — again and again and again. At the time, Shane McMahon, Vince's son, was going through a similar education, and many times when I was at the studio Shane was appointed to produce the announcers.

●   ●   ●

Next to his father, and perhaps *Raw* executive producer Kevin Dunn, Shane McMahon is the third hardest-working man in sports entertainment today. With youth on his side, Shane has an energy that can only be compared to a blaring K-Mart blue light, racing from department to department to promote the next sale, running 24/7 and juiced by 100,000 watts! This kid has more drive than I've ever seen — he's simply a machine. The guy can't stand still. I swear to you, while he's standing in one spot he jumps in place just to keep moving!

From day one, I admired him. Just imagine what he must have gone through growing up. I know personally from working for Vince McMahon, he expects *everything* from you — not just 100 percent, but every ounce of energy in your body, every single day. When you work for Vince McMahon, you are expected to hand him your life on a silver platter. I did, but just had nothing left to give after five years. Now multiply that by six, and you have Shane McMahon.

I don't think Shane will ever live up to his father's expectations — nobody could — but that doesn't mean the kid won't die trying. What he may have lacked in book smarts and common sense, Shane makes up for 10 times over in street smarts, heart, hard work and determination. But you just have the feeling that, in his father's eyes, Shane is always going to come up just a little bit short. I'm not saying Vince isn't proud of Shane — he is. I'm just saying that Vince may just expect too much from him.

It was my idea to put Shane McMahon on television. On one hand, I knew he was a natural performer — he's got charisma. On the other hand, I wanted to give him the opportunity to prove to Vince that when that red light came on, he could go toe-to-toe with the old man. And Shane didn't disappoint. To this day I'd say he is one of the top-five talents in the World Wrestling Federation. Right now, they're not even using him. Why? You tell me and we'll both know.

Who will ever forget Shane's first pay-per-view match against X-Pac (Sean Waltman) at WrestleMania xv? (Shane wrote the entire match out on paper and handed it to Sean weeks before the event. Needless to say, the ring veteran wasn't happy.) You've got to be kidding me! The guy went bell-to-bell like he'd been doing it his whole life. He was flat-out unbelievable. He not only stole the show . . . he made it. Shane never disappointed me; whatever I asked him to do in front of the camera he did, and did it like a pro.

I'm no psychiatrist, but sometimes I still have to wonder what's going on in Shane's head. There's a big part of me that just feels sorry for him. On the outside, a McMahon will never let you know that they're hurting, but on the inside . . . I have to wonder. Can anyone be happy with all that pressure, all those expectations? In my opinion, Shane should just concentrate on doing what he does best — being Shane McMahon.

●　●　●

So everything was going hunky-dory — right? I had the dream job, I was working with people I liked, I was pulling in 60K — what more could a man ask for? Well, buckle up for the next chapter. Little did I realize that I was smack in the middle of the calm before the not-so-perfect storm.

Chapter 28

I SHOULD HAVE TAKEN HEED IN WHAT JOHN MELLENCAMP WAS SAYING; OR, "WHEN THE WALLS COME CRUMBLIN' DOWN"

One of my all-time favorite songs is, "Crumblin' Down." To this day, John Mellencamp is just one of the coolest cats I've ever seen. And I hate to use the word "cat" — what am I, a black jazz legend? But no other word can describe him — the guy's a . . . well . . . *cat!* He's the guy that, deep down inside, I wanted to be. The guy is just so cool, especially when he's up on that stage. I've always fantasized about being a rock star. Can you imagine being up on a stage in a sold-out Madison Square Garden, with 20,000 females screaming at your every move? Is there anything more powerful than that? That's the ticket, man. Forget everybody and everything — I want to be Angus Young!

But anyway, you must be asking yourself, "Self — what do John Mellencamp and 'Crumblin' Down' have to do with this story?" Read on.

Some time, just months into my tenure at Titan, Vince hired some foreign guru "genius" to head the International Department. It seemed like every time Vince had a little bit of money to play with, or just got bored, he would add five or six new VPs to the payroll. All of which, I might add, in my opinion, may not have been worth the money he paid them. These guys appeared to talk a good game — but they rarely seemed to deliver. I don't know where Vince found this particular guy (whose name I won't mention, so from here on in I will borrow from Quentin Tarantino and refer to him as Mr. White), but maybe the "Human Mask" (this woman made Tammy Faye Baker look like the Ivory Snow girl) who headed up the human resources department was getting monetarily greased. Who knows, but every few months these holier-than-thou "leaders" would show up in their Armani suits, their heads nuzzled neatly against Vince's bosom. The sad thing was that Vince and Linda bought their goods hook, line, sinker and the whole pole! Clearly, this was none of my business — it wasn't my company — but I did find myself involved when Vince, for whatever reason, turned the publishing division over to Don Juan the Mark-o!

Reworking this book has been tough. Today, as opposed to before I was saved, I try my best not to gossip about or judge people. But in writing this — you must understand who I was, where I was and the conditions I was working under. I've left in some of the language of the old Vince, simply to paint a picture of then versus now. You can't truly understand who I've become without taking into account who I was.

Back then, when I felt as if somebody had crossed me, there just was no forgiveness. Put in that same situation today, I pray for the person. Gossip and judgement are handled a bit differently. I believe gossip is saying something behind somebody's back that you wouldn't say to their face. But as far as judging goes, I feel I can call you out on the carpet, as long as I am living up to the standards I am questioning you about. If you're cheating on your wife and you claim to be a Christian, I'll call you out on that. If you drink or take drugs, as a Christian — I'll call you out on that. I recently called somebody out claiming to be a Christian, who wrote a book totally burying and discrediting me. Did I have the right? Absolutely. Why? Because my book, this book, was just like his book — I shoveled dirt on a lot of people. But due to my new spirit, my new life, my new being, I completely reworked things, because hurting others was no longer a part of my nature.

This is where Mr. Blue comes in. Not having a clue, there were some rumblings that Mr. White might have been thinking about shaking up the publishing division. Tom Emanuel catches wind of this and he's gone. Tom was never one to play political games. He was way beyond that. Tom was the publisher because he excelled at what he did — he was a pro. So now, with Tom having left, Mr. White replaces him with Mr. Blue, an accountant. Do you get that? A bean counter was now going to play the role of Joe Publisher. So, let me tell you the supposed reason Mr. White hired Mr. Blue. . . .

I guess during his downtime — when he wasn't counting his change — Mr. Blue came up with this great publishing concept: "Let's develop a series of *children's books* based on the WWF Superstars." Mr. Blue even went as far as to actually have drawings made up presenting his ideas. Do you get the full picture here folks? Some accountant who has a drawing of the Undertaker offering some little girl a fistful of caramels is now actually running the magazine! What's the deal? The deal was this — politics, plain and simple. A nasty little game played by those who are incapable of getting the job done — those that don't want to get ahead through hard work, but rather by putting their snouts where no *real* man dares to go in order to find a shortcut to the top. The truth is, in the long run, there are no shortcuts. Sooner or later, they will have their judgement day — when they'll stand alone. Whether it's in this life or another — every one has his or her day.

How scary is that? I wrote about judgement day two years ago, with no worries I'd ever come face-to-face with my maker. Was I kidding myself or what? I was saying that everyone else was going to have to answer to God — but what about me? My maker would have had a blast with me back then: "Hey, Vince — when's the last time you came over to the house [church]? When's the last time we talked [prayed]? When's the last time you told me you loved me and thanked me for everything you have [never]"? I thank God that he saved me in time!

Writing this in my back office, I'm listening to "An Evening with John Denver." I tell you, when I hit 40, a lot of things changed. For one, I started listening to John Denver, and have become a big fan. You know, you get so wrapped up in the day-to-day "noise" that you forget about the things that really do matter. This book — everything in it — in the end doesn't matter. But, John Denver . . . man, John Denver. Take three minutes out of your day and listen to the words of "Rocky Mountain High." I swear to God, when all is said and done, I'm retiring to Colorado. Listen to the words — so much meaning, so much emotion, so much truth. I guess I'm just growing older and wiser.

When I hit the big four-oh, I was also suddenly overcome with a fascination for cats. Yeah, kittens. My whole life I despised them, the way they hunch up their backs to scare you. . . . Curse them, and curse their leader, Garfield. But now I love cats. For one, they don't mess the carpet. The first day you bring one home — even if they are only a week old — the first time they have to whiz they head straight for the litter box. To me, it's unbelievable. How do they know to go to the litter box right out of the womb? Does their mother tell them? And here's the great thing — unlike dogs, they decide when they want attention. Dogs pee all over themselves when you come home, lick you, want their bellies scratched — they're idiots. But cats? They won't give you the time of day until they decide to — which, I might add, is usually in the middle of the night, while you're sleeping. I respect that. Right now I have two cats, Crystal and Rainbow. I'm looking to add a third, but again, Amy thinks I'm nuts!

Back to Mr. Blue and Mr. White. So now Mr. Blue moves into Tom's office. Yes, he put the children's drawings up on his wall. I knew this was bad, I just didn't know *how* bad. The most dangerous thing for anybody is trying to be something they're not. It's another big pet peeve. When you try to be something you're not, it eventually catches up with you. One way or another, it will get you. You can make believe you're that person all you want, but if you're not, the truth will eventually come out and expose you to the world. Mr. Blue was an accountant. Always was, always will be. He was as far from being a publisher as I am from being a redneck! But in his own little mind, he actually thought he was a publisher. Or rather, I think the title they gave him was "general manager." Regardless, my opinion didn't matter. Remember, I was just a few months into my tenure, and I didn't mean zip.

I think it was on the same day that Mr. Blue moved down to the second floor and into Tom's office that I got word that he wanted to see me. Was I nervous? Not really. What, was this guy going to write the magazine, too? No matter how arrogant and uninformed he was, he needed me — I knew the product. Plus, how could I be fired? I'd just moved my whole family across the water from Long Island to Connecticut. So I walk into his office, and this is what I'm told. . . .

"Louie's fired, and you're lucky you still have a job, because I had no plans for you. Now, go get Louie."

You ignorant !@#$%, I thought. You clueless !@#$%. You didn't have plans for *me?* At the time, I didn't care whether I was fired or not. I knew then that even if I was kept aboard it was going to be a nightmare. But to have to fire Louie? You miserable !@#$%, this guy was the heart and soul of the magazine. This guy was the wrestling business. He knew more about running the publication than this accountant ever would. !@#$% you, the horse you rode in on and the cavalry behind you!!!

Telling Louie was one of the toughest things I ever had to do. I just knew how much he loved working at Titan. It was his whole life. Man, this is the company politics I've been telling you about— at its worst. Screw the little guy who makes the least and does the most. When I walked into Louie's office, the kid, he just knew. Maybe it was because I was whiter than Edgar Winter (the albino who was a one-hit-wonder with "Frankenstein" back in the '70s). The truth was, I was sick to my stomach. This was so wrong. Louie had never done anything to anybody. Where was he going to go from here?

Being street-smart, Louie wasn't surprised. I think he may have been expecting it. Like a man, he just walked out. I remember he once told me: "Vince, you see this office here? You notice I have nothing on my walls? You know why? Because every day could be my last day working here. That's just the way the business is. And when I go, I want to go the same way I came in — with nothing."

Louie indeed left with nothing. From that day forward, I never forgot his words. It was the most important thing anyone in the wrestling business ever said to me, including Vince himself. (Today, his words carry even more weight.) From that moment on I treated every day at Titan as if it were my last. And I didn't care. Why would I want to work at that kind of place anyway?

Chapter 29

"HEY, LOOK AT ME — I'M 13!"

The title of this chapter is a famous line from *The Honeymooners*. And it summed up the situation best. Mr. Blue was serious about his children's books featuring wrestlers. Not only that, he brought the same philosophy to the magazine! His model was *Sports Illustrated for Kids*. He wanted to turn the WWF *Magazine* into *Sports Illustrated for Kids*. What a poor, clueless general manager. . . .

At this point, there was no doubt that the wrestling business was going in the other direction. ECW (Extreme Championship Wrestling) was on the rise, and the fans were into hardcore reality. The writing was on the wall. The millennium was just around the corner, and sports entertainment was about to change. I've said it once, I'll say it a million times — you've got to *evolve* the business. All sports evolve, as does entertainment. Remember the old days of college basketball? No shot clock, the players weren't allowed to dunk. Can you imagine that game today? Same with the NBA — the three-point arc has changed the face of the game. Then there's baseball, with its designated hitter. You've got to *evolve!*

Entertainment is no different — it too has evolved. Today it's all about sex. Halle Berry flashed her chest, and a bomb of a movie, *Swordfish*, made millions at the box office. It's all about T & A in the entertainment business. *American Pie, Sex and the City,* Austin Powers, Gwen Stefani, Lil' Kim, adolescent language, nudity — people eat that stuff up! At the time, the WWF was going in the wrong direction. Doink the Clown was a major player. Things were bad, and Mr. Blue was set on making them even worse.

We would have department meetings — with women from the department involved who had no business even being in the building — and we would brainstorm ideas for the upcoming issue. I'll never forget this one time where the art director suggested we do a story about the WWF superstars . . . *gardening!* Man, what a cluster. We even put Bret Hart on the cover of the mag with Bart Simpson. It was an absolute disgrace. And, day by day, minute by minute, the WWF was losing money with no idea why. The ratings were going into the outhouse, house shows were down and merchandise was sitting on shelves. Vince was in trouble.

Yet another pet peeve — yes-men. Back then, I didn't know what was worse — yes-men, or suits, though you could argue they're all one and the same. Vince was surrounded by yes-men, telling him everything he wanted to hear whether it was right or wrong. Vince's yes-men were killing him. There was nobody in that company at the time who would tell Vince like it was. And that's what he needed.

For months, the magazine continued to go down this path. What could I do? I can even remember when Sid Eudy, a monstrous no-good heel, was brought back to the WWF and I asked Mr. Blue, "Sid isn't kid friendly, how can we represent him in the magazine?" Mr. Blue simply said, "Don't." Vince had just invested hundreds of thousands of dollars to bring Sid back to the WWF in an effort to gain viewers, and this *jabeep* (an Italian slang term for somebody "slow-minded") is telling me not to promote him in our own magazine.

With thick, permanent black spray-paint, the graffiti was on the wall. I wasn't going to last. I thought every move this guy made was asinine, and it was only a matter of time before my big Italian mouth would go off. The fact is, I really cared about the welfare of Titan Sports and the WWF. I liked and respected both Vince and Linda McMahon, along with Shane and Stephanie. Plus, there was a part of me — as corny as this sounds — that really wanted to repay Vince for all the years of entertainment he gave me as a child, teenager and adult.

This is where Corporate America really gets dangerous. My future, my career, the well-being of my family, was in the hands of an accountant who wanted to send Mankind (Mick Foley) up the hill with Jack-'n-Jill, just to make sure they "didn't do anything adult-like" while they were up there. On top of that, the money man had a chip on his shoulder that would fill the Snake River Canyon. He used to walk with this swagger that just killed me. With my fate sealed, I knew I had to do something quick to gain as much leverage as possible. So, at this point, I made an effort to form some kind of a relationship with Vince's two top guys, the two guys in the know — Bruce Prichard and Pat Patterson.

Let me say this — I love Pat Patterson, flat out love him. I haven't seen Pat in about three years, and I really miss him. A former wrestling legend in his own right (and the first WWF Intercontinental Champion I might add), Pat served as Vince's "Tom Hagen" (Robert Duvall's role in *The Godfather*), more or less the family advisor. Pat had been with Vince since the '70s, and the boss trusted him more than anyone else. Pat was one of the most colorful, energetic, enthusiastic, funny, caring and understanding individuals I've ever known. That Canadian accent just floored me. Pat always had a smile on his face, and from the moment I met him I was drawn to him. You never had to worry about Pat screwing you for personal gain — he just wasn't that way. He was always honest and sincere. I learned so much from him, and I think back then he was drawing from my energy. Pat and I always use to bounce ideas and angles off each other. To this day, I don't think he realizes what a thrill that was for me.

My relationship with Bruce Prichard was a bit more suspect. Bruce and I were better "friends" per se than Pat and I were, but call it instinct, I was always leery of him. From the beginning, for whatever reason, I never trusted him. You see, Bruce had been working for Vince for years, mainly writing television. Let me put it bluntly — whereas Bruce's ideas might have been okay for the "good ol' days of rasslin,'" they weren't in tune with 1996. Time may have passed Prichard by, and here I was, the new kid on the block, with fresh ideas that would change the business for years to come. In my opinion, Bruce may have known that; he also may have suspected that I was perhaps a bit more creative than he was. So in an effort to play the game, he "took me under his wing," almost as a defensive strategy, to hide my talents from the big guy himself.

But let me go on the record here to say I learned a lot from Bruce Prichard, and I genuinely liked him. Bruce and I spent a lot of time together, as did our families. It's tough to write about it, because to this day I still don't know . . . was Bruce Prichard ever sincere? Did he truly want to be a friend? There's a part of me that says yes, and another part of me that says how can I still be that naïve? It's the wrestling business. It's so sad to say, but there aren't "true friends" in wrestling. I learned that quickly when I was on the outside looking in. You see — when you're in that good spot everybody calls you, everybody is your buddy. But the minute you can no longer do anything for their careers, they forget your name. That's just the way it is. It was a hard pill to swallow — but then you realize, it is what it is.

So now I was positioning myself around a few guys who have some clout. I wasn't kissing up or looking to get anywhere — I was simply trying to save myself from getting fired by Mr. Blue. You see, the more I knew, the more he needed me. He was clueless when it came to what went on behind that curtain. I, on the other hand, was getting all the dirt from Prichard. He also had to be careful about the way he treated me, because Prichard and Patterson were Vince's right-hand men at the time. Suddenly I had some protection.

Man, I'm so bad with times, dates and places. I've made a habit of only storing in my mind information I need to know *now*. Some guys can tell you what match took place at what arena, what day of the week, what happened and what color the guy's jock was that night. Me, I block it out immediately. I remember the big stuff — but those little details, dates and things, escape me. What's past is past — I don't think about it. But at some point I found out that a decision was being made by Mr. White and Mr. Blue to farm the magazine out. In other words, to no longer do it at Titan Towers, but hand it over to a third party. In the transition, everybody would lose their jobs and the magazine would suffer greatly, but the bean counter insisted it would save the company a few bucks. This was wrong — *all wrong*. Handing the magazine over to a third party would only mean that we would lose control. At that time, Vince was still keeping angles and story lines close to his vest. I don't think it would have been in Vince's best interest to turn that inside information over to non-Titan employes. Like me, Vince is a control freak, a hands-on kind of guy who feels that when push comes to shove, he can do the best job. Truthfully, at that point the last thing I was really thinking about was my job. I felt my newly formed relationships with Prichard and Patterson weren't going to be enough. Whether or not the magazine went out-of-house or stayed in, I felt I was done.

The deal was literally days from going down. Still, something inside me made me feel so committed to the McMahons. What it came down to was they were the ones signing my paycheck — my loyalty was to them. Having run my own business for six years, I'd always looked at things through the owner's eyes. If an employee felt that there was something drastically wrong, I think it would be his or her duty to inform me. This situation was no different. Could it backfire? No question about it, but it was the right thing to do. So, without almost any contemplation, I scheduled a meeting with Linda McMahon.

●　　●　　●

Prior to writing this book, I told myself that if I was going to put the time and effort into doing it, it was going to be 100 percent truthful, unlike the other sports entertainment books I've read. Not to take a shot at the Rock, Mick or Joanie (Chyna) — three individuals I have the utmost respect for — but their books were published in conjunction with the World Wrestling Federation, so there was only so much they could say, regardless of what they might have really wanted to say. That being said, nobody is governing this book, so I can say what *needs* to be said. This book is based on what happened to me during my tenure in the business, and how I honestly viewed various situations and certain individuals. In many ways the truth hurts, but the truth is the only way I know how to tell my story.

So with that in mind, let's talk about Linda McMahon.

Okay, here's the "dirt" you've all been waiting for — there is *nothing* negative that I can say about Linda McMahon. Deep in my heart, I will always admire Linda. Business aside, to me she was and always will be the backbone of the McMahon family; the calm of the big top. A strong woman, perhaps one of the most honest human beings I've ever met in a world populated by con men, Linda McMahon was someone you could always trust. Face-to-face, she was always honest with me — always — and that was probably what I admired about her the most.

There were some people, both inside and outside of the Tower, who used to say that Linda had no right being in the position she was at Titan Sports. Some said she was only a vice-president because, obviously, it was Vince's company. To me that statement is ludicrous. Linda is one of the few people I met in the business who could exist — and exist nicely — in the outside world if she chose to. She is an extremely intelligent woman, and the mighty Tower just wouldn't be the same if Linda wasn't there to anchor it.

One rumor that circulated around the office said Linda had as much, if not more, power than Vince at Titan Tower because, following the steroid trial, Linda threatened to take Vince to the cleaners if she didn't get equal share of the company.

Now I'm not going to pretend to know if that's true or false, because honestly I don't have a clue. But I will say this: Linda was right there next to her husband in a federal courtroom when the whole truth came out about Vince McMahon, and let's just say some of those "truths" were personal . . . *very* personal. Add to that the mudslinging in the media at the time, and Linda was hearing things about her husband that perhaps she wished she never had. Some things, I might add, that may indeed have been true. But Linda stood tall — for her own reasons she decided to stand by her man. Some respect her for that, others question it, but regardless, Linda McMahon is 100 percent a class act. I don't know of any other woman who could be so poised, so classy and so strong while governing the "Island of Misfit Gimmicks."

I miss Linda. I miss talking with her, I miss all the McMahons. They were all such a big part of my life. No, everything wasn't always hunky-dory, but at the time they felt like family. Since I left . . . I don't know, there's just a part of me that's missing. Every week I have dreams I'm back there — man, it's crazy. Feeling this way you must be asking yourselves why doesn't he just go back? There's a reason . . . one that I will get into later.

• • •

So somehow, some way, here I was with everything on the line, having a sit-down with Linda McMahon. You know, one of my weaknesses is that I'm such an emotional guy. Man, I wear my heart on my sleeve, my collar, my pants, my socks. . . . In other words, you are going to know how I feel. I poured my heart out to Linda.

I had nothing to gain and everything to lose. I had no idea what Linda would say, or how she would react, but it didn't matter. All I was trying to do was the right thing. I felt it was my responsibility to let her know how I felt. There is no doubt in my mind that I could have been canned after that meeting, but the consequences didn't matter to me. I did what I felt I had to do.

As I look back on my words and my actions — I was always about "doing the right thing." There is no doubt, that should be attributed to God.

Even though at the time I had no idea where it was coming from, I always felt this presence of protection and guidance. I was always kept out of trouble on the road, always kept in a safe place, and always trying to do the right thing. God was there — he was present inside me from day one. The problem? I just wasn't paying attention. I was so wrapped up in myself that I just took my guardian angel for granted. That is, until he would no longer put up with it.

Following our discussion, Linda didn't take long to react. Within a couple of days she pulled the plug on the plans to farm the magazine out. I don't need to tell you that Mr. Blue and Mr. White were *fuming*. Not only were their plans squashed, but this was going to leave a huge blemish on their credibility as far as Linda McMahon was concerned. To be honest with you, I never thought Linda would make that decision. But give Linda credit for being a good judge of character. She knew I had nothing to gain. I made it clear to her on several occasions that I had no desire to run the magazine. My business sense stinks, because I don't care. I hate that side of it and always have. I'm a writer, a creator, a producer, a director. Give me a spreadsheet, I'm worthless. It was obvious I wasn't looking to take anybody's job and she recognized that. The only motivation I had was to try to do what I thought was the best thing for business and the McMahons.

But Mr. White and Mr. Blue . . . they were hot. After Linda informed them of her decision, I was summoned to Mr. White's office, where Mr. Blue was also there waiting for me. The message was simple, "If you ever go to Linda behind my back again, you will find your stuff out on the street." Inside, I was cracking up. The truth was, this decision had severely scarred their reputations and their business relationship with Linda. They were scrambling, and I knew it. They could sling all the threats they wanted towards me, but what were they going to do? If they chose to fire me, Linda McMahon would know exactly why. Without ever planning it, I now clearly had the upper hand. I was getting in tighter and tighter with Prichard and Patterson, I was more visible to Vince and Linda McMahon had sided with me in what clearly was the biggest decision ever made concerning WWF publications.

About a week later, I ran into Linda backstage at one of the events. When she asked me how things were going, it just came out: "Well, aside from being threatened. . . ." I told Linda the whole story. She took it in stride, poker-faced like she always was — but only weeks later, both Mr. Blue and Mr. White were "let go." It went down as Black Friday, and the village people were dancing in the streets. Vince and Linda McMahon took their company back with a vengeance, and it was party time in Stamford, Connecticut.

One thing that stands out in my mind about that day was that at about 5 p.m., Mr. Blue's assistant came into my office crying. She told me that they were taking Mr. Blue out for drinks after work, and asked if I would I like to come. Without missing a beat I said: "Would I like to come? No, I'd much rather give myself an enema!" What's ironic is that about a year later, due to her large heart, Linda McMahon hired back Mr. Blue. At the time I was the golden boy of the company. Man, when Mr. Blue came back, he treated me as if he was working for me! But you know what? Now that he had been humbled and his ego was swept aside — Mr. Blue wasn't so bad a guy after all. As a matter of fact, shortly afterwards, we became friends.

Chapter 30

I'D RATHER READ THAN WATCH TV

Man, I hate reading. Is there anything more boring? Well, maybe going to church — but that's about it. I'm a TV guy, always have been, always will be. I love TV, my kids love TV — it's all about the boob tube. However, there was a period of time at Titan when I'd much rather have read *Advanced Calculus* than watch the USA Network at 9 p.m. on Monday Nights.

Two years ago, I dreaded the two things that mean the most to me today, reading the Bible and going to church. What? There's no God? Read on.

With White and Blue now gone, I was running almost all the creative aspects of the publications department. Linda handled the business side of things. At that time, we had just launched *Raw Magazine*, a cutting-edge, in-your-face, "real" look at the business of sports entertainment. Shoot interviews based on reality and not fiction laced the pages, and we were taking the fans to a place they had never gone before. During those days, I knew the business was changing. You could see it on a daily basis. People just had so many more options, and kids were more sophisticated than we ever were. You couldn't just force that fake rasslin' down their throats anymore, they were much smarter than that. I used to sit back and just watch my two boys at the time. They were bored with something that was blatantly fake, yet some announcer wearing a ridiculous cowboy hat would try to convince them that it was real. It was an insult to anybody watching. Those were the days of the Goon, Freddy Joe Floyd, that crack-showing plumber (whose name escapes me) and who could forget — Who — a story I will get into later. And, ah yes, there was Mantaur. I'm still trying to figure that mess out. Half man, half buffalo. Would you believe that when they first threw that character out there, he actually wore a pâpier maché bison head that I swear to you wasn't an inch under five feet, and had to weigh at least 25 pounds. Unfortunately, overcome by all their excitement over the character, the brain-trust forgot one small detail: how the !@#$ was Mantaur going to get through the ropes and into the ring with a head the size of a small state? Man, you had to see this mess to believe it. The poor victim inside the costume practically tipped over trying to balance the weight of that enormous head! The television product was embarrassing to me; so outdated, so unhip — so ridiculous. This is why I sometimes chuckle when I hear and read about Vince McMahon, the *creative genius*. Who do you think was behind the buffalo? Yeah, Bruce and Pat were writing it — but Vince was approving it. So, rather than follow that cluster, I went the other way.

We started to tell the truth in the magazines — what was *really* going on behind that curtain. The meat the fans really wanted to know. We were ahead of our time, doing something that had never even been dared before. Shoot interviews, blood on top of blood, and oh, those girls in swimsuits!

Chapter 31

SMITTEN

I'll never forget the first time I met Rena Mero, a.k.a. Sable. I remember it so vividly. I was introduced to her by her husband Marc, someone I had formed a rapport with via the internet and telephone during my Vicious Vincent years. Rena was — and still is — the most beautiful woman I have ever seen. At first sight, I was like a wide-eyed child experiencing his first grade-school crush. She was so beautiful, I couldn't even look her in the eyes. And those eyes . . . they sparkled like a glass of fine champagne.

What, am I a freaking poet now? Snap out of it already!

I'll try, but it's hard when it comes to Rena.

Even though I was only the magazine editor at the time, the moment I saw Rena, I knew she would be a huge star, and that she would become even more popular than her husband. The sports entertainment world had never seen anything like her before. Yeah, there was Precious, Baby Doll, Elizabeth and Sunny. But there had never been a Sable. God, I sound pathetic, but man she just had it.

You know IT? You either have it, or you don't.

Sable definitely had it. But there was so much more to her than that. She had a presence I'd never felt around a female performer before. She walked into a room and it not only lit up — it exploded with blinding gamma rays.

There's so much more to get into concerning Rena, she was a huge part of my WWF history. In later chapters, I'll explain.

The *Raw Magazine* was everything *Monday Night Raw* should have been, but wasn't. (By the way, it just came to me, the plumber's name was T.L. Hopper.) The magazine was *dangerous* — perhaps even a little too dangerous for my own taste.

There is one story, in particular, that stands out in my mind concerning *Raw Magazine*. Bret Hart had just announced that he was staying with the WWF, despite a lucrative offer by the vice-president of WCW, Eric Bischoff, for him to join their organization. A few days after that show, I did a shoot interview with Bret that was perhaps one of the best I'd ever done. During that sit-down we discussed many things, including WCW and Eric Bischoff, who Bret put over (talked about positively). I threw every controversial question I could think of Bret's way, and the Hitman answered each and every one of them with nothing but pure honesty.

Knowing an interview like this had never previously appeared in any WWF publication, I showed Bruce Prichard a rough draft — to get his opinion before showing it to McMahon. Well, Bruce being Bruce, took it upon himself to show the man himself before I had the opportunity. So, I was called into Vince's office, where he sat at one end of a table and I sat at the other.

"What are you trying to do to me!" he screamed. "Put me out of business?"

With one sweep of his right arm, Vince cleared the table that was adjacent to his desk of everything that was on it. I sat there in total shock. I wasn't scared or intimidated, just in shock. All I was trying to do was sell magazines — a point which I tried to convey to Vince —

but he didn't want to hear it. I left his office asking myself only one question, if he was that hot, why wasn't I fired?

Well, I'll tell you why. At the time I realized Vince actually needed me, perhaps more than I needed him. Mind you, I was making 60 grand a year — as Mike Myers' Linda Richmond would say, "Big Whoop." I mean, the truth was I'd been making almost $50,000 with the Appliance Giant. So what would I have lost monetarily if Vince had canned me? On the other hand, Vince knew than that he needed someone like me around. He didn't know for what — but he knew that he did. Anyone who had the spaldings to put the name Eric Bischoff on the pages of a wwF publication had to have the spaldings to do . . . *anything*. Remember, Vince was surrounded at the time by people sporting *no* spaldings, yes-men who simply told him what he wanted to hear. I won't name them — but they're reading this, and they know who they are. People don't understand, but deep down, Vince really is a nice guy. He has many people on his payroll he simply keeps around and takes care of. Many of these individuals bring *nothing* to the table. Just recently, Vince let go an announcer I used to refer to as the Man from Bland, only to take him back after he submitted a novel to Vince stating what he had done throughout his career as a Titan employee. Now, Vice knew that this stickman probably wasn't worth the paper he'd typed the letter on, but Vince being Vince he took him back. He was always generous that way, sometimes too generous. That's why I still can't figure out his actions toward the end of our relationship. But we'll leave that story for later as well.

•   •   •

It's 8 p.m. on a Tuesday night. As my 12-hour monster day winds down, I'm sitting in my office watching a basketball game as I write. I have but one question for you: how ugly is TBS basketball commentator Hubie Brown? Is this man the ugliest human being on the boob tube, or what? How do you put a guy this hideous on television? I mean, I don't care about his knowledge of the game — who cares? I have to look at him for two-and-a-half hours! I'm begging you —

give me a hot broad. What ever happened to Jayne Kennedy? Do you remember Jayne Kennedy — one of the first women to actually break into the male-dominated world of professional sports? But don't kid yourself — Jayne broke in because she was drop-dead gorgeous. It didn't matter that she didn't know a nickelback from a humpback, what mattered was she was hot. And, that's what it's all about today, though TBS has yet to get it. Hubie Brown? You've got to be kidding me.

It's no different with the news. When are the networks going to understand that if they put hot broads out there to read the news ratings will go up? Hot broads are money in the bank. There's no way you're not watching *The Today Show* on NBC in the morning in hopes that little Katie Couric's skirt hikes up over those sweet little thighs. But noooooo — ABC still gives us Barbara Walters and Diane Sawyer. *Please!* What are these women, 80? Do you know how many more young people would be tuned into the news if they just gave them something to look at? How about Carmen Electra doing the weather? She doesn't need to know about the Doppler Radar System — just tell her what to say. Better yet — how about Cindy Margolis doing the sports in a teddy? What, are young adult males not going to watch that? Wake up people, it's what the normal person wants. Why in God's name am I watching ABC's Sam Donaldson at 7 p.m., when there might be a *Three's Company* rerun on Nickelodeon?

Give me T, give me A, give me the whole enchilada! Regis gets it. You think we're watching *Live with Regis & Kelly* for Regis? The tighter Kelly's sweater, the longer I'm tuning in. That's why *The View* is such a let down. Here's the opportunity to give us something totally hot. Give me five scantily clad models in a very cold studio and I'm yours for the hour. But noooooo — they give us Star Jones. They dumped the only good-looking broad they had on there because the rest were all jealous of her. I mean, why — in the good name of God — would I want to roll out of bed in the morning and have Barbara Walters be the first thing I see?

Sorry, Barbara, I just can't believe I wrote that stuff. I can't believe where my head was at. Today, my favorite TV personality is Joyce Myer, a mid-to-late 50-something, female television evangelist who has taught me more about God and the Bible in the past year than I had previously learned in my entire lifetime. Joyce takes the hands-on approach, by taking the word of God and teaching us how to implement it in our everyday lives. She represents precisely everything I was against only two short years ago.

●   ●   ●

Let me give you another perfect example of why Vince McMahon needed someone like me. Here's one of my favorite stories from my magazine days. . . . I was backstage at King of the Ring the year Stone Cold Steve Austin won it in 1996. Moments before making his acceptance speech, he ran it by me. I must admit I wasn't paying much attention at the time. Man, I suffer greatly from tunnel vision — I have my whole life. When something is on my mind, I focus on it 100 percent — I don't let anything else get in the way. I just don't believe in wasting brainpower. I deal solely with the matter at hand, when the matter's at hand. So Steve ran this promo by me, and I honestly wasn't paying much attention because I was preoccupied with something else.

Then he went out and gave it.

HOLY !@#$!!!! Right then, right there, it hit me with the impact of a Catherine Zeta-Jones lap dance.

"Austin 3:16 says I just whooped your ASS!"

I don't know . . . it was just magic. As the words sprayed out of his mouth, I just knew that that phrase was going to make Steve a star. It was just one of those things. Maybe I have a good instinct for the business, but I just knew — kind of like the first time I met Rena. . . .

The following day I couldn't wait to get back to the office. "Austin 3:16" was going to be the cover line for the new edition of *Raw Magazine*. Along with the photo editor, I searched for a picture that would best fit the phrase. We agreed on a black-and-white, up-close shot of Austin immediately after winning the event. We would then add a grainy texture to the picture, and use red as a third color on the cover to highlight the blood that dripped from his lip and nose. Excited that I was on to something, I took a mock-up of the cover over to the television studio to show Vince. I remember this like it was yesterday. . . .

Vinny Mac: "What does Austin 3:16 mean?"

Me: "Austin said it during his King of the Ring promo. It's going to be *huge*, Vince!"

Vinny Mac: "I don't get it. Change it."

Do you understand how much money that short phrase, "Austin 3:16," has made Steve Austin, Vince McMahon and Titan Sports over the years? More money than you and I will ever see in our lifetimes. Yet at the time Vince McMahon couldn't see it.

I've got to say this — I respect and admire Vince. But while he *is* creative, I don't necessarily agree that he is the "creative genius" everybody thinks he is. Vince's true genius is that he surrounds himself with geniuses. And no, I'm not referring to myself. Have you ever heard the name Kevin Dunn in association with the World Wrestling Federation? Kevin is the executive producer of *Raw*, and has worked for Vince for well over a decade. As a matter of fact, Kevin's father worked for Vince Sr. Now let me be the first to break the news to you . . . without Kevin Dunn you would not see anything *near* the production quality that you see every Monday night. Forget Vince — without Kevin Dunn the show probably would not go on, *period!* Kevin is by far the MVP of Titan Sports, more valuable than anyone on the roster — and yet you never hear of him. Much like I was, Kevin was, and still is, one of Vince's best-kept secrets. I guess Vince may think that if he went public with what Kevin brought to the table, then every network out there would be looking to woo him. And he's right — they would. But Vince has to give credit where credit is due. Think about it. Why aren't there any credits at the end of *Raw*? It's a television show, isn't it? Why isn't anyone else being given credit?

For a long time, it didn't bother me that Vince kept me under wraps (after I worked my way up the ranks). As long as he paid me, I really didn't care who knew what I did. But I'll never forget, as ratings grew and the company became bigger and bigger, there was Vince, on television and in print, taking credit for everything, and never once putting his people over. I mean, following a championship have you ever heard Phil Jackson say, "Yeah — it was all me — all my coaching, all that Zen nonsense. Forget Kobe and Shaq — it was me." Well, Kevin Dunn and I were Vince's Kobe and Shaq and we, along with many, *many* other all-stars, made up that team.

Man, it just started to get to me towards the end, especially when I picked up the copy of *Cigar Aficionado* with Vince on the cover. I have to admit — this time he did give creative props to somebody . . . his son Shane. Vince referred to Shane as a creative force behind the scenes at the WWF. Not to take anything away from Shane, but where was Shane when I was spending eight to ten hours writing the shows every Friday? Man, not only did that trigger me at the time, but later in my career it would hurt me, because many people didn't understand my contribution to the days of the 7 ratings. I'm talking about people in Hollywood, where I might have had a real opportunity, if only they'd known. But I don't want to sound bitter — what's done is done. In my opinion, Vince just should have done the right thing, that's all. Give credit where credit is due — not just privately, but publicly.

Another favorite magazine story concerns Tammy Sytch, a.k.a. Sunny. The competition between the women of the WWF was vicious. Sunny hated Sable, Sable hated Sunny, Luna hated Sable, Chyna hated Sable, Luna hated Sunny — it was a soap opera. A television show depicting that side of the business would make Rachel, Monica and Phoebe's Thursday night *Friends* look about as lame as the goody-good plain-Jane sisters of *Little Women!* And the girls were so open about it, too. Unlike the guys, who would quietly and methodically stab each other in the back, the "divas" would scream at each other, curse each other out, physically attack each other — it was, as Regis would say, "Out of control!"

Yes, the girls were quite public with their spats. I'll never forget the time when I stood in front of Sunny to protect her from a charging Luna. Now I was considered "office," hands-off, but that didn't stop Luna. She came at me like a bull seeing red — dumping me butt-first in a laundry cart. I swear to you, Luna Vachon could kill you. I don't care how big and tough you are, she'll rip out your eyes and eat them in front of you. So when it came to the swimsuit editions of *Raw Magazine* you've got to know where I'm coming from.

We were planning on doing a Sable and Sunny bikini bonanza in *Raw Magazine*. Sable would be on half the covers, Sunny on the other half. I believe we were promoting them as "collector's editions," but what a crock that was. It was basically a marketing ploy to make readers buy two copies of the magazine instead of one — which they did.

Now while we're on the topic, what's the deal with magazine companies putting hot chicks on the cover of their pubs, and then shrink-wrapping the book so we can't look at it on the newsstand? What is that? *Stuff* just had Leah Remini from *King of Queens* on the cover, scantily clad and teasing us about the other photos inside. !@#$% you, teasing me like this! I want to look at this magazine right here, right now — and not buy it. Yeah, I ripped open the thing. Man, this Leah Remini is hot — and the real deal I might add, straight from the streets of New York. Do these newsstand geniuses think we don't rip open the freaking bag? Come up with a better gimmick. Like those pill jars that *nobody* can open.

Vince Russo: Bad Boy! It's hard to believe how juvenile I was only two years ago. I don't know, I just felt this need to impress you. To come across as cool, to go against the grain, to be the "bad boy." Why? I have no idea, to be honest with you. Today all of those things mean nothing to me. I swear to you, I can't even pick up a magazine like *Stuff* any more. Realize, I didn't make a conscious effort to stop looking at magazines like that, I just no longer want to. That is what I mean about the "change." Everything in your life changes when God takes over — *everything*.

So, we shot Sable first. Man, I can't tell you how many times I looked at those pictures. Just one glimpse of something I wasn't supposed to see, that's all I was asking for — one nip-slip, that's all. God, the pictures were gorgeous — you knew then that she was *Playboy* material. What can I say? She was, and still is, the perfect woman.

So now it was Sunny's turn. Now remember, Sunny was no idiot. Somehow she got a hold of Sable's pictures so that she could see exactly what she was competing against. Now, though beautiful in her own right, if I were Sunny I wouldn't have wanted to see those pictures, because the truth was, I wasn't going to win. So we proceeded to shoot Sunny — and the pictures were indeed hot in their own right. Though Sunny had a different kind of beauty than Sable, any way you look at it, you're not turning away either one.

I chose a shot of Sunny for the cover that was hot — very exotic. I think she had her hair thrown back, her mouth open, a look of ecstasy in her eyes — and she was on her knees. Now, I've got to tell you — if I'm a guy, I'm buying the magazine. Well, on the second floor of Titan Sports, Sunny sees this cover shot and she's not happy. So, she starts throwing a hissy fit. . . .

"I'll sue for sexual discrimination! I'll sue for sexual discrimination! That's not me on the cover! That's not me!"

I couldn't pass up the opportunity to ask Sunny, "If it's not you — then who is it?"

•   •   •

Let's talk about sexual harassment in the workplace (I think I'm looking at pet peeve number whatever now). This is the biggest injustice known to us men. Constantly dealing with women in both the WWF and WCW, I was always scared to death of being hit with the sexual harassment deal. Basically, it's the easy way to get what you want. Whether it be money, a promotion, a buy-out — you cry sexual harassment and your boss is shaking in his corporate loafers. The whole idea of this is insane. Being in the power position I was in both

WWF and WCW, do you know how many women came on to me in an effort to further their careers. It was frightening! You see me claiming sexual harassment? If women want to be our equals and stand tall with us in the workplace, no problem — then treat *us* as equals. Don't assume we're looking at you as anything other than our workmates. If a guy puts his hands on you that's one thing — but if you "think" he's looking at you in a certain way — come on, think twice — give us the benefit of the doubt.

•   •   •

My experience at the magazine was invaluable. Not only did I learn a lifetime's worth about the wrestling/sports-entertainment business, but I also learned how to write. Some months I would literally write the entire magazine myself. It was all about discipline. I knew every day what I had to do, and I did it. But at the same time, once I had conquered it, I quickly grew bored with it. I wanted to do more for the company — especially since it was foundering badly. I had so much more to give, but I just couldn't crack that starting line-up. Yeah, I was given more and more to do. But what I was given to do wasn't going to have an impact on the big picture. Man, it was so frustrating — I knew I could do a better job than the people creating the product. But at the time I just went with the flow.

One of the first real breakout opportunities I received was when Vince asked me to start writing some of the promos the boys would cut to help sell tickets for upcoming house shows (untelevised wrestling events). I more or less became the voice of many WWF superstars, from the Smoking Gunns, to Bret Hart, to Kevin Nash. Some of the guys used my stuff, others didn't, but it was a great learning process. From there, under the tutelage of the great Jack Lanza, a former WWF superstar, I began to produce the boys as well. I can remember spending hour upon hour helping Sean Waltman, a.k.a. X-Pac, with his promos. Later, Sean would finally hit his stride. But in those early days? *Ouch!*

During that time I grew very close to Lanza. I was a sponge around him — I wanted to learn everything from Jack. The guy had been a legend in his day, and I was thrilled to have the opportunity to work under him. As time went on, I would begin to tell Jack about my frustration in the company. I'd tell him how I had so much more to offer than Vince could ever realize. Jack used to tell me every week, "Be patient, and just keep doing what you're doing." Man, I loved the guy; we grew extremely close. So close, in fact, that years later, when I flew down to Atlanta to interview with wcw, I called Jack from my hotel room to let him know what I was doing. Under circumstances we will get into later, Jack knew I was unhappy, and he told me I had to do what was right for me. Now here's the sickening part of the wrestling business, the part that I loathe — the reason I am writing this book from the back of my own store and no longer a part of an industry that is very hard to get out of my blood. To make a long story short, I took the job with wcw and I called Jack to thank him for everything. I got his voice mail, so I punched in my phone number and left it. About 15 minutes later, Jack called back and Amy answered the phone.

"This is Jack Lanza, did somebody page me from that number?" Jack said.

Amy was pleasant to Jack because she knew how I always ranted and raved about him.

Amy said, "Hi Jack, this is Amy Russo." Then Jack Lanza hung up the phone. Now obviously I was thinking Jack was probably on his cell phone, or maybe in a car with a bunch of guys so he couldn't talk to me at the time. So a few days later, I call his house. I explained to his wife what had happened and I said to her, "I just hope Jack isn't not taking my calls because I'm with wcw now."

"Oh, no, Jack isn't like that," Jack's wife said.

I never heard from Jack Lanza again.

That's what I'm talking about. That's what's tough about the business. There are no friends — only people that butt up against you when you're somebody. Some may say that maybe Jack was showing his loyalty to Vince by not talking to me, but I question that. Jack didn't seem to be worried about loyalty when he told me to go for the job at wcw. It's just cold. You never know who your friends or your enemies are. You learn to trust no one, and that's unfortunate. It took me several years to really see things for what they were, because I wanted to believe that this was the chocolate factory, and Vince was Willy Wonka. But it wasn't, and neither was he.

And yeah, you can say whatever you want about Vince Russo, but after I rose to a position of power in the wwf, the first thing I did was bring back Louie. You know — it's that Italian thing.

Chapter 32

"YOU WILL NEVER
FORGET THE NAME . . . GOLDUST"

I've said that I was going to expose everything and everybody. Cleanse the soul. Nothing is off-limits — not even me. I'm a hypochondriac.

My whole life I've had this fear of dying — it's just morbid. I think it started when I was about six. I remember discovering a blood blister on the bottom of my foot. At the time, I didn't know what a blood blister was — I'd never seen one before. However, we did have little grayish-blue stones that surrounded the outside of our four-foot pool. So in my mind, one of those stones had lodged itself into the sole of my foot. I was too petrified to tell anybody about this — I thought I was a goner. At six years old, I actually calculated the years in my head as to how long it would take that little, grayish-blue pebble to pass through my entire body until it reached my brain and killed me.

I swear to you, that's a true story.

Then in my teen years, after I'd learned about blood blisters, I had to come up with something else I was afraid was going to take my life. This time the deadly killer was the brain tumor. Again, I swear to you, every week I thought I had one. One time, I even went as far as to call my parents — who were at a wedding — and make them come home because this was the one that was going to kill me. I later discovered I had the flu.

I've just always had this fear of dying . . . I don't know why. After the brain tumors, I went through that bad stretch after getting married. Man, I didn't know what disease I had, but it was *surely* the end. Then came the wrestling business. Every week I was on the verge of a heart attack — I just knew it. God, how awful would it be to die on the road . . . my poor wife and kids. That's my greatest fear today, missing them. What would I do if I didn't see them every day? Then the funniest thing happened. Once I was out of the business, no more chest pains. I guess it was called S-T-R-E-S-S!

Once I hit my 40s? Prostate cancer, colon cancer. Now I'm back to the heart thing. Oh, I've been having some minor aches and pains — you know pains in my left arm, can't catch my breath, palpitations, that kind of thing. But now what's even worse is that I have to worry about something happening to a member of my immediate family. That's *four* more people to worry about. That's the whole reason I started talking about this in the first place. . . .

Three days ago, my daughter Annie discovered a bump on her head. So, for the past three days I'm feeling this bump. I'm feeling both sides of her head — bump on one side, no bump on the other.

"Annie, did you hit your head playing?"

"No, Daddy, I don't remember hitting my head."

Panic sets in. Brain tumor again — I diagnosed it right away. I was sick for three days because we couldn't get Annie into the doctor right away — she'd discovered the bump over the weekend. I'm looking brain tumors up on the internet. I'm feeling her head while she's sleeping. I'm a *wreck!* Last night, I took my sons to see the Nets and left after only three quarters because I was worried sick about my daughter.

Today we find out Annie has cat scratch fever, which until now I thought was just a Ted Nugent song. The tumor turned out to be a swollen lymph node.

As far back as I can remember, I've been like this. I can never enjoy the moment because I'm always worried about tomorrow. Even my success in the WWF. . . . You think I ever enjoyed it? I didn't — I was always worried about the "unknown." One day there will be a logical explanation to all this, but for now . . . there goes my chest again.

The logical explanation is simple — if I died back then, I knew I was going straight to hell. At the time I wrote the above passage, I hadn't acknowledged God in my life. Sure, I would have told you that I believed in God — but I wasn't living it. Today, I fully understand. It's not enough to believe, you have to *live it*. Your entire existence has to be about him. Everything you do and everything you say is all geared towards glorifying him. Yeah, it's hard to live your life that way, but in the end, you'll be the one living in eternal peace.

Tonight, if I went to sleep and never woke up I'd know that I was going straight to heaven to be with God. I'd know that I would be loved and protected as I waited patiently for my loved ones to join me. I know that I would be side by side, working hand, in hand with the one who matters most — Jesus Christ.

●　　●　　●

I was with Kevin Dunn over at the television studio when Vince conferenced us in on a call. Vince told us he had an idea for Dustin Rhodes, a new character named Goldust. Vince described Goldust as an eccentric individual straight out of Hollywood. Goldust would recite lines from movies, as well as put every situation and opponent into a Tinseltown context. Vince then broke into this deep, somewhat effeminate voice, a voice he wanted Dustin to master. When Vince hung up, I couldn't quite put my finger on what he wanted, but I went back to my computer and started writing for Dustin — I mean Goldust. I bought a few books with famous movie quotations and tried to fit them with the various WWF superstars who would be foes of Goldust. Immediately I came up with the phrase, "You will never forget the name . . . Goldust."

In the first vignettes promoting the arrival of the new character, you never saw what Goldust looked like, only a graphic that read, "Coming soon to the WWF . . . Goldust." So the anticipation was built up for weeks. Then finally, the curtain parted and out he came, literally. In perhaps one of the most glamorous entrances in the history of the business, Goldust graced the runway in a gold sequined robe trimmed with glorious golden feathers. His long platinum-blond wig caressed his golden painted face as the fans immediately began the infamous chant of "Faggot, Faggot!" Hearing this — we just went with it, not blatantly, but through innuendo. The promos I wrote for Dustin were some of the best work I'd ever done. If you listened, you would have found them hysterical. Just imagine what he said when Jake "the Snake" Roberts was his opponent. . . . In no time, Dustin became the character — he *was* Goldust. His wife Terri was added as his valet, Marlena, and as Jim Cornette would say, we had "the hottest heel in the territory!"

Goldust was on fire. Everybody was talking about him — not just the fans, but also mainstream media. He became so popular, I even had the opportunity to write and produce a skit between Goldust and Conan O'Brien on *Late Night with Conan O'Brien*. Predictably, Vince started to get a lot of public flak over the character, so he came up with the notion that Goldust wasn't in fact gay, but simply playing on the homophobic fears of others. A great concept at the time — and it made all the sense in the world. There is no doubt people weren't forgetting the name "Goldust." Man, it was magic. I wrote it, Dustin played it, and it was the hottest thing on WWF programming. No question this character was ahead of his time. At that point nobody knew what was around the corner. Nobody realized that in about a year wrestling would be out — and sports entertainment would be in.

Not to be arrogant — but I knew. Goldust was the kind of heel the fans wanted, the first heel of the 21st century. It wasn't the Goon, it wasn't T.L. Hopper, it was Goldust. So what did Vince do with it? He killed it . . . stabbed it right through the heart. Man, I could feel Goldust's pain. Why would you want to kill the hottest thing you had going? The outside pressure was just too great — especially in the overseas markets. The controversy over "Was he . . . or wasn't he" just became too much. There was nothing I could do, there was nothing Dustin could do — the character was put to rest.

I've got two Goldust stories that I've got to get in. Two stories you've never heard before and may not believe even after I tell you. But trust me, they happened.

At the height of Dustin's run as Goldust, an entertainment photographer who did some freelance work for the magazine pulled a few strings and got us passes to work the red carpet area of the Dorothy Chandler Pavilion the day before the Academy Awards. Now understand this — we had no business being there, but the camera clicker knew some people who turned the other way upon our arrival.

On the day we showed up it was nothing short of a mad house — hundreds of people working frantically to set up for the Tinseltown glam fest. Along with Marlena, Goldust and I sat in the back of a limo and picked our spots. When any area became clear, we would dash out of the car, rearrange a few things, and roll camera. In an hour's time, we had about eight vignettes in the can, but were still looking for that one with the 20-something-foot Oscar statue that stands at the door where the stars enter the pavilion. It was beginning to get dark — we had to get the shot. Seeing a crack in security, Marlena, Goldust and I headed to the area where the Big Oscar lay ever so gently on the grass. With no time to spare, I picked the Oscar up and stood it erect. Goldust then got in position and we rolled camera as he said a few words. Once all the words were out of his mouth, we turned around and headed for the limo. Maybe it was a message from God, or the devil, but as soon as we turned to leave, a strong gust of wind came — knocking the huge Oscar on its gold butt, *Ba-boom!* The magnificent statue cracked in about five places. All of a sudden somebody screamed. Hundreds of people came running to the scene, as if somebody had been shot. They dropped to their knees and fawned over this thing as if it were their own child.

"Let's get out of here," I said as I grabbed Dustin by the arm.

Unfortunately, as I was grabbing Goldust, someone was grabbing me. This secret-service-looking guy — suit, ear gimmick, the whole nine yards, took my arm and said, "You're coming with me."

Okay, so I accepted the fact that this was going to be my first arrest. I took one for the company — no big deal. It was a little scary that I was 3,000 miles from home, but what the heck? Let's just get this thing over with. So, this secret-service guy leads me into a building and down the stairs. What, am I going to get interrogated now? Is this *Midnight Express?* Is a strip-search next? Just tell me! Okay, so now I'm staining my pants a little. Finally Joe Secret Service speaks. . . .

"We've got a problem," he said.

I'm thinking — "It's a statue, get over it." But then I'm also thinking — "This is Hollywood, that golden bald man is like God out here — I'm *done!*"

"Did you touch anything you weren't supposed to?" he asked.

Long pause. . . . "Well, I . . ."

He fired back, "Well you nothing! You moved a piece of carpet, didn't you? The set designer saw you! You picked up a piece of the red carpet and you moved it."

Holy Hollywood — these CIA agents had no idea that we'd been responsible for crippling Oscar.

"Yes, yes I did it!" I confessed. "I'm sorry — I won't touch another thing. As a matter of fact, we were just about to leave."

I was then released in my own custody. What a great story. The next one, however, is not so great.

Here is an example of how we all get caught up in this business:

When Vince decided to Dr. Kevorkian Goldust, both Dustin and I were desperately trying to come up with alternatives for the character. That should explain the mess that was "the Artist Formerly Known as Goldust." Hey, desperate people do desperate things, what do you want me to tell you? What a cluster. It got to the point that I didn't even know what Goldust was — we'd just stick him out there every week looking whacked, and maybe something would stick. But it never did — so now we had to shut down the life-support altogether.

However, moments before we were about to pronounce the character dead, I get a call from Dustin.

"Vince, I've got an idea," he said. "Tell Vince if he pays me one million dollars, I will get implants."

"What?" I said. "A penal implant?"

"No," answered Dustin. "Breasts."

Let me break that down for you. Dustin Rhodes was considering getting breast implants for the wrestling business. Mind you, I'm sure Dustin was reacting out of panic. I'm sure if he'd really thought this through — a man walking around with women's breasts and all — he would have come to his senses . . . I think.

And yes, McMahon did contemplate it. But that's what the business does to you. It makes sane men go nuts. I reached that point one night when I was with wcw. At a *Thunder* taping, I asked Kevin Nash to gig (cut with a razor blade) my forehead. Kevin looked at me like I was nuts — and I was. But that's what the business does to you. That's why it has a shelf life. If you're normal, you can only do it for so long. I knew that only a few months after I was hired. It wasn't going to be the rest of my life. It was just too screwed-up.

Again, when you look at the business from the outside, it can blow your mind. After I left the wwf Vince and Shane McMahon had a wrestling match in which both of them bled like pigs. Now let's step back and look at that. Here you have a *father* and a *son*, first off, taking ridiculous bumps that, if miscalculated by a fraction of an inch, could easily confine them to wheelchairs for the rest of their lives. Keep in mind these are not Hollywood stuntmen, they are merely two grown kids getting their wrestling high. In the past, both father and son had competed in the ring — but on those occasions they were always in there with a seasoned vet, someone who would protect them from hurting themselves. Wrestling each other, they were performing without a net. But that's not enough. From there, the two — FATHER and SON — proceeded to *mutilate themselves*. In your wildest dreams could you ever ask your own flesh and blood, your son, to cut himself with a razor blade for the sake of a wrestling match? And even if you didn't ask him — could you ever allow it? It's so disturbing. . . .

•   •   •

March 2002: Vince had just brought in the NWO (New World Order) — Hogan, Nash and Hall — in an effort to revitalize plummeting ratings. He's spent well over a million dollars on players that might arguably be past their prime. So here we are, less than two weeks before WrestleMania, we've got the "Primetime Players" in place, and what happens? The ratings go down two-tenths of a point. Vince must be pulling out his hair. Well, if he doesn't get it now, there's just no more defending him. . . .

It's all in the writing, my friends — plain and simple. You can have the biggest stars in the world, but if the story stinks, the fans ain't gonna buy it. It's been proven time and time again — yet Vince McMahon still may not be getting it. Okay, let's break it down. DeNiro? Arguably the greatest actor of all-time. *15 Minutes?* Bomb. *Jacknife?* Bomb. *The Score?* Take it or leave it. *Godfather II?* Epic. *Goodfellas?* Epic. *Casino?* Epic. So, the question is, how can an actor go from Bomb to Epic? The answer is simple: the written word. An actor is only as good as his part — plain and simple. You want more proof? Look at the *Seinfeld* cast. Explain how Jason Alexander, Michael Richards and Julia Louis-Dreyfus went from the greatest sitcom of all time, to individual shows that were cancelled in the amount of time it takes you to get up and relieve yourself during a commercial break. The answer is obvious. Larry David, one of the cofounders of *Seinfeld*, is a genius. The guy could make a star out of anybody — just by putting them in the right situation, with the right words. You think Jerry Seinfeld was a good actor? Stars don't bring ratings — at the end of the day writers bring ratings.

Look at some of the guys that were so over during my stint as a writer — Val Venus, Goldust, Mark Henry. Where are these guys now? They're dead, because nobody knows what to do with them. "Sexual Chocolate" is your best-case scenario. You think the fans really cared that Mark Henry couldn't work (wrestle)? No, but they cared when he put on the charm to get down with Chyna. Same with Val Venus — you think his "work rate" got him over? What show were you watching? "Work rate" (wrestling ability) today is less than 50 percent of the formula, in my opinion. I was hated at wcw when I was on tv — did I know how to work? People who still think "work rate" is everything are 25 years behind the times.

The day Shawn Michaels left the wwf because of a severe back injury I said, "Shawn Michaels will never have to work another wrestling match again — because he will be over forever." And that's the truth — Shawn is an "entertainer." Put him in the right situation, with the right script, and he's the hottest thing you've got. I'm so sick of people not understanding the significance of good writing — not only in sports entertainment, but in television and movies as well. Look at shows on hbo. Why do you think they're some of the best in the history of television! Listen to the dialogue — some of those programs are so well-written it makes me want to cry. Those writers are the real stars.

And, since we're on the subject of writers. . . .

* * *

Man, when I knew Stephanie she was still so innocent, so naïve. Having just recently graduated from college, Stephanie McMahon was moved into the Titan Tower offices to learn the business. After his graduation, Shane went through a somewhat similar process. During that time, Vince kept Stephanie close — walking her through every step of the way, protecting her from the evil known as the "wrestling business." Vince guided her with marshmallow hands, much the same way I would have handled my own daughter. Stephanie's office was even adjacent to Vince's, on the fourth floor. Vince wanted to know what his little girl was doing at all times.

And what a sweetheart Stephanie was. Just the warmest, kindest, funniest woman you'd ever want to know. But like her mother, Linda, Stephanie probably had no business being in this business. If she hung around long enough it was going to scar her, you just knew it.

After her education inside the office, Vince introduced Stephanie to life on the road with the wwf superstars. For a few months, Steph traveled everywhere with us, just looking, listening and learning. God, it seemed like she was still a little girl back then. I can remember winter hats pulled around her childish face — she was everybody's kid sister.

So I guess in a lot of ways, I feel responsible — even though it would have happened anyway. I was the one who proposed to Vince that we put Steph on television. Vince was doing an angle with the Undertaker at the time. Again, reality tv. If 'Taker really wanted to get to Vince McMahon, who would he go after? His most prized possession — his little girl. Even though the television audience had never seen Stephanie, at the time it was a no-brainer. After days trying to convince Vince, he caved. He gave the green light, and Stephanie McMahon was suddenly appearing on television.

God, those early days were awful. Remember how Vince used to make her dress? Sneakers, pigtails — it was horrendous. Stephanie was a beautiful young woman — why not portray her as one? But no way — in Vince's eyes she was still his little girl, and she was going to dress, speak and act the part.

And like a McMahon, Stephanie was good. Like her father and brother, she was a natural. (No disrespect to Linda, but she could use a few lessons.) I was so proud of Stephanie — to throw her out there and have her perform the way she did, what a bonus for the company.

What a difference a year makes.

I couldn't believe it when a grown-up Stephanie McMahon showed up on wwf programming months after I left. In the story line she had married Triple H and gone from daddy's girl to bitch from hell in light speed. But it was okay. I always thought Stephanie was beautiful — why not take advantage of that? I liked Stephanie's role on camera — it's her current role behind the scenes that I question.

Why would Vince feed his own daughter to the savages the way he has? The only thing I can compare it to is putting Stephanie at third base, without a glove, against a Yankee lineup consisting of nine right-handed hitters who usually pull the ball. In essence, Vince replaced me with Stephanie, as she now heads the creative team of the WWF. All I can say is — wow! What a position to put your own daughter in.

That spot is thankless — it's a no-win situation. Dealing with the politics, the paranoia, the insecurity of the boys, it literally takes years off your life. And I was a male, and about 15 years older. Man, I'm sorry, but Vince put Stephanie in an impossible position. She has been the target of everyone's attacks as the WWF product continues to suffer. What a shame.

But I will tell you this — for those who want to blame the bulk of the company's problems on Stephanie, look again. First of all, she is surrounded by a mixture of wrestlers-turned-writers, and writers who lack a real knowledge of wrestling. Add to that the fact that at the end of the day, it's Vince's business, and that Vince makes the final call. Lighten up, it's not her fault.

The failure to generate ratings goes a lot further than Stephanie McMahon.

You know, it just dawned on me. You must have read that last line and thought, "That's great, Russo — you're the Tuesday-morning quarterback now. Anybody can make the show better on Tuesday morning." You know what I believe? There is no question that I could make *Raw* a better show — *tomorrow*. What blows my mind is how Vince has forgotten what actually brought us to the dance. It's not rocket science, but as day after day goes by, and you're listening to yes-men who don't (and never will) get it, your product is going to suffer. Do I have the answers? I sure do. But if you think I'm going to spell them out for Vince for the price of this book, hey, my friend Howard Weiner has a bridge, a book and a building he wants to sell you. . . .

It's funny, but when TNA was starting up and they were talking with me about joining them, I caught wind of a comment made by one of the people in charge, "If Vince Russo was that good, why isn't he still working in the business?"

That attitude has always been fascinating to me. People associated with the wrestling business actually have this notion that there is nothing outside of it. If you're not in it, it's because you're not good enough. Let me ask you this — could there even be the *slightest* chance that I'm no longer in the wrestling business because I choose not to be? Is that possible? Is it possible that rather than being at an arena every Monday and Tuesday night, I'd rather be at home watching *Everybody Loves Raymond* with my kids?

Just a thought.

• • •

So, as I was saying before I rudely interrupted myself, a lot happened for me during the Goldust era. It was probably the turning point of my career. What I took away from that time was confidence — now *I knew* I could do it. I knew I could create new characters and feed them story lines that no one in the business had ever seen. I knew I was light years ahead of the rasslin' business. But at the time, all I could do was take Jack Lanza's advice: "Be patient." So, during that time I worked my butt off for the company. I did everything that was ever asked of me. I was overseeing two magazines, writing promos for the boys, writing and producing vignettes introducing new characters (this is where I first meet Jeff Jarrett — but more on him later), sitting in on voice-overs — I lived at Titan Tower. I was a man possessed! Looking back now, I don't know why. I was so caught up in the moment that I just couldn't see or hear anything else . . . including, again, my own family.

Today I sit here embarrassed, realizing how much I sacrificed my own family for a wrestling company. During that time they were not my priority. Work was. And I'm ashamed to admit it. One thing I regret deeply — that I can never make up for — is that my son, Will, went from the age of seven to twelve while I worked for Vince. I don't remember a single day from those years. Mentally, physically and emotionally I was not there for him. Fortunately, since my son VJ turned nine a couple of years ago, I have been able to be with him every day. My relationships with my two sons are very different, simply because of the fact that I was there for one and M.I.A. for another.

I can't get those five years back. My family was deprived, especially Will, who probably needed me there more at that point in his life than at any other. Shame on me. Shame on me for being so selfish; shame on me for tuning Amy out — for putting her on the back burner. And for what? To be sitting here a few years later a bitter old man. What was she going through? What was I *responsible* for putting her through? Never being there, never returning her phone calls, missing every function at the kids' schools — I was failing our marriage. I just hope that if the boys read this, it gets through to one of them. I've said it a million times — when you work for Vince McMahon, *he* makes all the money. And in any case, the money you do make means nothing. Man, growing up I can remember being told time and time again that money doesn't bring happiness. Yeah, right — because you make peanuts at your manual-labor job? I was so arrogant about it. I thought money was everything. Man, was I wrong. I've gone from making $535,000 per year to about $250 a week — and guess what? No stress, no politics, no !@#$% — and somehow, someway, the bills still get paid.

It's such a blessing to be able to sit back and reflect on my own words, written just two years before Christ saved my life. Above, it appears that I was halfway there. I was starting to get my priorities in order. Through experience, I was able to understand my mistakes and make a conscious effort to never repeat them. But even though I was growing wiser, there was still definitely something missing. There was no fulfillment — there was still that empty void. You are getting a first-hand look at God at work. At that time God was working on my heart, my soul, my mind and my very existence. He was preparing me for something much bigger, something that would come just one short year later.

As the story goes, it's one thing to think patience, but it's another to be patient. I had no patience — my time was now. The product the

WWF was putting out at the time was absolutely horrible. Vince finally wised-up and realized he had to make a decision creatively, so he turned to . . . Cowboy Bill Watts.

My first instinct was, "You've got to be kidding me."

First of all, in New York, we hate cowboys. Cowboys just weren't, aren't, and never will be, *happening*. They're right down there with NASCAR.

How can racing a car be considered a sport? Anyone can drive a car around a track. All you need is hand-eye coordination. It's no different than playing a video game. You want to be a professional driver? Buy Playstation's Gran Turismo and you're a professional race car driver. And the same goes for golf. Who watches golf on TV? Who plays golf? Hitting a ball in a hole? *Who cares?*

(I still feel the same way about NASCAR!)

And how does a grown man go by the name of "Cowboy"? That's how Jim Ross always used to refer to him, "The Cowboy this . . . the Cowboy that." But, regardless of the moniker, it *was* a positive sign that Vince realized something had to be done.

Coming from New York, I hate to admit this — but at my advanced age, I'm suddenly into Willie Nelson. It's called a midlife crisis, and if you haven't experienced it yet, don't worry, you will. How cool is Willie Nelson? The hair, the bandana — the guy's got the whole gimmick going on. I'm just discovering Johnny Cash, too.

Come on, a guy who dressed in all-black can't be all bad.

Man, what is wrong with me?

Chapter 33

YIPPE-KI-YEA!

Great line. Bruce Willis? Great in *Die Hard*, forgettable in *Hudson Hawk*. Not having room for Bill Watts on the fourth floor with the big hitters, the Cowboy was stationed on the second floor, right down the hall from yours truly. For those of you who don't know, Watts was a legend in the wrestling business both inside and outside the ring. He's known as a guy who had a solid wrestling background, as well as a good creative and business sense. As a matter of fact, he was "the guy" for a while in wcw, when I was running around as Vicious Vincent. I can even remember going to wcw's Halloween Havoc, I guess around 1992, and seeing the Cowboy walking among the people. Now here he was — about 100 steps from my office.

During his first few days on the job, Watts spent a lot of time in the publications conference room watching videotape after videotape, trying to familiarize himself with the product as quickly as possible. One day I decided to walk in on him just to pick his brain.

Contrary to popular misconception, I *loved* spending time with the old-timers. The insights, the stories, it was an education. Guys like Jim Myers, a.k.a. George "the Animal" Steele, Bob Backlund (who in my opinion got better with age), these guys were a fountain of knowledge. I used to be the first one in the pre-tape room to ensure that I could produce Bob Backlund. The guy was off the charts when that red light came on. His promos were the best I've seen to this day. I still say my most enjoyable, creative experience in my 10-plus years in the wrestling business came when I took the straightlaced, bow-tie wearing "Mr." Backlund on Spring Break, where all the young animals were partying. Clad in a wool suit while sporting white sunscreen on his nose, Mr. Backlund read the young partygoers the riot act — in a hot tub, with his pants rolled up. It was, by far, one of the best things I ever did. I loved working with Backlund and even had the privilege of forming a relationship with him outside the ring. Man, I miss him. Other life lessons came from "Dirty" Dutch Mantell. I rode with Dutch for just one hour, and in that short time I learned more than in grade school, high school and college. That was the joy of riding from town to town with one of the legends. It's where wisdom is passed down — somewhere in the middle of the night, on a desolate highway between Terre Haute and Paducah. And, there were many others like Dutch. I could sit there and listen to Arn Anderson talk *forever*. Arn Anderson? He should write a new edition of the *Bible* or something. I had the utmost respect for those guys. Without them paving the way, I would have still been selling Amanda washers and dryers.

It's fascinating. When I look back on what I wrote two years ago, there are several references to God and the Bible. What's ironic is that at the time I wrote that last section, there was nothing biblical on my mind at all — nothing. Or was there?

Without my knowledge, I now know God was living inside me, through everything. As a matter of fact, he was probably hanging out on his beach chair, kicking off his sandals, sipping cold water and just waiting patiently for the time to strike. There is no question that God was my conscience at the time — good and bad, right and wrong, do's and don'ts. My problem was that I wasn't "submitting" to him. I was being a typical male — macho and bull-headed and believing I could do everything myself. Well, that worked for a while. . . . Until I eventually hit rock bottom — until I reached the end of myself. And that's when God gingerly bounced from his beach chair and said, "Are you ready now?"

All I ever wanted to do was carry on what the old wrestlers had started. But, in order to do that, the business needed to evolve. Getting back to the story, I popped into the conference room and introduced myself to Mr. Watts. For the next few days, he and I spent a few hours together, watching the tapes, talking about ideas, where the business was headed, yadda yadda yadda. Then one day, Bill called me in his office and said, "Vince, I've heard a lot of good things about you, and I myself am impressed with you — how would you like to start sitting in on the booking committee meetings with me, Pat and Bruce?" It seemed like at that moment, everything just froze. In rapid fire my mind replayed every event which had brought me to this point: Arezzi, Vicious Vincent, the Appliance Giant, Ed Ricciuti, Mr. Blue and Mr. White, Jack Lanza, Goldust. Man, very few times in your life do you have a moment like that — a moment where it all just happens for you. It was like getting that call up to the big show. All my hard work and dedication had paid off.

I should have realized then that it wasn't going to be that easy.

It's been a while since I first met Cowboy Bill Watts, and the story of my being able once again to spend time with him is astonishing. Over the years, the Cowboy has become a born-again Christian, and through his son (and now a good friend of mine), Eric Watts, I was led to the words of Bill through the internet. Every day I am moved by the words of Cowboy Bill Watts, and through the Lord, he is even more of an inspiration to me today than he was back then.

Chapter 34

COWBOY SCALPED!

It was so comical; bucking the system as only a true cowboy can, Watts did the old "end around" and extended the olive branch my way without clearing it with the Make-up Monster down the hall in Human Resources first. Man, she was wild at Watts — but if it weren't for his nerve, I'm sure I would never have gotten that opportunity. I will be forever grateful to him for that.

For about two weeks, Watts got me involved in the booking meetings with Bruce and Pat. As a matter of fact, we were all at Pat's house when the O.J. Simpson "not guilty" verdict came in.

Digest this. Immediately after the O.J. not-guilty verdict, Bruce informed me that Vince was seriously kicking around the idea of bringing "the Juice" to the World Wrestling Federation to wrestle Rowdy Roddy Piper. As you read that now, it probably doesn't come across as a big deal. But at the time, it was insanity at its best!

Let's play "Time Machine" for a second, shall we? Do you remember how furious the entire world was when O.J. got off? As a nation, there were very few who believed Simpson's story and even less who could comprehend how badly the LAPD had screwed up the case. Ron Goldman's father was on TV every day just breaking your heart. The entire country was in a state of shock, and the WWF wants to pay this guy, from what I was told by Prichard — *one million dollars* to wrestle? Now, perhaps Bruce was exaggerating, I don't know, but my suggestion to him was that this idea could work . . . with one modification: replace Piper with Ron Goldman's father. Then let Mr. Goldman use the weapon of his choice — bat, gun, machete, hand grenade, whatever he wanted — while O.J. had to work the match handcuffed.

During those sessions with Watts, Bruce and Pat, I would pretty much sit back, listen and learn. I enjoy evaluating people; one of my stronger points is that I'm a very good judge of character. During those writing sessions I was picking up a feeling of uneasiness in the air. It was nothing obvious — just an uncomfortable feeling. The way I read things, Prichard and Patterson weren't accepting Watts with open arms. Again, given the players and personalities involved I had to figure that Jim Ross might have been partially responsible for getting Watts into the WWF. Now (pardon the pun), Bruce and Pat were saddled with him — and they didn't appear to be happy.

Let me rephrase that slightly: I don't think Pat really cared. Pat wanted to help Vince out of loyalty — but the guy was ready to retire and hit the golf course. I mean, anyone who worked that closely with Vince for that long . . . as I stated earlier, there's a shelf life there, past which you find yourself bouncing off the walls of a padded cell. Pat was at that point, so I don't think he was really concerned about who Vince brought in. Bruce, on the other hand — that might have been another story. In my view, Bruce may have been intimidated by Watts — and rightfully so. The Cowboy's experience made him wiser and more knowledgeable than the younger booker. If Watts had stuck around, Bruce might have viewed him as a threat to his job. Whether he was or wasn't, we'll never know — but again — that was the paranoia of the wrestling business.

Watts was a smart man; he'd been around the business too long. After being involved in the booking for just a couple of weeks, Bill called me into his office.

"Vince . . . I'm done," he said.

"What?" I answered, surprised.

"Nobody's called me back all day. Not Bruce, not Pat, not Vince. The three are nowhere to be found. I know how this works. I'm done."

Man, it had happened again. Months earlier I had seen Jerry Jarrett, another old-school wrestling entrepreneur who'd been brought in to help Vince, suffer the same fate when he was on the verge of cracking the inner circle. This is how people tend to keep their "spot" for so many years in the wrestling business. Shovel dirt on those who may be a threat, those who were perhaps better than they were. I knew it was only a matter of time before I would be in the exact spot that Jarrett and Watts found themselves in. Though they both had light years more experience at the game than I did, I knew that somehow, some way, I had to be smarter. I had to beat them at their own game.

Chapter 35

THE CAKE IS ICED . . .
GET ME OUTTA HERE!

Rock bottom. When you hit it, you know it. There's no place else to sink. When the creative team wrote in Fake Razor and Fake Diesel (the former WWF characters of Scott Hall and Kevin Nash, who we'd lost to WCW), that was it for me. "Embarrassed" isn't the word — I had moved on to ashamed. What really boggled my mind was the fact that Vince himself was going along with it. At the time, I felt it was a total disgrace. How Vince could ever have thought that this was going to work was way beyond my comprehension. It's kind of like the Mets deciding to trade Mike Piazza, replacing him with *me* . . . and then trying to pass me off as Mike Piazza. It was inexcusable. At times I thought Vince had lost his mind. He was nearing desperation, if not already beyond it. I was told at the time that the WWF was tightroping that thin monetary line between black and red. Many inside Titan Tower suspected that Vince was in financial trouble — even though that was kept hush-hush.

Me? I had given up. The product was unwatchable. I had to laugh when the Fake Diesel/Fake Razor angle became such a disgrace that, in the story line itself, they wound up putting the heat on Good ol' JR. The Okey was bringing these guys into the Federation to get back at Vince McMahon for firing him a couple of years earlier. The good thing? At least the writers were starting to use some reality in their story lines. The bad thing was they couldn't figure out the best way to execute it. It was pathetic. I'd seen better Corey Feldman movies. It was getting to the point that I didn't even want to be associated with the company. I had to take some kind of action — and I did. I called my friend over at wcw, the *real* Diesel, Kevin Nash.

But before I get to that monumental phone call, I've got another story — one that clearly paints a clear picture of the *wwF Titanic.* This was the iceberg that literally sunk it for me. Even the band that played till the bitter end on the legendary cruise ship wouldn't have been able to find harmony on this one — they would have been pushing the women and children aside to be the first to jump off the ship.

Right around the corner from my office on the second floor of Titan Tower was the costume department, where this woman, whose name now escapes me, would work-up drawings of concepts for new wwF characters.

Rummaging through her office when she wasn't there was a great way for me to keep up with what creative ideas they had in store for the poor, innocent, unsuspecting fans. At the time there was a character running around the Federation by the name of "Who." "Who" was Jim "the Anvil" Neidhart under a mask — but nobody was supposed to know that. Bruce once explained to me that Who was supposed to be some sort of cheap-shot directed at Hulk Hogan, who was then with wcw. To this day I fail to see the connection — but then again, Bruce may have seen many things that other people couldn't see. Anyway, Bruce continued on with the character "Who" to mainly entertain himself. The real joke was, however, *nobody else was getting it!* But that wasn't bad enough. As I'm sifting through drawings on the designer's desk, I come across a sketch for Who's tag team partner — *What?* Ah, Bud and Lou would have been proud!

More than anything else, this should represent just how far apart the two companies were at the time. The wcw was doing Hall and Nash, "the Outsiders," and we were doing Who and What — the Bumble!@#$. There's no doubt in my mind that Who and What would have appeared on television if the landscape hadn't changed. Then, when the rating had collapsed to a 1.5 — Vince would have been saying, "What!" and Bruce would have been answering, "Who? Not me."

● ● ●

Prior to leaving the wwf, regardless of who will admit to what behind the scenes, the "Kliq," a.k.a. Shawn Michaels, Kevin Nash and Scott Hall, were running the wwf. In my opinion, Vince had little or no control of his locker room. Bruce made it known to me that he despised these three individuals, primarily because they thought of, and treated him like a joke. When Nash and Hall left for the greener pastures of wcw, it should have been a blessing. And it many ways it was — the locker room was better anyway. The problem was, Vince needed to create new stars — and it was almost like he'd forgotten how. Don't take that the wrong way — in the '80s, Vince was a star-making machine, but this was the '90s. The formula had changed . . . and Vince didn't have the new one.

I had to chuckle when Vince recently brought Hall and Nash back to the wwf. My, how we forget.

Let's call a spade a spade. I never, not for one day, enjoyed working with Scott Hall. From the minute I met Scott, he was difficult to deal with. Whether he was just kidding or that "was just him," it was a chore. The guy just liked to make your job harder — plain and simple. Now that's okay once in a while, but with Scott it was *all the time*. The sad part about it was that when you finally got Scott to do what you wanted him to do, he was without a doubt one of the best in the business. Unfortunately, those times were rare — for me, anyway.

Regardless of what anybody tells you, Scott could turn it on and off. The reason I say that is because when I saw him around kids, Scott was a different person. He acted as a hero to them — I saw it in person when he took some time with my own nephew many years ago. Around a child who only knew him as a star, Scott lived up to the billing of "hero." But when I worked with Hall he chose to be difficult, primarily because he saw it as part of his gimmick. Still, even though I don't know Scott well, I believe, inside, he has a heart of gold.

Kevin Nash? He'd drive Freud nuts. The guy is one of the greatest manipulators I've ever seen. And I'm not saying that in a negative way. Kevin is street-smart, probably more street-smart than anyone I've ever met. He can read people . . . and own people. Combine his mental ability and his physical presence, and Nash is an imposing force. Many people are intimidated by him — Kevin knows that, and he enjoys it. The guy is just so sharp. You see, wrestlers usually speak before they think, but not Kevin. His mind is always working, always playing a game of chess with you. I always admired him for that. I guess I admired it because I was onto it and just loved to watch him at work. Kevin would eat the Bruce and Jim Ross's of the world for lunch in one bite. That's why they were smart to just stay out of his way.

Kevin takes a lot of undeserved criticism from those claiming to be in the know. They accuse him of being the best politician in the locker room. I can tell you firsthand — Kevin is no politician — he just uses his mind to play the game better than everybody else. Kevin also takes criticism from those same "smart marks," simply because he tells them where they can go, rather than kissing up to them like so many others.

If I have one criticism of Kevin, it's that at times he can be moody. When he'd show up for work I never knew which Nash I was going to be dealing with. But at the time I was also probably one of the moodiest guys you'd ever meet. But I just want to say this about Kevin Nash: when he worked for wcw — he did *everything* I ever asked him to do, period. Yeah, many times he screwed with you before he did it, but that's just Kevin. And another thing that separated him from the pack: he's one of the most devoted fathers I've ever met. Kevin Nash would do anything in the world for his son, and he puts him above almost everyone. It's rare in this business.

There's a difference between "money" and "business." The majority of guys in wrestling will do *anything* for the almighty buck — regardless of what they have to sacrifice. Not Kevin — he'd sit home for the next 10 years if he didn't get the money on his business terms. Kevin Nash would never deprive his own flesh and blood to headline just one more WrestleMania, or for one more paycheck, or just to shine in that glamorous spotlight. Unlike others, none of that ever meant anything to him. It was always about business. You know, it's ironic, but for a wrestling fan watching week after week, the way Kevin comes across on television you would think the guy had a Madonna-like ego. But the reality of it is — he has none. I never realized how little ego Kevin had until I just thought about it now.

So for those who would bury Kevin on a personal level, it's only because you don't know him. And, for those who'd bury him on a professional level — yeah, you may know him, but you also know you're not smart enough to beat him.

CHAPTER 36

THE PHONE CALL THAT
COULD HAVE ALTERED HISTORY

Amy posed the question to me when we were lying in bed, "Vin . . . are you ever going to be happy?"

My immediate answer? "Yeah, when I'm dead."

The truth is, I haven't been happy for more than two decades. The last time I can literally remember being happy was during my college years. Since graduation, life has sucked — the whole journey has sucked. Oh, there have been some high points — my kids being born, the Giants going to the World Series in '89, but aside from that, life has blown. I'm telling you, looking back, I never thought it would be this hard, this unenjoyable — *never*. Sometimes it just seems to go from bad to worse. When does it get easy? When will I find peace with myself? Oh, don't give me that religious B.S. Yes I believe in God, yes I find peace in God, but right now, God isn't putting 70 hours a week into this business — *I am!*

Bono says it best, "I still haven't found what I'm looking for." The only problem is that after 41 years on this earth I still don't know *what* I'm looking for! All I know is I'm not happy. There's something missing. Sometimes it scares the hell out of me that it could all end abruptly, and that maybe I'll never find that peace within myself. Then again, maybe that peace is on the other side — I'm sorry, it wasn't my intention to bring you down, but the grind sucks.

Those last few lines sum up this entire book . . . this entire journey. Never mind you, the reader — for me to sit here and see first-hand my feelings, my thoughts, my emotions from two short years ago; to experience once again the loneliness, the depression, the despair, the reaching out. . . . And what's most mind-blowing are my comments about religion and God. Why did I even bring that up? Who'd said anything about God, or religion? That's what I mean when I talk about the subconscious. God was there all along, he walked every step, spoke every word, felt every emotion and waited . . . and waited, and waited.

At the point of that last log entry, I hadn't yet hit rock bottom. What was happening was that I was becoming more and more aware of my situation — not being happy, not feeling fulfilled — and trying to fill a void with no idea how. Without me even knowing it, my words were a plea to God. I was talking to him indirectly, but that's not the way he wanted it. In order for me to be blessed, I had to talk to him man-to-man, face-to-face. I had to ask for my salvation, my forgiveness. I had to thank him — but most importantly, I had to glorify his name. At that point in my life I just wasn't there.

But in time . . . I would be.

Before I get into "the phone call," there's one other thing I need to hit on, another bone that was thrown my way — Vic Venom. I created Vic Venom strictly for the *WWF Magazine*. You see, Vic was the kind of wordman who would basically say whatever was on his mind, regardless of the circumstances. Make no bones about it — Vic Venom and Vicious Vincent were one and the same. During my "everything sucks" period at Titan I had a meeting with Vince where

I brought up the newest show on usa, *Live Wire*. Again, I gave Vince my honest opinions on the show — and they weren't pretty. At the time the show was hosted by Sunny and wplj New York's dj, Todd Pettengill. To be honest, I wasn't a big fan of Pettengill, simply because I felt that he wasn't a wrestling fan. He was a radio dj doing a wrestling show. Nothing against Todd personally, but I took offense to that. In my view, a wrestling show should be hosted by a wrestling guy. So I took my concerns to Vince. Well, much to my surprise, the boss challenged me by saying, "Why don't you do the show?" Now keep in mind, at that point I had never even been on television. But that didn't matter to me — I wasn't afraid of the notion. So that Saturday morning, I went down to the television studio and I appeared on *Live Wire*.

Yeah, it was my debut on television, but it was no big deal — I just wanted to make the show better. Under the moniker of Vic Venom, they seated me in a studio separate from Sunny and Todd, and when the red light came on I did my thing. On the air, I told Todd where it was, where it is and where it's going. With rapid fire, I threw verbal bomb after verbal bomb his way. As I continued the assault, I could see the collar around his neck getting tighter and tighter. Man, he was getting hot, but what was he going to do? I loved this business, and at the time, right or wrong, I felt this guy was clearly in it just for himself and the money. I went on to do a couple of shows with Sunny and Todd — that is, until I po'd Vince.

Remember I told you Bret Hart made a public decision on *Raw* that he was staying with the wwf? Well, soon after that, the Royal Rumble was coming up. You and I both know how predictable wwf booking was at the time — Bret was going to win the Royal Rumble, no doubt about it. So that was my prediction on *Live Wire*. The scarecrow from *The Wizard of Oz* would have guessed the same. If I had said anything different, I would have looked like a buffoon. Well, Vince was in the studio that morning. As I walked off the set, there he was waiting for me. By the veins protruding from his neck, I knew he wasn't happy.

"Vince — why would you give away who was going to win the Royal Rumble? Why would you do something like that?" he asked. Without hesitation I answered his question.

"Vince, nobody told me that Bret was going to win the Royal Rumble — it was just so obvious."

Looking back, where did I get my spaldings? After my response, Vince didn't say a word. However, the finish to the Royal Rumble was changed.

● ● ●

Back to the phone call.

Feeling I had no other options, I called my old friend Kevin Nash. I told Kevin of my absolute disgust with the WWF product, and how the NWO was no question the future of the business. WCW was doing reality TV, while the WWF was doing Mother Goose. Kevin told me he would talk to Eric Bischoff, then get back to me. I also asked the same favor from another old friend, Double J Jeff Jarrett. Along with Shane McMahon, I had done some of Jeff's first vignettes when he came to the WWF. Not those ridiculous ones, where his gold tooth sparkled, but a series we did in Vegas promoting a match between Double J and Razor Ramon. From there, Jeff and I really hit it off. Like Kevin, I think I was drawn to Jeff because he was just so much more intelligent than everybody else. Even though I viewed him as a bit old-school at the time, Jeff knew the wrestling business better than anyone in that locker room.

A classic story? Jeff, myself and Road Dog (Jeff's story line "valet" and real-life friend, Brian Armstrong — a tremendous talent in his own right) went to L.A. during the height of the O.J. Simpson trial. This was the game plan: we were going to take photos of Jeff and the Dog right in front of O.J.'s house. While Jeff was striking his natural pose — Road Dog was going to have a look of shock on his face — as he found "O.J.'s mystery suitcase" behind the bushes at Rockingham.

So with Road Dog and Jeff in full costume, we drive to O.J.'s house, only to find the cops circling it every five minutes. Again, like "O.J. in the night," we picked our spot and did our thing. To this day, that photo is one of my favorites — unfortunately it never found its way into the pages of the wwf *Magazine*.

What can I say about Jeff Jarrett? Ours was the closest friendship I formed during my 10-plus years in the business. From the first time I ever met him I knew he was sincere. He just doesn't have it in him to be a . . . (long pause) . . . (cough) . . . bad guy. From day one Jeff was all business — he never gave me a hard time about a script, or a story line. If anything, he put in his two cents and made it better. Jeff was just smart that way — he was always looking to make things better.

And Jeff got it. It took a while for me to shake some of the old school out of him, but when he started seeing results, he understood. Jeff wasn't afraid to make the change from rasslin' to sports entertainment. He was smart enough to realize that the latter was the future. And did we have a blast nailing people with that guitar. Howard Stern's Beetlejuice may have been a nine on a scale of ten — but Mae Young, that was off the Richter scale! Think about it — he hit a 70-plus-year-old lady over the head with a guitar! That was television at its best. To this day, Jeff and I still talk about it. But then again, we coaxed a lot of celebrities into doing a lot of crazy things. When it came to Jeff, his southern charm may have been instrumental in talking them into it. We put Cindy Margolis and Ben Stiller in the figure-four, and of course, there was Gary Coleman. Man, "Arnold" was a hustler. He nickeled and dimed us to death over taking that guitar shot — but he took it.

Some of my best wrestling memories are from my time working with Jeff. We had our differences — but we also had a deep understanding of each other. If there is one guy who could ever talk me back into the business again, it would be Jeff Jarrett.

So, after weeks of waiting to hear something — anything — on a Sunday night, the phone rang. It was Eric Bischoff.

First impression? Not having ever met or spoken to him, Bischoff came across as a bit arrogant, maybe a bit full of himself. But in his defense, keep in mind, at that point, Eric was at the top of his profession. With the purchase of Nash and Hall, and after uniting them with Hulk Hogan to form the NWO (New World Order) — Eric had changed the face of the industry forever. His *Monday Nitro* was in-your-face, cutting edge, unpredictable and dangerous. If he was cocky, he had a right to be.

Eric told me that, unlike what other people thought, Turner wasn't an ATM machine. He said he would only be able to pay me so much, then asked what I was making. At the time it was a modest $75,000. I told Eric that I wasn't calling about the money, I was calling because I wanted a shot — something I wasn't getting in the WWF. Eric then said he'd see what he could do, and call me back.

To be honest with you, regardless of how bad the product was and how badly I may have wanted out of the WWF, I went to work the next day feeling dirty, like I had been unfaithful to the one man who was the reason I ever wanted to be in this business — Vince McMahon. God, I felt so guilty, even though I knew that I had to do what was right for me. I couldn't go on with a guilty conscience, but I needed an absolute answer as to whether or not I was going to get my shot to show what I could do for Vince, Linda and the entire company. Inside, I knew I didn't want to go and work for Eric Bischoff and WCW, but I also knew that I had to move to that next level. I had done the magazine, written promos, directed vignettes, helped create successful characters. I'd had somewhat of a hand in getting my booking ideas in, and I'd even appeared on television. I was ready to be Vince's go-to guy, and there was nowhere else to go. I knew that I had to meet with him and Linda to find out just what my future was with the company.

So here I was again, spaldings in hand, ready to take a giant step forwards . . . or back. I hope you're starting to see a pattern here. It's all about taking chances. That's the only way you're going to get any-where in life. Take your manhood and your confidence and just go for it. Like I stated earlier however, you've got to be prepared to lose it all. If you're not willing to take that chance, put your spaldings back in your jeans and go home. I was prepared to lose it all. At that point, it really didn't matter to me. If I wasn't true to the McMahons and myself, the company was going to crash and burn.

Knowing what was on the line, I hid under the covers a bit. I set up a meeting with Linda. There was a part of me that was scared to death, and I guess I believed just meeting with Linda would be a little easier. But I wasn't fooling anybody — I needed to tell "the man" face-to-face. As fate would have it, five minutes into my meeting with Linda, Vince walked into her office and sat down.

Picture it. It was a real tough situation. My mouth was so dry I could barely speak. It would have been so easy to give them a bogus reason as to why I was there, but I couldn't. It needed to be said — every word.

Looking back at that situation, there is no doubt that I took credit for *everything* that was happening in my life. There was no divine intervention, no Holy Spirit and there certainly was no involvement from God whatsoever. No, all that was put into play was about me and my glorious "spaldings."

Again, this is where the question of coincidence comes in. Was it just a coincidence that I knew deep down inside that I really needed to talk to Vince, but was too intimidated — and then he just to conveniently walked in? Or was this entire scene orchestrated by someone else? Knowing what I know now, there is no question in my mind that God himself was holding the conductor's baton, calculating every move and every word. In other words, it was meant to be. It was all part of God's plan, all a way for God to bring me around to the only thing that should, and ultimately *did*, matter — him.

●　　●　　●

Why did they !@#$ up the *Springer Show?* It was the best thing on television, and they went and screwed it up because of outside pressure. What — they stage fights now? What is this, *wrestling? Springer* was Americana. Trailer trash, rednecks, lesbians, midgets, homo truckers — everything we love about America — and they went and killed it.

Shame on them! The show is so obviously worked (staged) now it's difficult to watch. Why do some people think they have the right to determine what's good for my children? Who died and made them boss? !@#$ them and !@#$ Jerry Springer for caving. That's everything that's wrong with our country! Let me decide — and don't you dare try to decide for me!

Wow, wow and wow again! I read that and I want to vomit. I feel like Sunny now — "That's not me! That's not me!" I used to love the *Springer Show* — love it. I thank God every day that the old Vince is quietly resting in peace. Everything I represented was wrong. I was a fan of the *Springer Show* because that's exactly what I was responsible for writing at the wwf — "smut tv." Violence, sex, vulgarity, nudity, blasphemy — if it sold, I wrote it, without a care in the world. And what's even sadder than that was not only did I write it, I didn't even care if my own kids watched it.

I want to explain something. Being saved doesn't mean I've turned into some kind of a prude. What it means is that I now do everything in my life to glorify God — to please him. I don't think hanging the Undertaker from a "symbol" would have made Jesus too proud. I did a lot of things I'm not proud of now, but lowering the Undertaker on a cross is the biggest regret I have. At the time, I just didn't understand the implications. I just didn't understand the magnitude of what I was doing — of what Jesus had done. Years later, after Mel Gibson's *Passion* slapped me upside the head — I got it.

Man, it was all so wrong.

●　　●　　●

I talked about a lot of things that day in Linda's office — but the one thing that stands out is when I said to Vince and Linda, "If all you think all I'm capable of is writing the magazine, I need you to tell me that." They didn't — so I went on. I poured my guts out to them, telling them that I had so much more to offer than what they were currently getting from me. I don't know what was going on inside

Vince's head, but during my soliloquy he seemed to get hot. McMahon then basically told me that, in his opinion, I was being "selfish." To this day, I don't understand how he formed that opinion, but I didn't back down. I told Vince that I thought selfishness was the complete opposite of what I was doing. I told him I was offering myself to them at no extra charge. For a minute, I thought: "Am I nuts here? What don't they get? They're the ones in trouble, not me. Is this even worth the effort?"

I left Linda's office not feeling much better about the situation — but I was relieved. I'd shot straight with them, now the ball was in their court. They could either fire this bigmouth or give him the opportunity to back it up.

It was some time in early March, 1997. I could look up the exact date, but it doesn't matter. Like I said earlier — I can't remember yesterday's date, let alone one from years ago. But I do remember landmarks: times and situations that changed the course of my life. Someone, I'm not sure who, came up with the great idea of simulcasting *Monday Night Raw* from overseas and playing it live in conjunction with a *Monday Night Raw* shot in the States. In other words, some kind of a trans-global cluster — which it was. (Mostly due to the bad writing of not just one show, but two!) I'll never forget it — there were two different broadcast teams and we would go back and forth, country to country, bringing you nonstop action from around the globe! That doesn't even sound good on paper. What a mess — the worst show I had ever seen in my life. Wait . . . let me really think on that . . . no, *Battlebots* was *way* better! Man, to put it as nicely as I can, this show was *horrible!* I went to bed sick to my stomach. Remember, I had to go back to work for these guys in the morning.

When I showed up for work the next day, I wanted to put a bag over my head. But I didn't want to steal the "Unknown Comic's" gimmick. The minute I walked into my office the phone rang. It was Beth Zazza, Vince McMahon's assistant.

"Vince wants to see you in his office immediately."

I hung up the phone thinking: "What did I do now? A meeting

with the boss first thing in the morning . . . this must be bad." Immediately I took the elevator up to the fourth floor and went to Vince's office. Upon entering, Beth said to me, "They're in there," and pointed to Vince's conference room. "They?" I thought. "What — does he have human resources in there waiting for me? He can't fire me man-to-man? That's !@#$%."

So I walk into the conference room. Man, Vince had the ugliest office: red velour rug, a zebra-looking pattern on the walls. What was he thinking? Had he designed it? Or perhaps the "Crocodile Hunter" on an eight-ball?

To my surprise, there were no representatives from human resources to be found, but rather all of Vince's minions, sitting around a long table. There was Ross, Prichard, Cornette, Shane, Kevin Dunn — maybe even a few others, but I don't recall. At the head of the table there's Vince. He's standing, he looks mad, and he's got the *Raw Magazine* in his hands — the same magazine that housed the Bret Hart shoot interview that triggered the boss to clear his desk of all knick-knacks only months earlier.

The thoughts going through my head?

I'm done! He's mad about last night's mess and he's going to make an example out of me. I didn't write the show — Prichard and Cornette did. They're sitting right over there with their melons bowed in shame. It's their heads you want, not mine!

Vince slams the magazine down on the table.

More thoughts. . . .

Screw it, I'll call my buddy Steve. I'll be back on that sales floor tomorrow.

"This is what *Raw* needs to be like!" Vince screamed.

Come again?

"Last night's show was a joke! *Raw* needs to be like this magazine!"

I wanted to laugh and cry at the same time. First the laughter part — so much for politics. With one statement, I rose above all the creative brass sitting in that room. With one statement, Vince finally decided the days of mediocrity were over and it was time to shake things up. With one statement, Vince said, "You're out — he's in."

The crying part — this was a dream. Never had I expected things to wash out like this, in such a public display. Vince couldn't have stuck it to them any better. I had won — I had freaking *won*. All I'd wanted was a chance — and here it was. Man, I looked in the eyes of Prichard, Ross and Cornette that day, and never had I seen such hatred. They had to be thinking, "How did this guy pull this off?" I'll tell you how — by being honest, by not playing anybody to get there, by my own merit. . . . By just plain playing the game smarter.

I was on top of the world. I was going to be working *with* Vince McMahon, just like I had envisioned almost five years ago while sitting in Will the Thrill's.

Think and Grow Rich?

I had done it.

At that moment I never took the opportunity to reflect on the journey: where it all began, what I had to endure and where I wound up. In retrospect, it was a thrill ride. But that's me — I never take the time to live any moment to its fullest. Instead of stopping to smell the roses, I trample over them on my way to my next goal. I don't know, sometimes I just wish I could be different. I wish I could enjoy things more. Man, I'd pulled off a major feat, but the minute I accomplished it, I was already looking to what was next.

I guess that just comes with never being satisfied. Amy always tells me that. Sometimes I wonder if there is ever going to be a moment when I'm 100 percent satisfied and at peace. Why must there always be that next test immediately in front of me? Man, this is getting old — but I don't change. After wcw was sold to McMahon, I wanted to go back into business for myself and just be successful. Well, cd Warehouse has been open for less than six months and it is successful — so now what?

Okay, I want to get this book published. But once I do — and I will — then what? Damn it! Why am I this way? I just want to be normal.

Could I have asked for God's help any more blatantly? Could I have been crying out any louder? Reaching out? Pleading? Begging? It's just amazing that I can see it so clearly right now — but back then, I was a blind man walking in the darkness of the world.

In retrospect — *what if* Eric Bischoff had called me back? *What if* Eric Bischoff had offered me a job? *What if* I had taken it?

There is no question in my mind that the landscape of sports entertainment would be completely different. wcw would have become stronger, while the wwf got weaker. What would Vince have done? Would he have continued to go with the same hand? If not, who would he have turned to? Or today, some five years later, would Vince be the proud owner of wcw and everything associated with it?

I'm not so sure.

The wwf was about to crash and burn back then. Nobody had the answers, not even Vince himself. So he took a gamble — on me.

Vince had nothing to lose. Let's face it, his current creative team wasn't working. He was rolling the dice, and in the end, he came up with a seven.

Bischoff? Regardless of how he feels about me today (and that *is* another story, for another time), he has to be wishing now he did call me back. If it didn't accomplish anything else, at least it would have taken me away from Vince. But Bischoff didn't need me. He didn't need anybody — not until it was too late.

One return phone call could have forever changed the face of sports entertainment. One return call could have led all parties involved down a much different path — penning a much different story, with perhaps a very different ending.

One return phone call . . . but we'll never know.

Chapter 37

PUT ME IN A BOX, RUN ME OVER, TORCH ME, THEN THROW ME OVER A CLIFF

So this is how it broke down. Prichard was taken off the creative team and put back in his office, where he was to run talent relations, and myself, Vince and Jim Cornette began to write TV.

So there I was, back at Vince's dining room table — somewhere I thought I'd never be again. Man, Vince's house was phenomenal. Everything that you could ever ask for: a pool, complete gym, room after room and the CiCi Brothers manicuring the grounds 24/7. Man that was like a scene right out of Pacino's *Scarface*. What in God's name were those guys doing every day? But that's just the thing — when you have money like that, you have no idea where it's going. But heck, take nothing away from Vince, the guy worked for everything he has. Nothing was handed to him. Up until the day I left, Vince's car was *always* the last one to leave the office. I don't think there's another human being alive who has his work ethic.

Yup, I was living the dream . . . but there was one small problem.

I wasn't just working with Vince McMahon, I was working with Vince McMahon and James E. Cornette.

Man, was this a mistake. You see, at the time Jim Cornette and I went together like Ludacris and NASCAR. I wanted "attitude," he wanted Bullet Bob Armstrong (a legendary wrestler from the South). Jim was from the old school that said heels could only act one way — cheat, steal, spit, snarl — while babyfaces had to act another — smile, kiss babies and wink at teenage girls. Unfortunately, thanks to today's society, in the sports-entertainment game the heels are perceived as babyfaces, while the babyfaces are seen as heels. In other words — it's cool to be bad. The faces were perceived as phony, while the heels were looked upon as real. To give an example of Cornette's mindset, he actually used to travel around with a gun under the driver's seat of his car, in case he was attacked by fans — *because he was a heel!* We're talking 1997 here folks, not 1977. Man, it was ugly. We argued like Tom and Roseanne Arnold before, during and after the divorce. I'll never forget Vince's face during those meetings. He was getting so fed up with the both of us, he looked like his head was going to pop. Personally, I had nothing against Jim — I just felt his way of thinking, in 1997, was wrong. In my opinion, you can't book now like you did 20 years ago, because the fans are smart — they know it's a work (fake). Today's fans react to the product in a negative way if they feel their intelligence is being insulted. Old-school booking is based on one simple axiom — the fans are stupid, and they'll eat whatever you serve up because they don't know enough to question why you're booking what you're booking. In their minds, no one is "booking" anything — it's all happening for real. Years ago, you could get away with all kinds of corny and phony garbage, because the fans didn't know any better. Jim just didn't see that. The business was changing on a daily basis, and you were either riding the runaway train, or taking the third rail in a painful place! But I remained persistent. Even though we were driving McMahon nuts, I stuck to my guns, because I knew I was right. As a company, I knew where we had to go.

Some people mistakenly believe that my style and many of my

ideas came from watching ECW (I actually watched that show only a few times); my advantage actually came from studying my son Will, who was about 11. I used to make a point of seeing what was hip to him. What was he watching? What was he listening to? Yeah, he was a bit younger than our demographic, but he was the next generation — he was the future. Cornette, Vince, Prichard, Ross — none of them had that advantage. They were solely looking at the wrestling business through their eyes — what *they* knew. We're talking the Tom Green era here — it was cool to put poop at the end of a microphone and then stick it in an unsuspecting face for an interview. TV was becoming rude, crude, sexy and obnoxious. And that's what *Raw* was when it came down to it — a TV show competing with other TV shows. We had to be *Seinfeld*, not the 1970s National Wrestling Alliance. After a few weeks, I could see Vince was coming around more and more to my way of thinking. And then Cornette came up with the angle that would forever seal his fate on the booking committee.

Let me preface this by saying the following: when he isn't blowing a gasket, I like Jim Cornette. In his day, he was by far one of the best personalities in the business. The guy has a great mind — he comes up with things off the cuff that others couldn't come up with in a lifetime. He's a comedic genius — I once wanted to write a book on the thousands of sayings he would come up with on a daily basis.

In my opinion — and keep in mind, this is only my opinion — if Jim Cornette made the radical decision to adapt his way of thinking to the 21st century, he could be the man to take the WWF out of its current slump. For whatever reasons, however, Jim refuses to do that. Jim has chosen to live in the heyday of the late '70s and early '80s and that's his choice. Part of me respects him for sticking to his guns — the other part just doesn't get it.

Jim wanted to bring wrestling legend Terry Funk back to the WWF. I had no problem with this — I was, and still am, a huge fan of Funk. However, how Jim wanted to do this was a whole other story. . . .

Jim's idea was to have Cactus Jack, a.k.a. Mick Foley, wheel a huge box down to ringside. Week after week we would see this box, until finally Terry Funk emerged. When asked why, Jim answered, "Anybody who comes out of a box is instantly over." To this day, that's the greatest line I've ever heard. I've even considered using it for the title of this book. I thought Vince was going to die when he heard it. To appease Jim, Vince came up with the character of Chainsaw Charlie, who would chainsaw his way out of the box *immediately* upon his arrival in the wwf.

Man, it just wasn't going to work — Cornette and Russo. One of us had to go. All that arguing — all we were doing was wasting Vince's time and the company's money. I had a meeting with Vince and told him exactly that. I said one of us had to go, and if it was me, I totally understood. The next week, Cornette was off the booking committee.

Chapter 38

LAST CHANCE POLITICS

Also off the booking committee, Bruce Prichard was running talent relations. It was only a matter of months before Vince realized Bruce may have been in over his head. Understand, that's not a knock on Bruce. The job in itself is just so demanding — and thankless, I might add. So Vince soon replaced Prichard with Jim Ross, who even took over Bruce's office. Suddenly Bruce is a man without an island, so it was only human nature that he tried to get his old spot back — the one I was currently holding. One day, Bruce calls me into his office and tells me, "People in the office don't want to work with you — nobody!" He even went as far as to name names. Again, not believing a word of this ploy, I questioned everyone Bruce had fingered. Everyone flat-out denied the allegations. Who was lying and who was telling the truth? I really didn't care, I just didn't want to play this trivial game. So this time I took my case to Vince. What he said and how he said it to Prichard, I have no idea. But the Brother showed nothing but *love* towards me from that point on. (Yes, Bruce portrayed the old WWF character, Brother Love, at a much earlier time, in a much different place. . . .)

Chapter 39

SURVIVOR SERIES

I experienced many trials and tribulations during my tenure as head writer for the WWF, *all* of which we will get into a little later. However, in an attempt to keep things chronological, I'm going to turn to the infamous 1997 Survivor Series, because it was one of the last episodes in which Jim Cornette was involved as a member of the booking committee.

Believe me, the Survivor Series experience could be a book in itself. There are many aspects of that unforgettable day that very few people know about — including Bret Hart himself. Well, I was there every step of the way — besides Vince, nobody was more involved in the circumstances leading up to the event than yours truly.

To this day, many fans still have the misconception that behind the curtain, the good guys really have to hate the bad guys. C'mon, we all know it's a work — but there's got to be some animosity. A missed spot (move), somebody lands a potato (a real punch), there's got to be some "real" heat between the competitors? But the truth? There rarely is. When push comes to shove, these guys are professionals and act accordingly, even if they do have "real" heat with their opponent. Like I said earlier, with the girls it was different — but the guys, they rarely showed their true emotions.

That is, of course, with the exception of the Heartbreak Kid Shawn Michaels and Bret "The Hitman" Hart. For several reasons, many of which I'm not aware of — Shawn and Bret flat-out hated each other. On the surface, it was understandable — they're two completely different human beings. Shawn was flamboyant, arrogant and at times, downright disrespectful, while Bret was traditional, soft-spoken and a gentleman. Their personalities clashed — in a way, it was representative of old school versus new school. Inside, both individuals despised everything that the other represented, but being professionals, they pretty much kept things in check. Unfortunately, one night at *Raw*, Shawn carried things a little too far.

●　　●　　●

Man, the thing I miss most about New York is the talk radio. Howard Stern in the morning, Mike and the Mad Dog on the way home — it was a ritual. I can remember listening to Stern while driving the Long Island Expressway. The shock jock would say something that had me spitting my 7–11 coffee all over myself — then I would look to my right and some hot broad was spitting her Starbucks mocha latte all over herself. Everybody was listening to the same thing. Stern is a genius — I don't care what anybody says. Most of my inspiration as a sports entertainment writer came directly from Uncle Howie. Here in Atlanta the morning shows are just pathetic. Do these DJs know that they're just not funny? All they do is laugh at their own ridiculous jokes. How did these people get on the radio? Is anybody listening?

I just can't comprehend the things that were important to me two years ago. Did I have so little in my life that I agonized over such things as talk radio? Man, talk about a guy living with no purpose. I often wonder where I would be right now if God hadn't come knocking two years ago. Where would the road to nowhere on which I was traveling have led? If I was depressed then, where would I be now? Thank God those are questions I'm never going to have to worry about answering.

• • •

Anyway, one night at *Raw*, Shawn shows up under the influence of something. He cuts a live promo and hints at a "rumored" affair that Bret was supposed to have had with Sunny one night on the road. Now keep in mind Bret's married at the time, and whether or not Shawn's allegations were true or false, it's not the kind of thing you want the little wife at home hearing. So now things are really brewing — given that the two are supposed to work the upcoming Survivor Series. Well — at the next TV — the coffee was done.

• • •

I told you earlier that I was going to touch upon drugs — so I will. There is a drug problem in sports entertainment. However, we're not talking about your recreational drugs here (even though there is some use). No, we're talking about prescription drugs. Painkillers and muscle-relaxants are a serious problem in the locker room. They were before I was there, while I was there and now, after I'm long gone. It's sad to say, but many of the athletes are addicted to pills.

Let me give you their defense — even though I personally think the theory is weak. Okay, they're on the road 300 days a year. They put their bodies through hell night after night. They go to bed in pain, they wake up feeling worse. So what do they do? They pop a few little pills and the pain goes away. . . .

Hey man, I'm sorry — I feel your pain, but I have more sense than that. I have a responsibility to my wife, my children, but more importantly, to myself. In my opinion, if you're hurt, you're hurt. Stay on the sidelines until you're healthy again. Nobody knows their bodies better than the athletes themselves. But in many cases I think it's just an excuse. I think many of the guys get hooked on the stuff and then try to justify it in their minds, "I'm doing it because I'm hurt and I have to put food on my table." Guess what? Your table's going to be empty if you wake up dead.

Once, with my own two eyes, I saw a wrestler — whose name I won't mention — wheel his tag-team partner through an airport in a wheelchair. Oh, and by the way, the guy in the wheelchair was coma-tose and foaming at the mouth.

It's a problem — not for everyone, but for some. More needs to be done about it . . . but nothing ever is. Somebody needs to wake up before it's too late.

I wrote that two years ago. The Big Boss Man, Ray Traylor, just died. But, he hasn't been the only casualty. Since I wrote the first draft of this book, Curt Hennig, Mike Lockwood (Crash Holly) and Mike Hegstrand (Hawk of the Road Warriors) have also suffered early deaths. When does this stop? When is a program, a mandatory program, put into place to help the boys deal with the many pitfalls of the wrestling business — espe-cially addiction? When is somebody going to step up to the plate and beat some sense into these guys? That was the main reason I started my ministry. If I can help one of the boys — just one — it will all be worth it.

●　　●　　●

We were in the backstage area only hours before *Raw* was about to go on the air when Pat Patterson comes running into Vince's office.

"Bret and Shawn just had a fight in the locker room — I think Bret ripped out a chunk of Shawn's hair."

Pat was almost laughing in disbelief. To prevent things from going further the two were sent home. Later, Shawn threatened to never return. On *Raw* JR mentioned that neither Bret nor Shawn was in the building, stating that there had been some sort of altercation. Of course, everybody thought it was a work — smart wrestling fans think everything's a work. But this wasn't — it was very real.

Forgiven

• • •

It's Easter morning, about 11 a.m. I'm in the back office of my store and I'm writing. And yes, we're open.

You know, there are some places I can't go in this book right now due to legal issues, but in the future I will go there because the truth needs to be told. But sitting here working on Easter Sunday, I must say this — I'm currently being sued for defamation of character. While I can't really say anything about that, I will say something about this — I wish some people knew what "true" character really was.

I'm working here right now, not because I want to, but because I have to. I have a family to support. There's nothing I wouldn't do for my wife and kids. And you know what? My own wife doesn't even understand that. She argued with me about going to work today — like I wanted to do it. But I'll tell you this — I'll wear the blue collar any day over the white one. Since I've opened my business, I've come across so many men making $25,000 a year, if they're lucky, working 60 hours a week just to put food on the table. On the other hand, I've worked with those white-collar egomaniacs who make more in one week than those other people make in an entire year. And the shame is, they don't even know what they've got. As a matter of fact, they just want more . . . more . . . more.

I'm not going to lie to you — it's much more difficult sitting on this side of the fence. But on this side, the grass is greener. I've worked for everything I've ever gotten. Since I was 22 years old I've worked an average of 55 hours a week — and most weekends. I've made many sacrifices; I've earned my battle scars. Yet some people want to talk about my "character." Some people want to take from me and my family. I say fine — go for it.

I've preached it over a million times in this book — look in the mirror. *Do you like what you see?*

Though I clearly understood what I was talking about back then, the truth is that I should have been taking a closer look in the mirror myself. Perhaps my struggles were ongoing because of my denial of Jesus Christ.

Perhaps everything was a battle because I was simply fighting the war without an army . . . a spiritual army. There is no question that the spirit was trying to do the right thing. But the flesh just didn't have a clue.

I know where many of you reading this are right now. You are saying, "Yeah, I believe in God, and all I need to do to get into heaven is just do the right thing." I had those exact thoughts. I was always conscious of doing the right thing. But unfortunately, that's not enough. Being one with God means sacrificing your whole life to him — by any means necessary, spending every minute of every day of your life glorifying his name and his kingdom. It's about change — a new lifestyle, a new heart. It's a decision, a commitment you can't afford *not* to make.

With the Survivor Series just weeks away, Vince had his hands full — but there was also an interesting twist to this story. When Vince coaxed Bret to come back to the wwf rather than sign with wcw, he promised the Hitman a *great* deal of money, over a *great* number of years. Vince probably did so in fear. Bischoff and wcw had already taken Hall and Nash. If they added Hart to that list, who knows what would have happened. So Vince made a lot of promises to Bret, promises he soon realized he couldn't keep. On paper, Vince just couldn't afford to pay Bret what he'd agreed to — so Vince told Bret that he had his blessing if he wanted to go back to Bischoff and negotiate. What could Bret say? He didn't want to leave the wwf, but if Vince couldn't afford the money he promised him what was he supposed to do? So Bret went back to Bischoff and the two parties agreed on a deal.

Here's where it gets interesting. Going into the '97 Survivor Series Bret is the wwf Champion. Vince has to get the belt off Bret, fearing that Bret could take the wwf trophy over to wcw. The only logical thing was to have Bret drop the belt to Shawn at the Survivor Series — which, I might add, was taking place in Bret's home country of Canada. Well — no surprise here — Bret refused to do the job (get pinned) for Shawn in Canada. Not because he was being unprofessional — but because according to Bret, Micheals had said that he wouldn't *do business* with him (the right thing for the company in the ring), due to the way he felt about him. In the days to come, Vince tried to come up with every possible scenario to appease Bret, but nothing was suitable for the Hitman. This is where I come in.

Cornette, McMahon and I were at Vince's house writing television only days before the event. Vince brings us up to speed as to what transpired during the week, telling us he is no closer to a resolution than he was a week ago. At this point, I need to admit that I was privy to a few things that put me smack in the middle of the situation — but out of respect for Vince, I don't want to get into details. Next thing you know, Bret's on the phone. For the next hour or so, Vince threw numerous scenarios by the Hitman, including one in which he would drop the belt to Shawn at an untelevised house show in the States a day or two before the Survivor Series. But Bret wasn't biting. He did agree to hand over the belt to Shawn the night after the Survivor Series on *Raw* — but keep in mind that McMahon really was worried that Bret was going to show up on *Nitro* that same night and give the belt to Eric Bischoff instead. Vince brought up his concern, and the Hitman assured him he would never do that. Vince explained that it wasn't Bret he didn't trust — it was Bischoff. Bret then told Vince that he wouldn't allow Bischoff to do that, and then went even further, saying he would call Eric and have him sign a legal document to that effect. Bret hung up, saying that he would call back after he'd spoken to Eric. Hours passed. Bret hadn't called back.

For what seemed like an eternity we sat at Vince's dining room table agonizing over what to do. At the time I didn't trust Eric Bishoff, and wouldn't believe a word he said even if he signed a legal document in his own blood. Bret wasn't going to play ball no matter what we did. That left only one option: double-cross him. We'd agree to his plan: he'd defeat Shawn at the Survivor Series, and then hand the belt over to him the following night on *Raw*. But our real plan was to have Shawn defeat him *at* the Survivor Series, without Bret's knowledge.

Was it dirty? Yeah, it was. But Bret gave us no other choice. I can tell you better than anyone that Vince had come up with every possible scenario to accommodate Bret — and Bret wouldn't agree to any of them. Vince was doing what he felt he had to do to protect his company and everybody in it. I backed Vince 100 percent on this, and still do to this day. Knowing all the facts and being involved to the extent that I was, I would have made the same decision.

Day turned into night and the three of us sat there, empty, until it just hit me. Sometimes the answers to hard questions are the simplest and most obvious.

"Vince — we're making this way too difficult," I said. "Why don't we just do this? During the course of the match, let's have a spot where Shawn puts Bret in his own hold — the Sharpshooter. As soon as Shawn clamps it on, have the referee call for the bell as if Bret quit. Thus, a new WWF Champion."

Vince pondered the idea. The meeting ended shortly thereafter — but we were still some three days away from the Survivor Series.

Over the next couple of days I didn't have much contact with Vince. I knew that he was still wrapped up in deciding what he was going to do, so I kept my distance. Whether you like him or not, the guy's heart was being torn apart by this. Vince sincerely loved Bret — regardless of what Hart might believe today. But business was business. I headed off to the Survivor Series on Saturday still not knowing what the final outcome would be.

There was something different about the Sunday of the big show. The atmosphere was quiet — very quiet. There was a chess game going on and all parties knew it. Vince, again, kept his distance from me — which he did on many occasions after that — in order to protect me. That was one of the problems when I would later go to wcw. I had no protection. I was Brett Favre without an offensive line — thrown to the wolves to be eaten alive. That was not the case with Vince. He made me almost untouchable, and I'll never forget it. You messed with me, you messed with him. I could tell that on this night he wanted me out of the loop — nowhere near the fire. I read it, and I stayed away. As the bell sounded to start the WWF Title match between Bret and Shawn, I still had no idea what was going to happen.

As the match began I took a seat next to Mark Calloway, a.k.a. the

Undertaker, in front of a monitor in the back. Everybody was watching closely, and everyone knew the implications and was curious to see the outcome. In the locker room there are no secrets. Everybody knows everything, that's just the way it is.

So the match began. At the onset it looked no different than any you've seen before. These guys have a way of being professionals once they set boot between the ropes. The contest went back and forth for quite some time — until Shawn put Bret in the Sharpshooter. I felt my heart swan dive into my stomach. It was exactly what I had laid out to Vince. The minute Shawn locked it in, referee Earl Hebner called for the bell. Vince then strutted down to the ring, to show Bret that he took 100 percent responsibility for what had just happened. The Undertaker immediately rose from his seat in disgust. Everybody knew that Bret had been screwed.

You have to be in the business to really understand how bad this was. There is an unwritten moral code in wrestling that states "the office" (the brass, the suits) will never screw one of the boys. Remember, the boys are the ones who go out there every night and put their bodies and livelihoods on the line. To take that risk, there must be no doubt that they can trust the office. They must feel like the office would never intentionally put them in harm's way, or do something that might taint, hurt or damage their careers. If that trust is breached, then the boys start asking themselves: "Why am I doing this? Is what I'm doing right? Should I be sacrificing my body like this? Why?" Once the office is second-guessed, and trust goes out the window, the whole foundation of the business is cracked. Well on this night, the office royally screwed one of the boys — live — before the entire world, in his home country. I'll never forget Bret's face after the bell rang. There was a grin that said, "How could I have been so stupid?" But Bret trusted Vince, and regardless of any reservations he may have had, he went along with the plan laid out to him, thinking he was beating Shawn that night. Once it sunk in, Bret was irate — and after nailing Vince with a thick, wet loogie, Bret proceeded to destroy the expensive television equipment that was located ringside. Shawn, on the other hand, played dumb. To this day I have no idea whether or not Shawn was in on it. If I had to guess I would say he was — but again, that's only my opinion.

Man, there was dead silence in the air — the only thing I could compare it with is a funeral. It was almost morbid — but you knew it was far from over. There was going to be an encounter in the back, because Vince wasn't going to run away from his responsibility. I can remember sitting backstage waiting to see what the finale would be, when Mick Foley walked past me and said, "Vince, you should be ashamed of yourself." My heart broke. Coming from anybody else, maybe it would have been different. But Mick? This is a guy I always looked up to and put on a pedestal. Mick was so distraught over the events, he didn't even show up to television the following day. But again, understand that very few people knew the whole story. Before I could rebound from Mick's heartwrenching words, Vince walked past me, followed by Shane, WWF head agent Jerry Brisco and Bruce Prichard. He was heading straight for Bret's locker room to get what he knew he had coming. Later I heard that Vince had told Shane to let Bret hit him once, then break it up . . . and that's exactly how it went down. To this day I respect Vince for doing that. A lesser man would have filled the car with gas and pointed it towards Mexico.

After receiving a black eye courtesy of the Hitman's hand, Vince emerged from Bret's locker room. I thought the worst was over — but for me, it was only beginning.

In the days that followed, Vince had a meeting with Bret's younger brother, Owen Hart, an established WWF superstar in his own right and a favorite in the locker room. Vince explained to Owen what had happened concerning Bret, and told Owen that regardless of the circumstances surrounding his brother he wanted to be sure that Owen stayed with the company. Vince offered him more money, but regardless of the raise, Owen's heart was with the World Wrestling Federation. The last thing Owen wanted was to be involved in this, and quite frankly, he shouldn't have had to be involved. Owen just wanted to continue to work around friends and people he considered family. What went down between Bret and Vince was between them. But Bret saw things a little differently. It became all about "sides" with Bret. Owen was either with him or with Vince — a tough position to be in — but again, understand Bret's frame of mind at the time. Maybe he wasn't thinking rationally — and in those circumstances, who would be?

It was about 11 p.m. — five days following the Survivor Series. It was still the talk of the industry, and perhaps getting hotter by the day. Man, I was just happy to be home — just to get away from it.

The phone rang. It was Owen Hart. He was on the verge of tears.

"Vince, you've got to help me," he said. "Bret is telling me that if I continue to work for Vince he is going to disown me as a brother. He's serious, Vince . . . I don't know what to do. I tried calling Vince and he's not home. Vince, you need to call Bret for me."

Understand, I would do anything in the world for Owen Hart. I sincerely loved the guy. But calling Bret — only five days after the fact?

"Vince . . . please. You have to call him." Owen then hung up the phone.

I had no choice — there was no way I wasn't going to be there for Owen. At first I tried to call Vince — I guess looking to get his approval — but Owen was right, there was no answer. So my next call was to Bret.

It was one of the toughest phone calls I'd ever had to make. Even though I never lost one ounce of respect for Bret Hart during the entire fiasco, he saw me as nothing more than one of Vince's henchmen. Thank God he had no idea the screwed finish was my brainchild. But I had to make the call — I had to do it for Owen.

I'll never forget it. At that time Bret was in a whole other place. For five days he'd played it over and over in his head, and he was just getting more worked up with each passing minute. He was over the edge — there was no logic you could sell him — but I tried anyway. I told Bret that Vince never thought that he would screw him by showing up on WCW with the WWF Title, but that Vince didn't trust Bischoff. I expressed to Bret that though he couldn't possibly see it now — Vince did what he had to do for the company, and that I supported him 100 percent and would have done the same. But Bret wasn't listening. Saying all I could say, I apologized to Bret, telling him I knew he would never understand. But before I hung up the phone Bret said to me: "Vince — you know what I felt like doing the next day? I felt like showing up at the building with a gun and blowing people away."

Obviously Bret didn't mean that — but those words characterize what must have been going through his mind at the time.

I was always a big fan of Bret; not only the performer, but the man as well. Hart was such a respected human being. He was always soft-spoken and sincere. With the exception of Shawn Michaels, I don't think Bret ever had a bad word to say about anybody. But his silence carried great weight. He was from the "speak softly, but carry a big stick" school.

Bret stood tall for everything he represented — and he took that role very seriously. With great pride he wore the mantle of "Canadian Hero," only to be ridiculed by others. But think about it — what athlete today really takes pride in being a hero and role model? It meant a lot to Bret, and where many thought that he was caught up in his own gimmick, I found it noble. He lived to be a hero — and in today's society there is nothing wrong with that. The fact is, we could use more Bret Harts.

That day in Montreal changed him. The mental and emotional scars he has to deal with — only he can understand. At the time, I never dreamed that one match could have the impact it would have on the rest of Bret's life. Add to that the tragic death of his brother — and the man was not, and perhaps never will be, the same again.

On a more personal note, Bret has nothing to be ashamed of. He was always a man of honor, standing up for his beliefs and values regardless of what others thought. Today, the business sorely misses him, and there will never, ever, be another like him. And even though he may sometimes feel he's forgotten as he sits back in his hometown of Calgary, Alberta — he never will be. In my opinion Bret simply was "The best there is, the best there was, and the best there ever will be."

In the week following the Survivor Series, the controversy would not go away. It was all anyone could talk about. It was a major event, and even those in the know were intrigued. Those fans who were 'tweeners — who weren't sure if it was "live or Memorex" — wanted to hear more about it so they could form an opinion. After things settled down a bit, we had a meeting before *Raw* to discuss the situation. Everybody in the room wanted to bury it under the mat: "Let's forget about it and move on." *Yeah — let's get back to rasslin'!* I couldn't believe what I was hearing. At this point, we were still getting hammered by wcw. Bischoff and the nwo were running rampant — and these bananas wanted to sweep the hottest thing we had going under the rug? No way. So I spoke up and basically said: "What, are you guys nuts? This is all everybody is talking about — we've got to go with this." I could see Vince listening . . . and thinking . . . and listening. He then spoke. . . .

"I agree, we need to take advantage of this."

Thus the infamous "I didn't screw Bret . . . Bret screwed Bret," sit-down interview with Vince McMahon that later aired on *Raw*. Sure, some understood, while others didn't have a clue — but those watching were intrigued. They knew something was going on even if they couldn't quite understand what. Regardless, they were tuning in to find out.

We had them.

Man, looking back, that was such an historic moment. To think that only months before Vince had cleared his desk of wrestling-related knick-knacks after reading my shoot article with Bret Hart. He had come a long way in such a short period of time. But the fact was — so had the business.

To be honest, at that moment I didn't fully understand the impact of what had happened. If something like the Montreal screw job happened in the past, it would have been kicked under the rug. But here we were, opening up that curtain and letting the fans in. Suddenly there was a level of sophistication surrounding the product. For the first time, we were telling "the truth" about the business. We were pushing the circus clowns to the side and presenting a new kind of high drama. Remember, this was before the "reality show" craze hit the networks. We were ahead of our time, and people were coming on board.

Chapter 40

PLAYING CENTERFIELD WITH WILLIE MAYS

When I was brought in to "help" write television for the WWF, the rating of the last show before my involvement — the "bi-global cluster" I talked about earlier — was 1.9, one of the lowest *Raw* had ever received. So I guess you could say there was nowhere to go but up.

And up we went.

You can read all you want about creative teams and booking committees, but during the time I was writing with Vince those were fictitious terms. There was no "team" and there was no "committee." It was Vince and I — period. To this day McMahon might not even admit that. For his own reasons, he wants you to think a group of writers gathered in a room every week to write TV. Well, maybe that's the case today, but back then it was just us. And the process worked like this. . . .

After we arrived home from *Raw* I would work on all 11 segments of the following week's show on my own. I would look at our roster of players and make sure that *everybody* was involved in a story line, or an angle. This was quite important to the process, because at the time all Vince cared about was what the top four guys were doing. My philosophy was the top four guys weren't going to be around forever, so we needed to start building the future. So that's how it all began — me, my brain and a computer. Once I had an outline of the 11 segments, I would go to Vince's house the following day. There I would pitch the entire show to Vince, and he would then add his ideas. That usually consisted of a 10-hour day — just Vince and I sitting at his dining room table. I think this is where we complemented each other so well. I would hit Vince with the "big picture," and he would fine-tune it. Regardless of what has been said or what you may think, Vince hardly ever made drastic changes — he more or less went with what I had, adding his two cents to make it better. Remember, it's much easier to tweak a show than it is to sit there with a blank piece of paper and make something out of nothing.

The next day, which was usually a Friday, I would format the show on my computer. That's what it came down to — me and a hard drive. Here is where I went over it with a fine tooth comb — from who would enter the ring first, to who would run-in (interfere in the match), to who would go over (win the match), to whose music needed to be cued after the match, to the loser getting his revenge while the music was still playing. The final format involved everything — pre-tapes, live interviews (with each one written out), vignettes, commercial breaks, everything. Man, writing that was so tedious, so demanding. It took me an average of eight to ten hours just to put the show on paper. From there, I would distribute it to everyone in the TV production department. Then, usually somewhere around 6 p.m. on Friday evening, I would go up to Vince's office with the formatted show and we would tweak some more. The tweaking would go on all weekend, and continue up to and even during the day of the show. But in reality, when we arrived at the building to shoot *Raw*, the show was 95 percent done. Vince and I used that system for the good part of two years — and, I must say, it was magic.

• • •

Growing up in Brooklyn, my father was a New York Giants fan. During his early life, he went round and round with the Dodgers, always remaining loyal to the black and orange. When then-owner Horace Stoneham up and moved the Giants to San Francisco back in 1958, my father remained loyal. He never changed colors, even though his boys were now roaming the diamond some three thousand miles away.

My father loved Willie Mays, the "Say Hey Kid." Hands down, Mays was the greatest Giant — if not baseball player — of all time. Willie roamed centerfield with the grace of no other — making basket-catches on balls others couldn't even get to. He had speed, power and an arm like Johnny Unitas. In his prime, he was the Michael Jordan of his era.

By the time I was eight, I was already following in my father's footsteps. Willie Mays was my lord and savior — and the Giants were my morning, noon and night. Every morning, my father used to leave me the scores from the west coast on my night table, so that the first thing I saw when I woke up was how the Giants did. Whether they won or lost, it would affect my entire day, even back then.

To this very day I am obsessed with San Francisco Giants baseball — it is my one and only pleasure. When the Giants are on, everything else stops. Don't bother me, don't talk to me, leave me alone. When the Giants lose — it's the same — don't talk to me, don't bother me, leave me alone. The Giants are my drug — I can't get enough of them. When it's not baseball season, it's just not the same. I'd rather watch a Giants game than do anything else.

You can imagine how bitter I was when the Giants were in the playoffs against the Florida Marlins in '97, and I had to miss the games because I was writing TV with Vince.

I mention Willie Mays and the Giants because that's what writing television with Vince McMahon was like — playing centerfield next to the Say Hey Kid. It was magical — everything I had ever dreamed of, and more. *Think and Grow Rich?* I was living my dream. Vince and I clicked on all cylinders — I knew what he was thinking, and vice versa. He trusted me, I think because he knew I was sincere. I had no ulterior motives — I just wanted to help make things better. But it was his trust that gave me the confidence and freedom to throw everything his way as quickly as he could digest it. That's how we worked. Vince rarely came up with the big picture — that was my job. And I was never insulted when he didn't like my ideas. Working that closely with Vince, you couldn't allow your feelings to get hurt. I mean, at the end of the day it was his company — if he liked something, he liked it — if he didn't, he didn't. Luckily, nine times out of ten he liked my stuff. Very rarely did we go toe-to-toe. I can only remember one time where I got really hot, and it was because he was caving in to the talent and I knew it was wrong.

It was the "Highway to Hell" Summer Slam, the main event being a match between the Undertaker and Steve Austin. 'Taker and Steve were hell bent on going into the match with a respect for each other, rather than a hatred. The reason was obvious — behind the scenes these guys got along. But the truth was nobody cared if these guys went out drinking after a long-day's-rockin'. They wanted to see them kill each other. Well, Vince caved, and the match sucked. It was Madison Square Garden — a full house — and *nobody* cared. After the match Austin and 'Taker were both disappointed; they couldn't understand the lack of crowd response. Hey, I could have told them . . . and did. I was from New Yawk — remember?

But all in all, being able to work with Vince on that level was a gift. There are just so many misconceptions about him, things that you would never know unless you'd worked that closely with him. When it comes to concepts, ideas and the big picture, McMahon may not be the master everybody makes him out to be. In my opinion, his forté, and the thing that constantly used to blow me away about him, is that he could always make things just a little bit better. He visualized things better than I ever could. It was his small tweak here and there that would turn a 50 million dollar picture into a 100 million dollar blockbuster. That was his genius: seeing things that nobody else could.

It was no surprise when, week by week, the ratings began to climb. One of the main reasons was patience. Vince knew the business was changing with every word we put down on paper — and success wasn't going to come overnight. Every week we would be sitting at his house when the ratings came in — and Vince never got excited one way or another. All he did was stay the course — *patience*. That was a big difference when I went to wcw. They wanted to see results the following week — and it just doesn't happen that way. It took the better part of eight months just to get the ratings out of the twos, barely touching the threes. I tried to explain that to the chiefs at wcw many times — but they didn't get it. In fact, there was very little they did get. But again, that's another story for another time.

When the first quarter of '98 came along, the ratings were in the mid-threes. Vince and I used to kid each other, saying, "We work damn hard for those threes," and we did. We wrote every show to be better than the last, and every show as if it were our last. You see, there was a formula. Along with patience, Vince and I took every traditional rasslin' outcome or finish, and went the other way. Whatever the audience was expecting — give them the unexpected. Immediately this brought *unpredictability* to the product — something it had been lacking for years. Babyfaces would do heel things and sometimes heels would even do babyface things. This was unheard of. It had been written in stone — a heel had to act one way, while a babyface acted another. Well, guess what? We dropped — no, threw — that stone off the Brooklyn Bridge. There were no more rules and regulations.

After throwing out the rule book, we concentrated on writing stories, shooting angles and creating characters that had a razor-sharp cutting edge — an attitude that the business had never seen before. We were standing up and screaming "@#!$ you!" at the top of our lungs and people were starting to pay attention. Without a doubt, we had become *dangerous*, and slowly, but surely, *Raw* was becoming the "in thing" to watch.

And yes — we had a little bit of luck on our side.

Chapter 41

THE BOTTOM LINE

There were many variables that led to the somewhat quick success Vince and I achieved, but a large part of it can be attributed to Stone Cold Steve Austin. Another little known fact is that when Austin was brought into the WWF and given the moniker "Ringmaster" (I swear to you, when Prichard first told me I thought it had something to do with the circus), Vince gave me direct orders: when writing for Steve, "Let Ted DiBiase [Austin's manager at the time] do most of his talking. And when Steve does speak, he should speak only in a monotone."

I could care less what Vince McMahon will tell you today — back then, he saw nothing in Steve Austin. The only reason we'd had a discussion about him in the first place was because I brought it up. When he first came to the WWF from ECW, Steve was viewed as one of those underneath guys, or "mid-carders," that Vince didn't have much, if any, time for. I had to laugh a few years later when Vince, on a biography special about Austin, said that he saw Steve at ECW and knew immediately he could be a huge star. First of all — Vince *never* watched ECW. The only thing he knew about the promotion is what others told him. And for him to say that about Austin . . . Steve would be the first to tell you that he practically had to beg Vince for a job. But to be honest, even I didn't see the success that lay before him. Yeah, I was a big fan of his over at WCW, but I never knew he would almost become bigger than the game itself.

Man, I can remember producing those early promos for Austin. He hated that monotone nonsense, but it was what the boss wanted, so he did it — no complaints. The character of the Ringmaster went on for a while, until Steve himself busted out of that shell and refused to be denied. As Vince and I were hitting stride and becoming comfortable with each other — so was Stone Cold Steve Austin. I'll never forget — right around the time he won King of the Ring, there was an episode of *Raw* in which Austin sat in on color for the first time. It was one of those true TV moments, like seeing Gene Simmons spit blood live and in person from the front row of Madison Square Garden for the first time when I was 16. My mouth hit the floor — what had we been we thinking?

But for as good as he was, Steve needed something perhaps even better to play off.

Give all the credit to Vince; it was his idea to portray himself as "Vince McMahon, owner of the Evil Empire." For years, Vince had made an effort to stay out of the limelight. Even though it was a known fact that he owned the company, he had never really been involved in a story line or angle. He had been untouchable and above the fray. It was unthinkable to involve him in the ring — he was just too important — and that's exactly why it was such a *huge* deal to see his character become part of the mix. I think what it came down to was this: deep down, he knew that if he was going to get the ratings back up he wasn't going to rely on anybody other than himself. Vince had the foresight to see that he could outperform 95 percent of the roster — and he did. In that character, Vince was amazing. He was the guy you just couldn't wait to boo every Monday night. There was no doubt — again in the words of James E. Cornette — "Vince became the biggest heel in the territory."

Through a natural progression, Stone Cold Steve Austin and Vince McMahon would cross paths — and when they did, we had them — the fans were eating out of our hands. Not only was the chemistry between them sweeter than Simon and Garfunkel, but they were telling a story every blue-collar worker could relate to. Every hard-working man who earns his pay 60 hours a week with his own two hands would love the opportunity — just once — to tell his boss to stick it . . . well, you know where. Steve Austin spoke for all those people. And Vince represented Corporate America — perhaps the biggest "heel" in the world. Whether you were a wrestling fan or not, you were now tuning in on Monday nights to watch *Raw*. Having a front-row seat through it all, I can now tell you that no two other individuals could have pulled it off. Vince and Austin *were* their alter egos — that's what made it so believable.

And I must say this — Vince was a gamer. Whatever was needed of him, he did. Probably one too many times I asked him to perform in the ring because the story begged for it, and whether he was banged up or not — Vince put on his black pants and muscle tee and went out there and did it. Remember, the guy was already in his 50s. Give him all the credit in the world — that's nothing short of incredible. I know. I first hit the ring when I was still under 40, and man, it was taxing. And I didn't do one-tenth of the crazy stuff the boss did. But again, Vince was leading by example. I'll never forget the time I made him chase a chicken in butt-deep snow, while he was sporting a horrible cold, just so I could get off on my *Rocky* fixation. But when that particular vignette aired — there was no doubt it was a Slammy Award winner.

I can go on forever about McMahon vs. Austin. A story like that only happens once in a lifetime. It was like seeing Pacino and Brando on the screen together — their story was the backbone of our success. But keep in mind, it was going to take more than one good story to pull us out of the grave that we had dug for ourselves.

● ● ●

It turned my stomach when weeks after I left the WWF for WCW, a WWF internet host poised this question to Shane McMahon on *Byte This:*

"How do you feel about Vince Russo taking all the credit for the success of the WWF?"

It really hurt. I have never once taken credit for the success of the WWF. I was put into a situation where a lot of good things happened at the same time. A great part of my success can be attributed to Stone Cold. Austin was just beginning to hit his stride when I began writing. It's no different than Dusty Baker managing Barry Bonds, or Scorsese directing DeNiro. Steve was such a pro — you gave it to him and he ran it in.

But on the other hand, please don't tell me it was a "group" of writers who were responsible for the success. After my departure, the PR mannequin at Titan sports said, "Vince Russo was one of a team of writers . . . blah, blah, blah." I have no reason to lie to you — there was no team — it was me writing a show (first alone and then with the help of Ed Ferrara, a former Hollywood television writer who was everything I wasn't — he could spell and use much bigger words), and handing it to Vince. So yeah — I'll give others credit all day long, but give me my props, too. Like I said, put Al Pacino in *Monkeybone,* and you've still got . . . *Monkeybone!*

Anyway, after Austin defeated Shawn Michaels at WrestleMania XIV, Vince gave me the order: "When at TV — mirror Steve 24/7. He is your priority. Be there for him at all times, nothing else is as important." And that's what I did. Those early stages with Steve as the new WWF Champion were vital. Vince knew then that he had something special on his hands, and he wanted the situation treated accordingly.

I spent a lot of time with Steve during that period — yet I never got close to him. Personally, I didn't make a habit of becoming friends with the talent, because, as I've said, I learned early on there are no friends in wrestling — only "business associates." But behind the curtain, Steve let few, if any, people in anyway. He kept to himself more often than not and he just preferred it that way. Don't get me wrong, he wasn't introverted at all — he even played the role of class clown at times — he had a great personality, his smile would light up the whole arena. What I mean is, he never really let you get close. But there was one occasion where I saw a different side of Steve.

Austin rarely showed emotion — he just wasn't a huggy-feely kind of guy. But I'll never forget the day after Owen Hart passed away — Steve could tell I was distraught. Man, I wrote the story. I'd written down on paper: "the Blue Blazer descends from atop the arena." I'll get more into that tragic day later, but Steve came over to me and said, "Don't blame this on yourself — it wasn't your fault." Then he walked away. Coming from Steve, that meant a lot. I'm certain he doesn't even remember it — but it was something I'll never forget.

Steve Austin knew the Stone Cold character better than anyone. It was his alter ego, his baby. So when Steve told you he "didn't feel it," you usually moved on to something else. When in the zone, Steve was awesome. Yeah, it's a stupid word to use, but I can't think of a better one. He just had it all. The one thing I respected most about Steve is that no matter how big he became, he worked every match as if it were his last. His work ethic was through the roof.

Sometimes it became a nightmare — but it's also totally understandable — Steve always wanted to know every aspect of his story line for the upcoming week. He wanted to be sure that every detail, down to the smallest thing, made sense. On occasion I became frustrated by this, because if you pick a story apart long enough, you're going to find something wrong with it. And sometimes Steve did that. The fact is, many times he drove even himself nuts. But I respected and understood that about him. It was a big part of what made that character so successful.

Steve got so much, so fast, that I think, in time, he became paranoid — always thinking that it could all end in a heartbeat. In my opinion, that's why he dissected everything. It had taken him a long time to get to the top, and now that he was there, he wanted to be sure he wasn't leaving before he was ready. But whether he was the Ringmaster or Stone Cold, our relationship never changed; that's one thing I learned from my experience with Steve Austin: treat everybody like they are the top star — because some day they might be.

One other thing about Austin — he was the most stubborn SOB I've ever meet. And if you crossed him once, you were dead in his eyes. Austin never forgave Owen Hart for dropping him on his head and causing a severe neck injury. Regardless of how bad Owen felt, or how many times he apologized over the miscalculated move, Steve wouldn't let it go. Again, with that sense of paranoia the business creates, Austin no doubt felt it was intentional. Then there was Jeff Jarrett's in-ring promo, where Double J made a disparaging remark about Austin's 3:16 T-shirts. Even though Jeff was a heel and actually putting over Austin's T-shirts (if a bad guy tells the fans not to buy or support something — they will), after Jeff's comments, Steve was waiting for him on the other side of the curtain. He proceeded to cut into him, feeling that Jarrett was hurting T-shirt sales (the boys make a profit from their merchandise). I could understand how Steve viewed it at the time, but he never forgave Jeff, and went as far as refusing to ever work with him again. And, maybe with the exception of Shawn Michaels, nobody could make Vince cave like Austin. If Steve didn't like it, whether he had a valid reason or not, Vince would change it. I once got into an argument with Vince — telling him that no one star is bigger than the WWF. Hogan wasn't, Shawn wasn't, Bret wasn't and Austin wasn't either. But Vince never listened — he would cave anyway.

Still, I have to say it was a privilege working with Steve during that time. It was special — an experience that cannot and will not ever be repeated.

Chapter 42

BREAK IT DOWN

With one piece of the puzzle now in place — it was time to create the others. Shane McMahon had a lot to do with bringing the idea of "Degeneration X" to fruition.

Degeneration X was the name of an upcoming WWF pay-per-view. At the time Vince and I were trying to come up with something to combat WCW's NWO. We realized that as much as the NWO was over at the time, you were talking about three guys — Nash, Hall and Hogan — who were probably already past their prime. On the other hand, as Vince said, we had "the real deal" — young lions who could go.

Three spots of DX were immediately cast — Shawn Michaels, Paul Levesque (a.k.a. Hunter Hearst-Helmsley), and his partner in crime Joanie Laurer (Chyna), who were connected through a story line. Probably more than anybody else, those three represented what was cool and hip in American culture at the time — in-your-face, screw authority, do what you want to do when you want to do it. Plus, all three personalities had a real sense of the business. They knew what the fans wanted and were ready to deliver it.

Just a side note: I'll never forget Jim Cornette sitting at Vince McMahon's dining room table and making the statement — "Triple H will never draw a dime in this business." No, Jim, he hasn't drawn a dime, he's drawn a *billion dimes!*

We would go with the duo of Shawn and Hunter for a while, but our immediate plans were to add two more guys to round out the group. It was Vince who suggested Road Dog Jesse James (Brian Armstrong) and Bad Ass Billy Gunn ("Kip" Sopp). I've got to be honest — I just didn't see it. Vince, however, did. He sold me on the idea — even though he didn't need to — and we had the final line-up for DX. During those early months, Shane McMahon, then in his mid-20s, brought a lot of energy to the project. He was the same age as the demographic we were looking for — and hip to what was going on. Shane was instrumental in bringing the whole concept together — from the look, to the music, to what they wore, to their ring entrance. His excitement really got me hooked into the concept.

Another little-known fact. . . . As I've said, we started with Shawn and Hunter, and slowly but surely DX started to catch on. But what really pushed it to the next level was the catch phrase, "Suck it!" The million dollar motto was never really planned. One day Shawn was walking down the aisle towards the ring with DX music blaring in the background. On his way towards the ring Shawn kept mouthing the words, "Suck it, Suck it, Suck it," while chopping his crotch. It was another Austin 3:16 moment for me — I knew he had something.

But really, the little-known fact I was talking about is this: as the gimmick started to get over, Shawn and Hunter were skeptical about putting Billy and Road Dog in the group. They were mid-carders at the time, and the main-eventers were afraid of being brought down. So, the New Age Outlaws were born. The plan was to build Road Dog and Billy as a team first, get them over and then marry them to DX. The plan worked like a charm. But then again, with the personality of B. G. James (Road Dog), how could you not get yourself over?

All of those successes were cooperative, with Vince and I creating the situations, and the talent doing the rest to pull it off. At that time everybody stepped up to the plate, and everybody was hitting Barry Bonds–type home runs. DX was over — but now we needed something to help put them over the top.

To me, it was a no-brainer. I firmly believe that when you are number one, ignore number two. Act as if they don't exist. However, when you're number two and you're doing the chasing . . . throw everything you've got at the top dogs. My idea for Vince: let's declare war on WCW. Let's go right after them publicly. Let's pull out all the stops.

The rest is history.

•   •   •

Last night I brought my kids to see Tenacious D.

Man, I've got to tell you — Jack Black and Kyle Gass are two of the most talented musicians I've ever seen. If you don't know who they are, Jack Black is an actor who recently played the lead opposite Gwenyth Paltrow in *Shallow Hal*, and Kyle Gass is an amazing fat, bald, comedic genius who can tear the house down with an acoustic guitar. Think about that — in the year 2002 a fat, bald guy with an acoustic guitar is tearing down the house! But that's just it — the D is a gimmick. They know it, they play it and the fans eat it up.

Today, however, my question: why were Will and VJ the only two kids in the house? Is something wrong with me? Or is something wrong with everybody else?

Man, parenting is a complex thing. How do you know whether or not you're doing a good job? You'll find out 10 years from now, but by then it may be too late. What is the right way, and what is the wrong way to raise a child? My philosophy is so different from a lot of people I know — especially here in Hickville. I believe in exposing my kids to everything and then letting them make the decision. I don't know — I guess being a creative guy I strongly believe in freedom of expression. I don't believe in shielding my kids from the real world. Hell, there's a lot going on out there, and sooner or later, they are going to be exposed to life. I don't want to draw them a Dr. Seuss cartoon just to have them find out that the Cat in the Hat is really Fritz the Cat — and he's out there pawing every animated feline he can get his claws on!

Is this wrong?

I don't know. I treat my boys with respect; I think they're old enough to handle it. I just believe in allowing them to be individuals, letting *them* decide who they are — not me. Amy and I go toe-to-toe over it, but I'd rather they be exposed to what's really out there.

Man, here in Atlanta it's so backwards. It seems that here in the South they want all the kids to be cut out of the same mold, with the same values, principles and goals. I *despise* that. Sure, you set boundaries for your children, but then you have to take off the leash and let them explore. If you've raised your kids the right way, with the right principles, they will remain within your guidelines, even when you give them the freedom to more or less find their own way.

Here I go playing Dr. Phil again. Kids want what they can't have — plain and simple. The more things you make forbidden, the more they'll want to explore those things. If you don't make it a big deal, it won't be a big deal.

Was something wrong with me . . . or everybody else?

Why are we programmed to think something is always wrong with "everybody else"? Here I was bringing my 11 year old to a curse fest (though comedians, the D used vulgar language and sexual content in spades to get a laugh). There are no other kids in sight, and I think something's wrong with everybody else?

You know, even though I've been saved for more than a year now, I still believe in letting your kids be exposed to the real world. Why? Simply because you can't protect them from it. You may want to, but you can't. You can't go to school with them every day, you can't be with them when they're hanging out with their friends. There's just so much that's out of your control. But back then, I thought I was being "hip" by letting my kids do what they wanted, I thought I'd be the "cool" dad. I put them in a situation where they'd "find out things for themselves."

Luckily, I didn't get burned — but it could have been disastrous.

Once God came into my life my kids could see a change. All of a sudden Dad was "different" and they wanted to know why. But something else happened along the way — they liked this new Dad. This new Dad was "cool" and "hip" without even trying to be. Suddenly, without saying much — they had an example to follow. Dad is happy now. We want to be happy — we need to be like Dad.

Today my kids follow Christ, and not only do they have a role model in me, they have the greatest role model of all.

• • •

In my humble opinion, one of the key ingredients to us overcoming WCW was DX's assault. We sent DX on missions to the CNN Center, arenas where WCW was playing, WCW headquarters — wherever WCW was, we got in their faces and wouldn't go away. Man, this was an exciting time.

Something of this magnitude had never been attempted. In the past, Vince refused to acknowledge the competition — you *never* mentioned them. But this was a new time — none of the old rules applied. For the first time ever the WWF was second best, and it was time to pull out the heavy artillery, regardless of the consequences. And I'm not taking about the Huckster and Nacho Man, childish and flat parodies of WCW that Vince designed and which fell short of the mark. This was: we're on live TV, daring you to do something. What are you going to do?

All we wanted was to get WCW to acknowledge us — and they did. There is no doubt that our attacks got under their skin. We made it clear to Eric Bischoff that we were coming, and we were coming hard. I later had the opportunity to ask Eric where he was the day DX drove a missile launcher to the back door of an arena where WCW was playing. Eric said, "I wasn't there that day."

Right Eric — and you're president of the Vince Russo Fan Club.

The tide was starting to turn, you could just feel it. If anything, the fan at home had to be saying, "Man, I don't believe the spaldings on these guys." People were starting to sit up and take notice. Meanwhile over in Turnerland, it was beginning to be same old, same old. The NWO angle was being hashed, rehashed and hashed again week after week. Suddenly everybody was joining the group. It was beginning to look like the Von Trapp family and they were starting to Do-Re-Mi, and everybody else, to sleep.

So now we've got two huge things happening at the same time. In one corner, the Texas Rattlesnake is quickly becoming a pop-culture icon, while in the other corner, DX was telling the American People to "Suck it" . . . and they were loving it. The question loomed, "How do we marry these two franchises?"

Vince had the answer.

Chapter 43

IRON MIKE

If Iron Mike Tyson had not bitten the ear of Evander Holyfield, I might be writing a much different story today. As bizarre as that incident was, nobody could have known the impact it was to have in the months and years to come for the World Wrestling Federation.

Due to his total violation of the rules, Mike Tyson's ban from professional boxing left the boxing pay-per-view business in a hole. For years, Mike had been their drawing card — the only time they made significant money was when he stood between the ropes. Now they were screwed. No Tyson, no buys — no money. The boxing world just wasn't the same. Say what you will about him, but people wanted their Iron Mike . . . any way they could get him.

Vince picked up on this immediately. The fact was, people paid money to see Mike Tyson on pay-per-view. He wasn't allowed to box anymore, so they weren't going to get their fix there. But if we could somehow, some way, get him involved in WrestleMania xiv — also on pay-per-view — would those same people pay to see Mike just for the sake of seeing Mike? It was a gamble, but Vince had a feeling. To be honest, I wasn't sold on the deal. But I did understand one thing: Mike Tyson would bring the WWF mainstream exposure.

So Vince went to work and Mike Tyson was soon signed. The story was covered *everywhere*. Most reports were negative — but who cared? There's no such thing as negative publicity in the wrestling business. If the outside world acknowledges us, *it's all good!* They were talking about Mike Tyson and the WWF in the same breath. At the time that Tyson was talking to Vince, Mike was having contractual problems with Don King. Knowing Vince, and with a few things I'd overheard, I think Vince was seriously considering managing Tyson's boxing career. Again, I'm not going to state that as a fact, but rather as a strong opinion. Man, could you imagine that marriage?

So now we had Tyson, what were we going to do with him? Again, all the ideas were the same — that old '70s wrestling !@#$%. "Tyson is a babyface in people's eyes — so let's buddy Mike up with Austin. An Austin rub may even help Mike with those burying him over the Holyfield incident." And again, I had to say something.

"Are you nuts? Forget Mike Tyson. Is this about what we can do for him or what he can do for us? Everybody is expecting what has just been laid out. Why don't we have Tyson go toe-to-toe with Shawn Michaels? Paint the picture that they're gonna go, then let Mike rip off his shirt to reveal a DX T-shirt underneath. Remember — *go the other way!*"

Vince bought it — and we did it. Nobody saw it coming, and now all of a sudden you had an issue between Steve Austin and Mike Tyson, perceived as perhaps the two toughest SOB's on the planet at the time. If you weren't watching WrestleMania before, you were watching it now. The momentum was building up — we were coming and nobody could get in our way. The WWF machine was firing on all cylinders — the tide wasn't just beginning to turn, we were a tidal wave.

Iron Mike Tyson provided just the punch we needed. Wrestle-

Mania xiv was a huge success. But let me also point out that *everybody* involved had a hand in our success. It was a period where everybody was at the top of their game. The entire locker room was working as a family, one unit, with the same purpose: to take back what was ours . . . that number one spot in the ratings.

Chapter 44

THE SECRET WEAPON

So there we were. WrestleMania xiv was a smash hit; Austin/ McMahon was on fire; and DX was in while the NWO was moving out in a hurry. Everything was going right. We had all the ingredients we needed — except, perhaps, just a little pinch of *sex.*

Now, I'm not going to go on another T & A rampage here, but the truth is, that's what our core audience wanted. I know the only reason I watched the movie *O* for two and a half hours was in hopes of seeing Julia Stiles naked. (Which, I might add, I didn't — so just pass on the freaking thing.) *Rock Star* would have been a hit instead of a bomb if only Jennifer Aniston had taken off her shirt for a few seconds. Sarah Michelle Gellar has a no-nudity clause in her contract — I'll save my eight bucks. I will go see Alyssa Milano in *anything* — even something that goes straight to video, as long as it's rated R and there's even an outside chance of me seeing something . . . *anything!*

Do I have a problem? Hell yeah, I'm a male! I'm the guy watching our show on Monday nights! I'll take anything — Jules Asner in a tight shirt with no bra, or Jennifer Love Hewitt in a tight bra with no shirt — *give me anything!*

We gave them something, all right . . . we gave them Sable.

●　　●　　●

I would just like to add that even though I am personally a huge fan of the boob and the butt, the bottom line is: it really doesn't matter. I've said this a thousand times, so I might as well say it a thousand-and-one — it was never about what Vince Russo wanted — or, for that matter, even about what Vince McMahon wanted. It was always about what *the fans* wanted.

That was the downfall of many a booker in the past. Before and after me, others seem to have a tendency to write what they like — what they enjoy. Well guess what? It's not about them — it never was and never will be. All that matters is what the fans want. During my days at the WWF, I used to go out into the crowd and just listen to the fans, to see what they were buying, see what they weren't. That was my most valuable tool. From there I would study the ratings inside out — to see what they were tuning into and what they were tuning out. If it was getting over with the fans, we went with it. If they weren't buying it, we canned it. It really wasn't rocket science, kids — as a matter of fact it was simple. But today you combine the "good ol' boys" writing network with their politics — and in my opinion you have a product that is almost unwatchable.

Two short years later, and what made me tick and why I made the choices I made, have become crystal clear. All that talk about Julia Stiles and Sarah Michelle Gellar was just that — talk. An effort for me to seem cool, hip, to impress you. I was 41 years old at the time. You think I really cared about seeing Buffy in the buff? I didn't — what was I trying to do was please you, please this world, to be accepted at any cost. And I pulled out all the stops — from sex, to violence, to drugs, to nudity, to homosexuality, to transvestites, to men beating women, to the killing of small household pets, to castration, to the unnatural love between a mother and her son, to demonic worship, to demonic sacrifices, to blasphemy, to the degrading of the cross.

If I thought you wanted it, I dished it up.

And that was my downfall. How was I glorifying God through that potpourri of smut? Is that why he put Vince Russo on this earth? That was my mistake — trying to please my fellow man. I wanted you to accept me and I wanted you to accept our product. That was my downfall in the eyes of God. Thus, the depression, the distant marriage, the darkness, the pain, the misery.

To make the situation more clear to you, let me show you a column Bob Ryder (now a friend) wrote for his website, 1wrestling.com:

RAW IS PORN
December 22, 1998

Did any of you seriously think I wasn't going to write about this?

I'm often asked to describe what it is about the WWF that prompts the criticism I throw their way. Last night's edition of RAW is PORN sums it up. What possible wrestling-related reason was there for the Mark Henry skit?

For those who were lucky enough to miss this, Mark Henry, Terri Runnels and Jacquelyn were involved in the segment, which spanned most of the last half-hour of the program. After removing Henry's clothing (except for his boxer shorts), the women lay him on a massage table, put a chain around his neck, oiled him down with coconut oil, covered him with whipped cream (which Terri licked off), stuck a ball-gag in his mouth, tied his hands and feet to the table, whipped him and (according to off-screen play-by-play from Jerry Lawler) proceeded to use a vibrator, gerbils and hot wax on him. All of this with a backdrop of moaning and groaning throughout the segment.

The segment reached its "climax" when D-Lo Brown yelled that it was time for his match and Henry screamed out, "I'm coming, I'm coming!"

After the match, a slimy Mark Henry appeared on the ramp to explain what happened to an angry D-Lo.

Was that segment really necessary?

word out for you — J-E-A-L-O-U-S-Y. How dare a female make it in a male-dominated world? How dare a female get more television time than one of the boys? In my view, they were simply acting like children. The fact was, I didn't care if a chimpanzee scratching his butt was pulling in numbers. If the fans wanted to see a monkey, I would send his hairy rear out there each and every week. Rena was drawing huge numbers, and the bigger she became, the more bitter the boys got. Think of the position that put Marc in. He's one of the boys — but he was married to Rena. Man, it was getting ugly. There was even an incident where Rena and Marc were working a tour overseas, and one of the boys actually defecated in Rena's bag. How sad and barbaric is that?

Despite Rena's success — Vince was being persuaded by the boys to diminish her role. I'll say it: I love the guy, but when it comes to women in the business, in my humble opinion, Vince takes on a sexist attitude. In his world, women are only going to make it to a certain point, and then they're gonna get chopped back down to reality. That's just the way it is. It happened with Sable, and it happened with Chyna. Behind that curtain it's a man's world, and if you're a woman and they start cheering your name, start looking for another job.

Due to all the childish politics, tension between Vince and Rena grew until lawyers were brought in. Eventually, the parties involved went their separate ways. I remember Vince being so proud, bragging to the boys that he had beaten Rena and Marc in a legal battle, and that the Meros were walking away with nothing. All I could think was: "What are you walking away with, Vince? You just lost a property that was earning you cash on top of cash."

But again — so goes the wrestling business.

I've got another favorite story about Rena. Sable was to be a participant in an upcoming bikini contest that was to be broadcast live on pay-per-view. About a week before the event, her husband Marc told me Rena had an idea. Instead of wearing the traditional bikini she wanted to wear only a G-string, with latex hands painted over her bare breasts. Now, you've got to understand, even though I would never have acted on it, I was still a male and I was smitten with Rena at the time. Marc knew it, I think everybody knew it. (That's probably another reason why she had so much heat.) So I told Marc, "Well, if that's what she wants to do — there's nothing I can do to stop her."

Man, I couldn't wait to see this. Let's face it, this was the closest I was ever going to get. You know how it is when you have that fantasy woman in mind, the one you dream about. We all saw *The Woman in Red*. Gene Wilder knew he was never going to get anywhere near a young Kelly LeBrock. . . .

Sunday and the pay-per-view couldn't come quickly enough. If Tom Buchanan, the head WWF photographer, missed this one, I was going to hurt him, personally. About an hour before show time, Marc tracks me down in the locker room and says, "Vince, come with me — I want to show you something." He leads me into Rena's dressing room.

I swear to you — I'm sweating. I'm flushed, I'm faint, I need air, I'm going to puke. Rena walks out of the bathroom — and there she is with nothing but a G-string and two hands painted onto her bare-naked bazooms! Marc asked, "Well — what do you think?" I was Ralph Kramden: "Humna, humna, humna, humna." What did Marc want me to say? Looking back on it now, he must have done that on purpose, just to see my reaction. I've got to tell you though — I tip my hat to Marc. He is so confident in his relationship with his wife that he never worries about things like that. And, make no bones about it, Rena adores Marc. But if that were my wife? Not only would she never leave the house, I'd deadbolt the doors and buy myself a pit bull that eats only human flesh!

To this day, I stay in contact with Marc and Rena. The only problem is that since Marc became Rena's agent, he doesn't let me talk to her anymore. That's understandable — after reading this *he's* probably not going to talk to me anymore! All kidding aside, the Meros are true friends, a rare breed when your booking days are over.

It's just mind-blowing what wrestling does to people. The security I just talked about between Marc and Rena — the fact that Rena adored Marc? Two years later — over, done. Rena found somebody else — in the wrestling business.

You know, I recently ran into Marc, after not having seen him for two years, and he admitted to me he knew where he needed to be in his life. But he wasn't there. Marc was clearly talking about his walk with Christ. Marc also told me that at a certain point in their careers, he and Rena chose money (Rena posing for *Playboy*) over what they knew was right. Obviously the outcome was not what I think either of them expected.

We can glorify him or we can glorify ourselves — the choice is ours.

Chapter 45

FORGET BURNS & ALLEN — IT'S
TIME FOR THE ROCK-N-SOCK CONNECTION

So now we were in the midst of a soap opera fueled by both high drama and sex. The only missing ingredient was comedy. Yeah, there was *some* wrestling, mixed in there — but to my taste it was always too much. Vince and I used to joke that our goal was to eventually have *no ring* at all. It just got to the point that it wasn't really about the wrestling anymore. Casual fans were tuning in by the droves just to get their weekly fix of this male-oriented soap opera. The masses didn't want to see 20-minute wrestling matches, they wanted to see all the stuff that went on in between. The bottom line was, and still is: hardcore fans are always going to watch the show as long as the word "wrestling" is somewhere in the title. That's what wrestling fans do — they watch wrestling. The key was to draw in that television viewer that wasn't a wrestling fan. And because we had a little somethin'-somethin' for everybody, that's what we were able to do.

In looking to add that pinch of comic relief — we really didn't have anything particular in mind — I guess you can say it just magically happened. Traveling two separate roads, somehow, Mick Foley and the Rock met at an intersection. Like Austin and McMahon, the chemistry between the two superstars was simply magical. If Austin/McMahon was the David Blaine New York Street Show, then Mankind/Rock was the *Wonderful World of Disney!* Man, an angel had to be sitting on our shoulder for all these things to work out the way they did. It was like everything came together at once. We weren't missing a beat — everything we touched was turning into gold. I don't think there'll be another time like that in sports entertainment history. And, what an honor it was to work so closely with two men I admire and respect — Mick Foley and the Rock. By far some of the fondest memories I have from my 10-plus years in the business revolve around them.

How could you not love Mick Foley? Here is a guy who would do anything — I mean *anything* — that was asked of him. He was the most unselfish person I think I have ever come across. Mick is the kind of guy you would want to bring home to meet the family, maybe play a couple of games of "Twister" and hope he'd never leave. He's everybody's best friend. That teddy-bear smile tattooed on his face is stuck in my mind to this day. You just always looked forward to seeing Mick.

Mick and I had a lot in common. We were both from Long Island, and we both knew John Arezzi. As a matter of fact, the first time I met Mick was on Arezzi's radio show on WGBB. From that first day until the last time I saw him, the guy never changed. No matter how big he got, ego was never an issue. Mick was one of those guys who, in my opinion, was just too damn good for the business. He was smart, intelligent and no doubt would have been successful in whatever he chose to do. But for Mick that choice was easy. By the time he was a teenager, Mick was jumping off the roof of his Smithtown, Long Island, house in a public display of his love and admiration for professional wrestling.

One of the most difficult things I ever had to do during my tenure as head writer for the World Wrestling Federation was to look Mick Foley in the eye and tell him that he wasn't going to be a part of the main event at WrestleMania xv. Mick's dream was to main-event a WrestleMania, and knowing that, I did everything within my power to make that happen. The story was written. WrestleMania xv was going to headline with Stone Cold Steve Austin, the Rock and Mick Foley competing in a three-way match to determine the WWF Champion. Vince agreed to it, and we were set.

The *Raw* that was already written for that week was to lay down the groundwork for the match. Well, when we arrived at the building, Shawn Michaels made an appearance . . . an unbooked, unanticipated, unexpected appearance. Man, Shawn could stir it when he wanted to — and he knew exactly what buttons to push. Shawn got in Austin's ear and somehow convinced Steve that the WrestleMania xv main event should be just himself and the Rock. Austin, who was on the surface a good friend of Mick's, then went to Vince (whether he sold Shawn's opinion as his own I don't know) and, as he had done before when it came to talent, Vince caved, or "changed his mind." Mick was out, just like that. I was nuts at Shawn — livid. If anyone deserved to be in the main event at Mania it was Mick. And of course, nobody had the spaldings to tell Mick he was out — so I had to. Looking in his eyes that day, he was crushed. We both knew it was absolutely wrong, but that's how the business is, most of the time.

Later on, I think I buried Shawn to somebody, probably Hunter. After catching wind of it, the Heartbreak Kid threatened to kick my butt if I said another word. I think his exact words were "I know I can take you." Whether Shawn wanted to kick my butt or not didn't really matter to me at that time. What mattered was that a good man took the hammer. But as always, Mick did business without ever saying a word — that's just the way Mick is.

Following WrestleMania xv and the headaches leading up to it, Vince never wanted to see or hear from Shawn Michaels again. He was just flat done with him. But there I was at Vince's house, every week, lobbying to bring back the Heartbreak Kid. Sitting here thinking back, there was yet another instance where I was threatened by Shawn. One day, after I'd called him and told him we needed him at television, Vince changed his mind. Shawn had made some public comments the boss didn't like concerning one of the boys. I called Shawn to tell him to stay home, but I couldn't get a hold of him. So when he showed up at TV and was told he wasn't going to be used — he came looking for me! Yeah, me, the same guy who was *begging* Vince on a weekly basis to put Shawn back on the air. . . .

But again, to me it was all about the product. If Shawn was difficult to deal with at times, so be it — deal with him! At the time he was the best, hands down. You couldn't shelve him just because there was some maintenance involved. What we gained by having him appear on *Raw* always outweighed the loss of time spent catering to him. And I don't mean that in a negative way — there was always some "catering" involved when it came to the big-time players.

I hope I can once again spend some time with Mick Foley. To this day, I don't even think he has the slightest idea of the influence he had on me. Mick taught me to never change — to always be true to yourself, no matter if you're on top of Mount Everest or at the bottom of the Hudson River. I wish some of wrestling's egomaniacs would take a page out of Mick's book and quit taking themselves so seriously. It's only wrestling, boys. Mick — I never had the chance to tell you then, so I'll tell you now — thank you. Whether you realize it or not, you made a difference in my life.

Inside the ring, Foley was a flat-out freak. With the body of Dom DeLuise, Mick would fly through the air like Peter Pan, crash on his head like Evel Knievel — then get right back up like Rocky Balboa and do it all again. We used to have this tiny Frenchman on the road whose name was François Petite. A character in his own right, François was responsible for putting the boys "back together," courtesy of manipulating bones and non-invasive medical procedures. If it weren't for François' work on the walking wounded, some nights we might not have had a show. While some swore by him and others swore *at* him, the colorful "artist" also claimed to be many things —

from a general in the Foreign Legion to a brain surgeon. We never knew whether this guy was the real deal or Walter Mitty, but I will tell you this — François also practiced shiatsu, and man, when he worked your back, it was the next best thing to getting a day off (which, by the way, was unthinkable). Though daggers at times, his fingers could put you back into a place where you were pain free. One of the few things I do miss about the road is having François put me through 15 minutes of agonizing ecstasy.

On the road every week, for what seemed like hours, François would work on Mick — "Let me put this here — and this over here." I used to just sit and watch in amazement. Then, after working himself into a sweat, François would collapse into a chair and say in his gay, French accent (make no mistake, François is not *gay* — he's married to a beautiful model — but his accent *is*): "Vince, I don't know what to do. His spleen is where his liver should be, his liver is somewhere up near his small intestine — he's a freak, Mick is a freak!" And Mick Foley *was* a wonder of science. How he's even able to walk today is beyond me.

I was backstage while François worked on Mick following his Hell in the Cell classic against the Undertaker, when Mick took those two horrific bumps. (A 15-foot drop from the top of the cell, through the announcers' table to the floor, and a straight-back bump from the top of the cage all the way to the mat. . . . The second wasn't supposed to happen that way. The top of the cage was supposed to collapse gradually, with Mick almost sliding down in an effort to break his fall. But as we all saw, the top of the cage collapsed with Mick hitting the mat with an impact only Wile E. Coyote could have survived.)

When Mick came through that curtain following the match, everybody in the back gave him a standing ovation. That's very rare in this business — I think I've seen it about three times. But stop and think about it: this guy nearly *killed* himself out there and the boys are giving him a standing ovation? Wow — talk about that in Abnormal Psychology class tomorrow.

As the Frenchman was working on Mick, Foley looked up at me

and with a smile on his face, asked, "How was it, Vince — was it better than Shawn's bump?" Mick was referring to a match from a few months earlier, in which Shawn Michaels took the then-most-dangerous bump in the history of the WWF off the same steel cage. Man, all I could think was, "Mick, what are you talking about? You have two small children at home." But Mick did what he did out of pure love for the sport. He thrived on hearing the crowd pop. To this day I can't watch the wrestling documentary, *Beyond the Mat*. There, a handcuffed Mick takes chair-shot after chair-shot to the head with his young children watching in the front row.

Luckily, after that brutal match Mick found another way to entertain the fans without killing himself. It came in the form of a sock and it was *Raw* at its finest.

After winding up in the hospital courtesy of Stone Cold Steve Austin, Vince McMahon received a visit from Mankind, a.k.a. Mick Foley, who had stopped by to lift his "friend's" spirits. Mick arrived at Vince's hospital room with an armful of gifts. Mankind even went as far as to bring a clown along, Yurple, to help brighten the boss's day. The skit was the funniest thing I'd ever seen on television, two of the best playing off each other in their finest moment. But just when you thought it was over, from beneath the bed, Mick revealed Mr. Socko — a sock puppet with a magic marker smile.

The next day when I went out into the arena prior to the show — there were Mr. Socko banners and puppets *everywhere*. Mick Foley had a new career.

There are so many things I could tell you about Mick, from the birth of Dude Love to the brutality of "Cactus Jack," but he's already filled up two books talking about his experiences — and I pray to God he fills up a third. Mick was, simply, the best. I miss him dearly.

But there wouldn't have been a Lewis, if there wasn't a Martin.

Man, they tried — as a matter of fact they tried royally — but the creative brass just couldn't screw up Dwayne Johnson's career. In his first WWF match, he single-handedly went through all his team's opponents to win his Survivor Series contest. Shortly thereafter, he "shocked" the world by becoming the WWF Intercontinental Champion. What you were experiencing was Pat Patterson's favoritism toward Dwayne. Pat was high on him — so let's just shove him down everybody's throats. Thank God, Dwayne got hurt and disappeared for a while. If he hadn't, Vin Diesel might be the Scorpion King today.

Dwayne Johnson is your perfect example of why the old school rasslin' "push theory" doesn't mean beans in today's world. In the past, promoters liked to claim that they "pushed" wrestlers they liked — in other words, *they* were the ones who decided if they were going to be stars or not. You know, the God theory. Unfortunately, you can't *push* anybody. When it comes down to the naked facts — you either have it or you don't.

In the sports entertainment business, you just can't make somebody a star. Regardless of what I think about her professional ability, even Britney Spears has some level of talent. Wrestlers in general are always talking about the "push" — getting a "push," waiting for a "push." Man, that's yesterday's news. Only one person is going to make you a star in wrestling, and that's you.

In writing television for both the WWF and WCW, my philosophy was simply to give everybody an opportunity. That's all I could do. From that point on, after I tuck the ball in their arms, it's up to them. You're either going to put six on the board, or fumble on the goal line.

Dwayne Johnson is the perfect example. With the role he was given early on in his career, the "Blue Chipper" Rocky Maivia, he should have been long gone and buried in the swamplands of New Jersey. But no, the Rock was great — and no matter how hard you try, you can't keep greatness down. Triple H's story is similar, but you'll read about that a little later on.

On the other side of that coin? If you're not great, no matter what story is written for you, or what situation you're put in, you're just not going to make it. There were certain guys in the WWF that we tried to make stars, but it just didn't happen. Because, in the end, they *weren't* stars.

So yeah, they tried everything to screw up Dwayne — they labeled him Rocky Maivia after his father and grandfather before him and put him in some Greco-Roman god-awful outfit. I still don't get that — was the guy supposed to be, Spartacus? It's a wonder they didn't give him a sword. When Dwayne was ready to come back to work following his injury, I was writing TV. At the time we were looking to do something — *anything* — with the Nation of Domination. The group had potential, but were missing something . . . like personality. To give credit where credit is due, it was Bruce Prichard's idea to put Rocky in the Nation. Granted, he didn't know why — but he did suggest it. I took Bruce up on his idea and Rocky was in.

Again, there is always that moment. It happened with Austin, Sable, and DX, and it happened with Dwayne. At first, Ron Simmons, a.k.a. Faarooq (that was another winner of a gimmick — remember that ridiculous blue helmet they put on him for his debut? Oh *that* was Spartacus — now I get it) was the leader of the Nation and Rocky always stood in the background. But without saying a word, the guy had an air of cockiness about him. You could just see it in his facial expressions, his eyes. Then one day, we told him to simply interrupt Ron while he was talking. Rocky did, and a loud "oooow" came from the crowd. At that moment, I knew we had something. Here was this arrogant, young, good-looking stud in the background — and you just knew he believed that he, and not Faarooq, should be the leader of the Nation.

The intensity grew. Then, on a day I remember as if it were yesterday, Rocky had to cut an important promo for the story line. For a while I had been thinking about Rocky using the moniker "the Rock," but I had mixed feelings about it because one of my greatest wrestling heroes growing up was Don "the Rock" Muraco. Some of the best things ever done in the history of professional wrestling/sports entertainment were the vignettes, or "skits," as they were probably called back then, by Mr. Fuji and Don Muraco in the early '80s. "Fuji Vice" and "Fuji Bandito" were light years ahead of their time — and a total inspiration to me for years to come. After much contemplation prior to his promo, I took the Rock aside and said, "Rocky — start referring to yourself in the third person, start refering to yourself as the Rock.

You know, the Rock said this, and the Rock said that." Rocky took my advice — and did the promo.

Let me make something perfectly clear — I am *not* taking credit for the success of the Rock. Did I make that clear? I gave him the idea, and he went out and did it. It could have sucked or it could have made him a movie star. . . . Dwayne Johnson turned it into a million dollars. From that day forward he ate, drank and pooped the Rock. In front of that camera he became larger than life — and he worked at it every day. He came up with his own catch phrases, and I thought they were just brilliant. "Roody Poo Candy Ass." How do you come up with that? Pure genius. Man, I became such a mark for the Rock — I had tears in my eyes when he cut some of those promos. Again, look at the pattern here: everybody had a role, and everybody delivered. It was like writing for the cast of *Seinfeld*. If you put it down on paper, you just knew that they were going to blow it off the chart.

There is no bigger fan of the Rock on this planet — and there is no bigger fan of Dwayne Johnson — than me. You've got to know the two personalities to know how different they really are. I've said it a million times to anyone that will listen: there never has been, and there never will be, a bigger star in the world of sports entertainment than Dwayne Johnson. And I'll tell you why. Yeah, he's got the looks, the physique and the rap — but so did a lot of others before him. What puts Rock heads and tails above the rest is his *brain*.

Highly educated, Rock is the most intelligent sports entertainer to ever play the game. And, the funny thing is he'll never let you know it. You see, in this business there are great "workers." I won't mention any names, because I might get sued for defamation of character again, but these are guys that get by their whole career just BS-ing people, lying and stabbing others in the back for their own personal gains. Rock doesn't work that way. He'll just read you and know what you're going to do or say before you ever do or say it. That's the difference — you can't BS the Rock. If you're sincere, he knows it — if you're not, he knows that, too.

Another thing Rock has going for him is that, unlike so many others in the business, he isn't the least bit paranoid. That comes from being confident in his own abilities and knowing that there is no one else out there better than him, period. And that's the truth — nobody else even comes close. Enjoy him now, because once his wwf contract is up, chances are you'll never see him wrestle again. Rock is a bona fide movie star — and one of the few guys who no longer needs wrestling. Like Mick Foley, the Rock is just too talented to have to put his body on the line every night for a paycheck.

Whatever he chooses to do with his life, Rocky will write his own ticket and be successful. Oh, and there's one other small detail — there is no ego in the Rock. That must be hard to accept, considering who he is, but believe me when I tell you — from Spartacus to Scorpion King, he was the same guy.

Man, it would be a dream to work with the Rock again, only this time on a different canvas. Who knows? Maybe after I sell the movie rights to this book, the Rock will play himself for me.

•   •   •

I've got to set this scene for you: I'm working desperately on this book in my back office at my cd Warehouse. I'm literally writing paragraphs between customers. All I want to do is get this book done so that I move to the next point in my life. My top priority right now is to get out of Atlanta. I hate it here — can't stand it — but the real reason I want to move back north is because my son Will just despises this place and I know it's affecting him, mentally and emotionally. I feel responsible for him going through such a tough period. It's my fault — I brought the family down here.

The whole place is whacked. I got a call from one of Will's teachers about a year ago, telling me that Will didn't have his shirt tucked in that day at school. I had to bite my tongue and just let it slide off my back. I despise the fact that in this God-forsaken state they want all the kids to be cut from the same cloth — look the same, act the same — screw that! If I wanted my children to be robots, I'd have moved to Stepford.

Will's biggest problem here in Atlanta is that he flat-out hates rednecks. I've got to be honest with you, these people are a freaking joke. They're living in some world from 20 years ago. And they're such simpletons. I swear to you, when I watched *Hee-Haw* as a kid — only for Barbi Benton — I never dreamed that there was such a place. It never even dawned on me. Now I'm living next door to Buck Owens and Roy Clark. And there aren't any Daisy Dukes either — that whole thing is a myth. I haven't seen a single one. Even though I whole-heartedly agree with Will, I'm the father, so I have to set an example. So, I humor these people. They come in, they want to talk NASCAR — I'll talk NASCAR. They want to talk Georgia Bulldogs, I'll talk Georgia Bulldogs. But keep in mind, all the while, inside I'm cracking up at these imbeciles. It's called amusing yourself — something Will is just too young to get.

But anyway, now I'm at the point where these people know me — they think I'm their friend, and they come in for three-hour clips! *Three freaking hours!* All I want to do is go in the back and write my book — please, getouttahere! Man, I've got this one guy who comes in that I've just labeled "the Talker." He goes on forever — and every other sentence he says, "People say I like to talk." *No !@#$, Sherlock!*

But today may have taken the ring-ding. This woman in her late 40s comes in every week with her son, who I would guess is about 17 . . . and weighs 300 pounds. Don't get me wrong — they're good people, but right out of a Farrelly brothers movie. Well today, the two come in, and for two hours this woman is telling me that she had to go to the hospital because she had *shingles!* Now, I don't even know what shingles are, but I do think they have something to do with the butt. Can you imagine this? Two years ago I'm writing a pilot for Fox, today some old bag is telling me about her butt problems! *Holy !@#$, amen!*

Another wonderful insight into the world of the "unsaved" Vince. Man, I was brutal — and to think that attitude was rubbing off on my own kids. Thank God I listened, just in the nick of time.

Overnight the Rock became huge — overnight. But, like Mick, it never went to his head — *never*. Dwayne Johnson is one of the nicest people you would ever want to meet, and he remained that way up until the last time I saw him. Some of my fondest memories of the Rock were when I'd call him prior to going to TV to lay out what we had for him and get his input. All the great ones did this — they wanted to know about their stuff beforehand. Rock, Mick, Austin, Triple H — they were constantly thinking about the next Monday night. And, from our viewpoint, the big hitters had to know what they were doing in advance. If they had a problem with the angle or direction, and we didn't find out until Monday, it might send the entire live show into a tailspin. Some of those conversations were so creative — these guys had brilliant minds and they all really cared. I used to get a kick out of the Rock referring to me as "Roo," because he knew how much I dug the phrase, "Roody Poo Candy Ass."

There was nothing better than putting Rock and Mick together. I lived for their entertainment. Whereas all Vince cared about was what Austin was doing, I made Rock and Mick my priority. Working with them gave me great pleasure — they were the best two human beings on the roster. One of my all-time favorite projects was when Mankind surprised the Rock with "Rock — This is Your Life." I'll put that segment up against anything that ever aired on television. Two of the best, in one of the best things I was ever involved in writing. I remember watching this from the gorilla position (the area on the other side of the curtain where the wrestlers gather before going out into the arena) — and never wanting it to end. However, in the corner of my eye I could see Vince, and he was getting antsy. After it was over and Rock and Mick came back through the curtain, I congratulated them and told them how much I'd enjoyed it. Once they left, Vince called me over.

"Vince — what the hell are you doing?" he said. "That ran for over 15 minutes." McMahon was hot. What could I say? I knew he was wrong and I was right — the rating for that segment was going to be through the roof.

Later that night I ran in to Mick again. He asked what Vince had thought of the segment. I told him and Mick seemed a little disappointed. The next day the numbers came in.

"Rock — This is Your Life" drew an ungodly 8.4, to this day by far the highest-rated segment in the history of *Raw*. Back then, an average rating for a single segment of the show would do somewhere in the five or six range — nothing to sneeze at. But an 8.4? The USA Network had to be beside itself. I couldn't wait to tell Mick. This was obviously one of those "I told ya so, Vince" moments. After I'd told Mick about the number I had to go to the day's production meeting. I could see Mick waiting outside the door pacing, just waiting to stick that 8.4 to Vince. The reason I remember that incident so well is because Vince never apologized — he never said he was wrong. I don't know, I just kind of expected him to, but sometimes there were shades of Vince that made me stop and say . . . "Hmmm?"

Chapter 6

STOPPING TO SAY . . . HMMM

I feel so corny saying this, but I have to. Vince and I grew really close. At times, he almost felt like a father to me. I cared so much about him, his family and his business — maybe as much as I cared about my own flesh and blood. I just really enjoyed seeing him overcome everything to once again be the king of the kingdom *he* created in the first place. Back in the days of writing the magazine, that's all I ever wanted to do — give back to him for all the enjoyment he had given me growing up. And I had done that. I have my critics out there, but the fact remains that without me attached to his hip, Vince never would have achieved the success he did during that time.

Financially, Vince took care of me. I never had to ask him for more money. My salary went from $60,000 to $350,000 in less than five years. On occasion he would even slip me a check with a lot of zeros, just for the sake of it. Looking back, I think Vince and I had a unique relationship. Vince used to tell me, "If you knew how I was back in the day you wouldn't want to have anything to do with me." I'm glad I didn't know that Vince — this one was a lot better.

I had many memorable times with the McMahons. One great story comes from when Linda McMahon first invited me into their inner circle of friends, even though I had no business being there. It was Vince's birthday, and Linda was throwing a party at the house. Linda invited Amy and I, and told me to "bring the kids." What a mistake. First of all I showed up like . . . well, me. Jeans, black construction boots — it's a birthday party, no big deal. Well, let's put it this way, I was the only one without an alligator nipping at my breast. Yes, the Clampetts were there — in full force! Vince had to be embarrassed and hysterical at the same time.

Now, in his backyard, Vince has a tremendous in-ground pool. My kids want to go in, so they do. I have Annie, who's about two, in a tube with VJ and Will watching her. Of course, the minute I turn my back for a second, VJ and Will get out. I turn around just in time to see Annie sliding right through the middle of the tube. What's a father to do? Combat boots and all, I dive into the pool and get her. As I emerge from the water, all eyes are on me. How could Vince ever explain this lunatic to his friends? But the truth is, I don't think Vince really cared. He let me be me and that's why our relationship worked.

Even though everything seemed hunky-dory on the surface, in the back of my mind I couldn't help but wonder whether Vince truly cared about me as an individual, or whether he cared about me because I was his cash cow and best-kept secret. It really began to bother me. I just couldn't figure out whether or not the guy was genuine. There were some instances that made me wonder. One came when we were working on a pay-per-view. For the life of me I can't tell you which one — I can only tell you that Rock had a match against Ken Shamrock. Sure, I could look up the exact event, but it'd be irrelevant. I flew out on a Saturday for a production meeting, and I was sick as a dog. I'm telling you I had only been sicker maybe once or twice in my life. I had no business getting on a plane and going to work — there was no question I had a severe case of the flu. But there was never any doubt in my mind — I was going. When I arrived at the meeting, I took a seat to the right of Vince at the head of the table. I was white as snow, shaking and had tissue stuffed up my nose to keep it from draining on the table. About five minutes into the meeting Vince looks at me and says, "What's the matter?" I simply said, "Vince . . . I'm sick." Vince looked me in the eye as serious as could be and said, "There is no sick."

I'll never forgot that line. At the same time, I should have been familiar with it. It always seemed so important for the McMahon men to be "manly." I remember on a few occasions, when we were traveling together, it would be freezing outside and Shane McMahon would refuse to wear a coat. It just wasn't "manly" to be cold, I guess. . . . Forget that — when I'm sick, I'm sick, and if that means putting on my feetie pajamas and going to bed. . . . Mommy, make the hot toddy!

The next day, at the pay-per-view, I literally kept my coat on the entire time. I was dripping with sweat and visibly shaking — teeth chattering, the whole deal. I had to remain seated, in fear that I would collapse. Following the event, Vince wanted to go out to eat like he always did, but there was just no way was I going to make it. I had someone drive me back to the hotel. I thought I was going to die. I'll never forget taking all my clothes off, getting into the tub, turning on the water as hot as I could take it and curling up like a fetus just waiting for it to be over.

About an hour later the phone rang. I got out of the tub and answered it. It was Vince. Despite how I was feeling Vince wanted to meet at some ungodly hour in the morning to go over that day's TV. I don't know how I made it, but I went. I got home the following day and I was in bed for a week.

That's how Vince was when it came to business. It was all about *his* company. I couldn't get that experience out of my mind. The guy really was insensitive at times — probably much like I was at that point. But I'm not just talking about a cold here — I probably should have been in a hospital. But Vince cut me no slack. I don't know, do you treat somebody you sincerely care about like that? Would he have dealt with Stephanie the same way?

You know what? He might have. But then, there was that other side.

I remember a time, during the glory days, when I was just flat-out exhausted. The day-to-day grind was wearing me down mentally, physically and emotionally. To put it as plainly as I can — I was shot, nothing left in the tank. The pressure of the beast we had created was eating me "Raw" and I felt like I was going off the deep end. On top of that, at the prior TV meeting Vince once again scrapped a good idea — one that I'd worked on for days — because a talent didn't like it. I used to hate when a talent didn't like something — but then they didn't have anything better. Nine times out of ten, when someone didn't like what I wrote it was simply because they didn't get it — it was too complex. You see, the boys rarely see the big picture, they only see what they're doing that night. And Vince would always cave. Forget the house-of-cards effect on the whole show when one thing got changed — if the talent didn't like or understand something, Vince went in what he called "another direction," which in my opinion was more times than not the *wrong* direction. Not many people realize this, but Vince hated confrontation when it came to the boys. On any other level, he seemed to thrive on it — but when it came to the talent, he seemed like the mother who just couldn't say no to her children. If a talent didn't like something, he changed it — even if Plan B stunk. Worse, when he did it with me in the room it killed my credibility. On this occasion, I was in the room.

I was hot when we got back to Titan Tower, so I scheduled a meeting with McMahon. As I said, I was on the verge of a breakdown, so maybe I was just using the incident as an excuse to clear my system of anything and everything that was poisoning it. To this day I still don't totally understand it, but as I sat down in a chair across from Vince, I started crying like a baby. I couldn't stop. My emotions — whatever they were — came out in a river of tears. The expression on Vince's face . . . I don't think he knew what to say. Inside, however, he had to know that perhaps the pressure of our success was getting to me. But Vince needed me to be strong — and he knew he needed to treat me with kid gloves. After I laid everything out, Vince said a few words, and then ended his thoughts by saying, "Vince . . . I love you."

As soon as those words came out — I'm thinking two things. 1.) HOLY !@#$ — this guy really does care about me. And 2.) Is he kidding me, or what? Would he stoop so low, and be so sappy as to make me believe he really does care about me?

I left Vince's office not knowing if he had been sincere. That's a shame, but that's what the business had done to me — you're always second-guessing, you're always doubting. To this very moment, I don't know if Vince meant those words, but then again if he truly did I would have heard from him at least once in the past two-and-a-half years.

Aside from often stopping to go *"Hmmm"* when it came to Vince's true feelings, on many occasions I had to put my finger on my lips and stop to ponder when it came to some of the boss's ideas. For every great idea in the wrestling business, there are 10 not-so-great ones. That's the way it works — you sift through the sand at times to discover that one real gem. Brain farts . . . we all have them. Including yours truly (even though I still say David Arquette *wasn't* one of them). To explore the lighter side of Vince, let's look at some of those brainstorms which made me stop and say, *"Hmmm."*

One that immediately comes to mind? When we were desperately trying to come up with a new identity for Goldust, Vince came up with the idea of dressing up Dustin in a full-body stocking and letting him prance around as the "Naked Guy."

Hmmm.

Then there was the time when Vince decided to put the most over female in the history of the business, Sable, together with the "Parade of Human Oddities."

Hmmm. (On second thought, maybe it was more about vindictiveness than being a bad idea.)

What about "Golga" — remember him? Vince's vision was to make John Tenta's character a humpback so that his opponents wouldn't be able to pin his shoulders to the mat.

Hmmm.

Or how about this gem? When Rena Mero exited the World Wrestling Federation, Ed Ferrara and I shot a series of vignettes with Stevie Richards and the Blue Meanie called, *The Blonde Bitch Project*. Stevie and Meanie are prime examples of two guys with all the talent in the world who just couldn't get a break. These vignettes surely would have gotten them over. Keep in mind, at the time *everybody* was talking about *The Blair Witch Project*. The low-budget film was rapidly becoming the highest-grossing horror movie in almost a decade. So I decide to take advantage of this thing while it's hot.

One rainy night, in the middle of nowhere (the woods next to Ed's house), we shoot the vignettes. Now anybody who saw the movie would know that the films we produced were nothing short of stellar. Vince, however, decided against airing them. He said, "Nobody will get it because nobody saw the movie."

Hmmm.

When Vince said things like that, it was best to not argue with him. The truth was, because *he* hadn't seen the movie, he assumed nobody else had. Sometimes I viewed that as a flaw in Vince's creativity. Nothing personal, but at the time Vince was in his early 50s and regardless of what he believed or what he tried to portray, he just wasn't hip . . . no man at that age is. Hey, it's no different with me. When I hit the big 4–0, I wasn't the same ol' 30-something kid who wrote Vince's TV. Regardless of what I said earlier, in my 40s, I may not be tuned-in enough to be successful in that way again. But a few years back, I not only had youth on my side, I also had the advantage of my kids. I was constantly looking through their eyes, taking notice of what was hot and what was not. Vince didn't have that advantage, and that's where I was a huge asset.

Today, Vince's product is so uncool, so unhip. Rather than evolve, the WWF has turned back the clock. Just the other day I witnessed one wrestler attempting to get heat on another by whipping him with a belt. In Sports Entertainment 101 you learn that the ultimate objective is to "suspend the disbelief" of the fan. Please tell me how I am supposed to believe that two monsters, both over six-nine and 300 pounds, are so mad at each other that they have no other choice but to proceed to beat each other with leather straps? See what I'm talking about? That just doesn't happen in the real world. That's like the Penguin poking at Batman with his umbrella in the heat of battle instead of shooting him right between the eyes! The only difference was Batman was campy — it was supposed to be funny. When it comes to sports entertainment, we are supposed to be "suspending the disbelief" of the viewer, making them believe what they are watching is real. A belt? I think the last time a belt would have sufficed as a legitimate form of punishment was when Oliver Twist asked for another bowl of porridge!

Chapter 47

GAME OVER!

═══════════════════

Within 18 months — we had won. The war was over. Eric Bischoff had not only lost the battle, he was "relieved of his duties" in the process. Eric rode the wave of the NWO story line until it became so watered down that it was nothing more than a warm, old, flat bottle of Coke. Nobody cared anymore. Over on the other channel, we had revolutionized the industry. And we didn't do it with one thing, we did it with a dozen — complexity, realistic characters, reality-based story lines, breaking the forbidden "kayfabe" and mostly, *heart*. Deep down we all really cared about what we were doing. There was no going through the motions — not on one single night. Man, Eric became so desperate, that he actually challenged Vince to show up at a WCW pay-per-view to fight him. I kid you not. And Vince would have shown up had Stephanie not been graduating from college that very same day. How interesting would that have been? One thing I learned was, unless you were Shawn Michaels, you did not challenge Vince. His ego was bigger than his arms, and if Eric wanted to fight, Vince was going to fight — and I promise you it would have been for real. I also promise you, despite Eric's training in the martial arts, Vince wouldn't have allowed himself to lose to *anybody* — especially Eric Bischoff.

Man, we were the darlings of the USA Network — and everybody was talking about "Attitude."

Let me talk for a minute about the USA Network. Those guys were awesome. Unlike the experiences I would have in Hollywood a little later on — USA Network was all about business, money and ratings. The person who was in charge of handling *Raw* has since gone on to head the Sci-Fi Channel — a woman by the name of Bonnie Hammer. This gal was sharper then Freddy Krueger's glove. She was so savvy, so hungry and she knew what sold. The more we pushed the envelope, the higher the ratings got and the more money *Raw* generated for the network — plain and simple. All we had to do was call Bonnie in advance if we knew we were going to be walking the tightrope, just to prepare USA for any phone calls they might get after the show aired. As the ratings began to soar, USA would look the other way.

Beautiful, baby, beautiful.

That's the way television should be — it's all about the numbers. Numbers equal money.

That's why I had such a difficult time over at Turner. In the first three months, I raised the ratings a full point. The next thing I know I'm sitting in a conference room being told all the things I'm doing . . . *wrong*. But guess what? That's another book.

Ironically, months before the phrase "WWF Attitude" was coined, I gave Vince a T-shirt that read, "Don't give me any of your attitude, I have enough of my own." And we did have attitude. We were in the driver's seat once more and nobody — no way — was getting rid of us again. The ratings reached ungodly heights. From a 1.9 we grew all the way into the sevens. It was storybook — David versus Goliath — and the mighty giant, WCW, was left for dead.

Vince was making money hand over fist — and getting into trouble, perhaps, just by wanting more. Merchandising — that was always an issue. I don't know, it always seemed like Vince never made enough money. When is enough enough? At the time, *Raw* had to be one of the most risqué shows on television, yet whether Vince wants to admit it or not the WWF *was* marketing to children. And in time, even though I was as responsible for that as anybody, I was beginning to struggle with the idea. I would tell Vince over and over again that I wasn't writing a television show geared for kids — I was writing it geared to an audience of 18 and older. Time and time again I would tell Vince that the merchandising was going to get him into trouble. In business, the philosophy is always to make as much money as you can. I knew Vince hated me harping on this, because in retrospect, it was all about the Benjamins!

I mean, how can you have an episode of *Raw* where somebody is looking to hack off Val Venis's private parts, Sexual Chocolate is "exploring" a transvestite and Goldust is goosing his opponent — and then go to Eckerd's the very next day and see Stone Cold Steve Austin lollipops on the counter? If that wasn't targeting kids, I don't know what was.

I became so concerned I told Vince I wanted to sit in on the merchandising meetings at Titan. Man, they hated me in there. There was this one bald guy, I think his name was Stanley, who used to work on commission. This guy was trying to sell a license for everything and attempting to pass it off as if it weren't for children! Remember Dan Akroyd many years ago on SNL? He portrayed a character named Irwin Mainway, of Mainway Industries, who used to market and sell "questionable" items to kids. One of his best-sellers was the unforgettable Bag-o-glass. Well, Stanley *was* Mainway! For example? The WWF Superstar . . . Slip-n-Slide. Yeah, a bunch of 20 year olds are going to get together, have a few kegs, couple of joints, and have a Slip-n-Slide party! It was flat ridiculous. Remember Pogs? Those small, cardboard circles that children used to collect? How were they not for kids? How many males in their mid-20s play with Pogs? It was a joke, and I knew the heat was going to come back to us — one way or another.

But back to the winning thing. There were so many individual stories in winning the war against wcw — everybody was stepping up to the plate and bombing ding-dong (my phrase for a home run) after ding-dong after ding-dong. But perhaps the most inspirational story, the story that exemplified courage to a level I had never before seen, came from the veteran of the bunch — the man they call the Undertaker.

You could never fully appreciate Mark Calloway until you'd seen him collapse on the floor of the locker room immediately following a match. Everything hurt on Mark — his back, his hips — the punishment he'd put his body through over the years was beginning to catch up with him. But when that red light came on, you'd never know it. He gave everything he had for the company, regardless of the pain — you just can't say enough about that.

Mark was the quiet leader in the locker room. Even though he was soft-spoken and didn't say much, when he did speak, it was deafening. The only way he knew how to lead was by example. If the squared circle was a baseball diamond, Mark would have visited the disabled list more times than Rosie O'Donnell frequents Krispy Kreme. And every match — regardless of the pain — Mark sucked it up and performed as if it were his last.

Courage: that's what Mark Calloway represented to me. He was on the all-Madden team — in the trenches, digging in, doing what he had to do to win. At times I was even guilty for writing Mark in when he was hurt. On some of those occasions I just didn't know, but on others I just should have known better. Mark would never say a word; he would just go out there and do it. Sometimes I really have a difficult time looking myself in the mirror when it comes to 'Taker. I needed him and I put him out there, even when I sensed that he may not have been 100 percent. That was wrong — it was selfish. But again, these were the things you did when you were possessed by the wrestling business.

In talking about the Dead Man, I must also mention Bill Moody, a.k.a. Paul Bearer, who was phenomenal in his role as the Undertaker's cryptkeeper. Bearer and I worked extremely well together; it was just a kick in the pants to see how excited he would get over giving one of his priceless promos. I always respected Bearer — but on one occasion he was surely second-guessing yours truly. . . .

On one unforgettable episode of *Monday Night Raw*, I decided to wheel out Howard Stern's "Whack Pack" in an effort to help get over our own Parade of Human Oddities. If you're unfamiliar with Stern's notorious bunch, they consist of Hank "the Angry Drunken Dwarf," who recently passed away, Fred "the Elephant Boy," who sported an unintelligible speech impediment and Crackhead Bob — no explanation needed. After making their way out to the ring, I positioned myself next to a monitor in the back to witness the train wreck that was about to take place. I noticed Bearer standing next to me with his chin somewhere around the floor. With an "I can't believe I'm watching this" look on his face, Paul turned to me and said, "Vince — you just slapped all the boys in the face."

Coming from Bearer, that hurt. I had always considered him a friend — because he was always honest with me. Well, this time his honesty was slapping my bearded puss. But I knew that Paul had no idea how those freaks would help change the business and the success of the WWF forever. It was just another stage in reshaping the industry.

But that's how it was for me early on — "Who is this guy, and why is he doing this?" There is no doubt that people were laughing at me in the beginning. There is no doubt that some people wanted to kill me from the start. But at the time, I had to stick with my instincts. I just knew I was right. Two short years later, those knives in my back were magically turning into pats.

Today, many people ask, "Vince, because you've changed, are you saying that if given the opportunity you wouldn't put that same brand of television on the boob tube?" The answer is simply . . . no.

In my prime at the WWF, I was aiming to please my boss, my critics and both the fans in attendance and those watching on television. In doing so I would receive some form of praise, which for whatever reason means everything to human beings. Unfortunately, that entire mindset is wrong.

Today, again with *all* of the glory going to God, I now understand that it is not about pleasing your boss, the fans or anybody for that matter — it's all about pleasing God. Gratification shouldn't go to the "self," the gratification should go to God. You see, without God, we are *nothing* — nonexistent. I didn't realize that until I came to the end of my life and he took over. God is responsible for everything we have. Every action we take should be an action to glorify God and his kingdom. I wasn't glorifying God with the "Whack Pack" — thus the depression, thus the anxiety, thus the misery.

Remember, you reap what you sow.

As key as the main-eventers were to our success, you can't take anything away from the "mid-carders" — a term I hate to use. In my opinion, if you made it to the WWF you were a bona fide star. And when those guys in the middle, looking to make it to that next level, were given story lines to execute — they all came through. From D-Lo Brown (A.C. Conner) to Mark Henry to Al Snow (Al Sarven) to Kane (Glenn Jacobs) to Hardcore Holly (Bob Howard) to Ken Shamrock — all these guys ever wanted was a chance. They deserved it, they got it, they did it. I knew it would be a sad day for the guys considered to be on that "next tier" when I left the WWF. When all Vince cared about was what the top guys were doing, I made sure that everybody had a story line. The day I left, I knew the majority of my pet projects would be lost in the shuffle. You see, when you're writing TV it's easy to write for the proven stars. The challenge is writing to create new ones. Today, the WWF doesn't know how to do that, and many talented young men and women are paying the price. I've been away from the WWF for a few years now, and during that time only one real new star has been created — Kurt Angle. If that doesn't tell you something, then your mind is already made up about me.

Also, let's not forget the WWF rookies. My passion was working with the young guys and helping them create characters that would one day become the foundation of the company. This is what it was all about for me — creating something from scratch and watching your project explode before your very eyes. Back then we were working a lot of new guys into the mix: Edge (Adam Copeland), Christian (Jay Reso), Gangrel (David Heath), Matt and Jeff Hardy (who I had to beg Vince to hire), Test (Andrew Martin), Droz (Darren Drozdov) and my favorite — Sean Morley, a.k.a. Val Venis.

Next to Goldust, Val Venis was my favorite creation. Usually when I would come up with a character for somebody, I would look at interviews they would do at the training facility and something would just come to me. With Sean all I could think of was, "Man, this guy looks sleazy." The porn star was born. Val's early vignettes were some of my best work. The guy was over before the fans ever even saw him work. In my opinion, Val would have been a *huge* WWF star, but again, outside pressure forced Vince to kill the character. Sure, he has since re-launched it, but like Goldust, it will never be the same.

Little-known fact: we used porn princess Jenna Jameson in some of Val's early vignettes. Vince refused to air them, stating that Jenna looked "horrifying."

It wouldn't be right if I didn't also point out two of the most underrated stars in the company during my tenure as head writer. "Old-timers" Pat Patterson and Gerald Brisco brought tears of laughter to my eyes on many occasions. Working those guys into the story lines was a treat, and those hams loved every minute of it. Man, they were spectacular. I will forever remember the motto, "Brisco's Body Shop — It's Worth the Drive." Now *that* is classic.

Recently, I thought it was horrible when the current writing team attempted to turn Kurt Angle and Steve Austin into two bumbling idiots. With Patterson and Brisco it was tailor-made — they *were* two bumbling idiots — but Austin and Angle? Steve Austin *spent* nearly five years being the toughest SOB on the face of the planet — and now all of a sudden he's an idiot wearing a cowboy hat? How did that happen? Where's the logic? Where's the "reality?" The answer is simple, there is none and that's part of the problem. I'll go into it more later.

Forgiven

Everybody pitched in — props to all. I know there are some guys — and gals — I'm forgetting, and I apologize. Everybody had a hand in the success of the WWF, from the cameramen to the pyro guy to Kevin Dunn's entire crew — Chris, David, Kerwin, Adam, Terry, Jen and Sue — and a host of others, all the way down to Richie. But before I get to "the Wonder Boy" himself, there's just one thing I'd like to add. There was literally no one in the entire company I didn't like — *no one*. Now don't get me wrong, at times I hated people, but by the end of the day there wasn't anything I wouldn't have done for any of them. I'm sure there are those who can't say the same about me — but that's fine. You see, I got most of my heat with the boys when I told them what I felt was the truth about their characters to their face. Some appreciated that, some just didn't get it. Let's call a spade a spade: Goldberg hates me, Hogan hates me, Bradshaw hates me, Bischoff hates me, Piper hates me, and I'm sure many others stand in that line. But if they're going to hate me for being honest with them — I can live with that. Understand, my job was thankless and it was impossible to make everybody happy. The hardest part was just looking the talent in the eye and telling them what your true thoughts and opinions were. That's not easy to do, and it's not easy to take. But I'll tell you what — I'd rather have a stand-up guy tell me to my face, "No, that's not going to work," than have him go around and not have the spaldings to live up to his responsibility. In the long run I was just trying to help them. But as the old saying goes — the truth hurts. Today, a lot of those guys I mentioned rip me in the dirt sheets and on the internet. But that's fine with me. Again, I can look myself in the mirror and know that I was a stand-up guy who never screwed anybody and treated everyone with the utmost respect.

I've got to backtrack on the respect thing. There was this one time when Shawn Michaels was backstage at a pay-per-view stirring it — and stirring it good. I became so frustrated that when Billy Gunn said something I perceived as wrong — I told him to go !@#$ himself. As soon as the words left my mouth I knew I had screwed up. You just don't disrespect the boys that way — and it was one of the few times

I spoke without thinking. I thought the Road Dog was going to lay into me — he was hot. Thank God, by the end of the day we all kissed and made up. But that's the way it was. As dysfunctional as the family got, we were just that, a family. . . . Maybe.

Now, about Richie. It was guys like Richie Posner — somebody you'll never hear or read about, that made the WWF *great*. Richie, I don't think he even had a title, was the "Gimmick Guy." You wanted a rubber sledgehammer that looked real, you went to Richie. You wanted a disappearing-corpse casket, you went to Ritchie. You wanted a trap door beneath the ring, you went to Richie. You wanted a female French poodle who could bark in German, Richie would find the pooch. This guy was a magician — he was literally a magician, he could pull rabbits out of hats, the whole thing. You don't realize what somebody like Richie is worth until you don't have a go-to guy like that anymore. When I went to WCW and was looking for my Richie — I got instead four misfits who couldn't hang a box from a pole without it falling in the middle of the match. There is no doubt that Richie, and Kevin Dunn, were the two MVPs behind the scenes.

One unforgettable high spot? Richie was responsible for "gimmicking" a table (rigging it so it would break on impact) that Vince was going to take a bump onto — from a 10-foot high steel cage. Understand the pressure on the poor slob? This was the first big bump the boss was going to take, and Richie had to make sure that not only did it look good, but that Vince wouldn't get hurt. Richie rigged the table, and you know he did it right — the guy did everything right. Well, Vince took the bump and rather than fall onto the table, he fell onto the edge. . . . The table didn't break and Vince ended up in agony — though he wouldn't dare let anyone know it.

When Vince came into the back, he ran into Richie. Vince was adamant, telling Richie that he didn't rig the table right. Keep in mind that a lot of the boys were around, and Vince wasn't about to take the blame for his own miscalculation. Now picture this. Here's Richie, about five-foot-nothing and maybe — *maybe* — 150 pounds. The guy had a Larry Fine haircut and always wore Hawaiian shirts.

He was a walking, talking gimmick. As Vince began to reprimand him, the gimmick guy, without knowing any better said, "No, Vince — everything was set up properly, you just landed in the wrong place." You could see Vince's face turn red. And remember, there was an audience.

"No, I didn't," said Vince through his teeth. "You gimmicked it wrong."

"No," said Richie matter-of-factly, "you landed wrong." At that point Vince didn't know what to say. I just wanted to tell Richie to get out of Dodge and go build something.

That night after the show, a few of us went out to eat with Vince, as we usually did. You had to see him try to sit down. It was hard not to laugh, but then Vince was laughing himself. A few days later, Vince showed me a picture of his butt and to this day it was the most horrendous sight I have even seen. It was like a black-and-blue giant plum. It was grotesque. But Vince never sold the pain he was in — never.

Chapter 48

RIDDLE ME THIS

This chapter is dedicated to the only person who survived the "Vince Russo Experience" through the trials and tribulations of both the WWF and WCW.

Bill Banks may not be a household name, but he is no doubt the glue that keeps the fragile world of professional wrestling together. Bill is every cliché you can imagine — the "go-to" guy, the guy "in the trenches," the "give it to Bill, he'll do it" guy. Even though he's gone unheralded — until now — Banksie is the kind of guy you realize is invaluable, the day after he leaves.

At the ripe age of 20, Banksie started with me as an intern at the *WWF Magazine*. With "unique" looks, I compare him to that lovable sloth from the *Goonies*, Banks was a workhorse who would do whatever you asked of him, whenever you asked him. He was *always* working — perhaps even more than I was. But aside from being a workaholic, Banksie had a few other . . . um . . . problems. The first one being that when you embarrassed the guy, his Spock-like ears would turn redder than Santa's suit. Now picture the contrast of "ears-o'-fire" to the rest of his face, which sported a flat, milk-like complexion. You get the picture — not a pretty sight! On top of that, there was his attitude. Banks was so negative, that he earned the name "Mr. Nego" after only a few months on the job. But the best thing about Banks was that he was the perfect victim for a practical joke.

Here's my favorite.

Having just started on the job, Banksie had an office just 25 feet across the hall from me at Titan Tower so I could make sure he would "stay out of trouble." Halloween was upon us, and with the help of former WWF stickman Kevin Kelly, we pulled what might have been the greatest prank in the history of the Tower. Of course the victim was Bill Banks.

Next to the television facility at Titan, there is a daycare center where workers can bring their kids, appropriately called "Titan Tots." Well, every Halloween, the tots get dressed in their costumes and come over to the tower for sweet, teeth-rotting treats. With Bill still new to the job, I told him the day before Halloween that it was Titan tradition that all employees dress up in full costume when the kids come for their goodies. Banks may have been a bit skeptical, but he became a believer when he picked up Kevin Kelly for work the next day and Kevin had his Halloween costume in a brown paper bag . . . or so Banks thought.

Now, some time around noon, Kevin Kelly calls my office to kick the prank into full gear. After I hang up with Kevin (remember, Banks was close enough to hear the phone ring), I told Bill the call had been from the receptionist on the first floor and the kids were on their way up. It was time for all of us to put on our costumes. With that, Banks got up from his desk and shut his office door to change. Once the door was secure I darted down the hall and corralled everybody from their offices. Once the mob was gathered we walked to Banks' office and opened the door. And there he sat in all his glory — The Riddler, question marks and all! Banksie had donned full Frank Gorshin regalia, from head to toe — including the purple mask. I thought the redness was going to explode from his ears! Can you imagine the humiliation? There we are in our formal working attire, and there he was looking to take over Gotham City! Man, we showed no compassion.

But all kidding aside, Bill was a guy I was really tough on. I would always tell him that my tough love was an effort to make him learn and understand the wrestling business, but the truth was I was usually taking the frustrations of the job out on him. To Bill's credit, he took everything I dished out — that's how much he loved wrestling.

People like Bill Banks are few and far between — but I can tell you right now, without people like him holding up and supporting the circus, the big top wouldn't be what it is. Without Bill doing this and Bill doing that, the dogs barking the orders would have to fend for themselves — and believe me, that would be a very ugly sight.

Thanks, Bill — you will never be forgotten.

Chapter 49

THE GAME

"The Game."

I gave Hunter that moniker and I cringe every time I hear JR scream it. Man, if I was paid royalties, I'd be living in San Francisco, retired and sitting in Pac Bell watching a Giants game right now. So many characters were my creations — their look, their name, their catch phrases. But, getting back to Hunter, all I ever gave him was the name, "the Game." Because in my opinion he was.

There is nobody more deserving of success in the sports entertainment business today than Paul Levesque, a.k.a. Hunter Hearst-Helmsley. Everything that Hunter has, he has because of Hunter. There isn't, and never will be, a harder worker.

I was with the WWF when Triple H worked his first match. I was even there when the brilliant writers made him wrestle in pig poop. When I first saw Triple H, nothing really stood out. But once I began working with him, his gift was obvious — he had heart. Hunter was determined to be a major force and was willing to do whatever it took. When I first started working with him, I wrote all his promos — you remember the ones, where he had a different rich girl on his arm every time you saw him. But it wasn't working — not because he couldn't do it, but because he was uncomfortable doing it . . . it wasn't him. But again, that's what the boss wanted. When Vince gave you a character you never questioned it. There was always this perception that Vince was a star-maker. There's some truth to it, about half of the time. The other half, you had Golga. But again, that's not a shot at Vince — simply a comment on the odds of sports entertainment. Hunter became a star only after *he* began to weave elements of his own personality into the stodgy, snooty aristocrat from Greenwich.

If my kids ever wanted an example of drive and determination, I would tell them the story of Triple H. It's a long one, but I've got some time — nobody's in the store right now.

Early on in his tenure with the WWF, Hunter was befriended by the "Kliq" — the group of Shawn Michaels, Kevin Nash and Scott Hall. The threesome took Hunter under their wing and more or less taught him the ways of the road. At the time, the "Kliq" had a lot of heat in the locker room — and as the saying goes, if you sleep with the dogs, you're gonna wake up with fleas. But Hunter didn't care. These guys were true friends and if he was guilty by association, so be it.

Well, days before Hall and Nash were to go to WCW, they were booked at New York's Madison Square Garden. After the matches were over, Shawn, Hunter, Kevin and Scott went back out, then climbed to the top of ropes (inside a steel cage) in separate corners as a symbol of friendship and to say goodbye.

Keep in mind — this is back in the mid-'90s when babyfaces and heels still weren't supposed to be seen together, let alone be seen celebrating together. At the time, I believe Scott and Shawn were babyfaces and Triple H and Kevin were heels.

Oh my God — *they broke the code!* The president's been shot! The president's been shot!

The next day, I was at Bruce Prichard's house and he was livid! He must have been on the phone with a hundred different people. Man, what these guys had done — I swear, it was as if they had raped someone. And in the eyes of Prichard and Cornette, they had — the rasslin' business. Well, now Kevin and Scott were gone. And Shawn, I believe, was the champion at the time. So what were they going to do to him?

Hunter was the new guy who was no doubt going to take all the heat.

For the next six months — or however long it was until I started booking — the office buried Hunter. They punished him like a third-grader who'd been caught wearing shoe mirrors to school. But that's the way the business was back then — the office punished you, tried to "teach you a lesson," when you did something they didn't agree with. I can tell you that wasn't my way of handling things when I came along. I didn't believe in those ancient "ways of the business." If somebody screwed up — tell them, correct it and move on. If they needed to be reprimanded a second time — then act accordingly — but to their face. Don't screw with them and keep them in the dark about what's going on.

So Hunter was in the doghouse. They tested him on every level to see if he was going to gut it out. And he did — he shoved it straight up their tails. What's even funnier is that the guy who, along with his three friends, almost ruined the business one night at Madison Square Garden is today married to the boss's daughter. We've come a long way baby!

Yeah, Hunter prevailed, and in the end became one of the biggest draws in the WWF. I spent a lot of time with him, talking over every match and every promo after it happened. He wanted to know what went right or what went wrong. He wanted every time out to be better . . . no, not better, perfect. In my opinion, Hunter deserves every penny and every accolade he receives.

●　　●　　●

If we're talking about Triple H, I must also give Joanie Laurer, a.k.a. Chyna, her due. Hunter and Joanie were dating when I was in the

WWF, and I must say they were one of the classiest couples I've ever met. Funny thing is, the first time I ever saw Joanie I swear to God I wasn't so sure she wasn't a man. I'm both ashamed and embarrassed to say that, because I would soon find out that Ms. Laurer was 100 percent woman. Joanie, in my opinion, truly was the "Ninth Wonder of the World" — as a matter of fact, I gave her that moniker. She could go toe-to-toe with any man on the roster, and often did. At the time she was taking close direction from Hunter; when I laid out a story for Chyna — Hunter had to be present.

Occasionally, that made things difficult, because at times Triple H was a bit overprotective — understandably so. But you have to wonder — how does Joanie feel about that today? Hunter is no longer a part of her life. Would Chyna's career have gone in a different direction if she had taken more control of it? The answer is we'll never know.

But I will tell you this — the bigger Joanie got, the less opportunity she was going to get. Again, it was the "Sable Syndrome." In this business, a woman is only going to be allowed to go so far. I kept wanting to push Joanie — I wanted to push her to the moon — but there was this underlying force that prevented me from doing so. Isn't it ironic how both Rena and Joanie had to take the same path — leaving the WWF — just so they could attempt to realize their full potential.

● ● ●

I admit it — I love reality TV, from *Survivor* to *The Real World* and everything in between. But last night I saw the best reality show to ever take over my boob tube. MTV's *The Osbournes* is hands-down the best thing to hit the airwaves since Goldie Hawn on *Laugh-In*. Whoever had the idea of putting a camera in Ozzy Osbourne's house while he plays Daddy is a genius. Watching the "Blizzard of Oz" try to turn on a vacuum cleaner when he doesn't have a clue is priceless.

That's the problem with TV execs today — they think too much for their own good. They have no idea how to determine what's good and what's bad, because they get so wrapped up in numbers and focus groups they lose sight of the objective — which is to entertain the audience. Give them something they can understand and relate to. It's such an easy formula. I've dabbled in Hollywood, writing a pilot for Fox — and the process was so unreal I thought I was starring in a bad sitcom. I'll get more into that later on.

Chapter 50

FROM THE FINK TO THE WARRIOR

I've got to say a few words about a couple of guys who remain in my thoughts even though I haven't been active in the business for a while: WWF ring announcer Howard Finkel and, perhaps the most intriguing player to ever hit the ring, the Ultimate Warrior.

Early in my WWF career, Howard Finkel was my traveling buddy. See, when you work the road, you usually travel up and down the highway with someone you like and can relate to. Okay, let's get this straight — I couldn't *relate* to Howard, but the truth is I loved the guy. You see, Howard is your perfect example of a "WWF lifer" — once you get the job, you're in for life. I've said on many occasions that when you work for Vince McMahon you are expected to hand him your life on a silver platter — that is the reality. I did just that for five years until I just couldn't do it anymore. Well "the Fink" has done that for over 20 years. How? I have no clue. But Howard lives and dies for Vince. On one hand, you have to admire his loyalty —

but on the other, you have to ask, "Why?"

But I could never bad-mouth Howard — I mean, he's just "the Fink." I spent so many road trips just bending his ear and telling him what a better job I could do of writing television than those who were writing at the time. Howard was a phenomenal sounding board as he searched the FM radio dial for classic rock stations — his passion. When he couldn't find classic rock, he would listen to the *Fabulous Sports Babe* — which drove me nuts. How in God's name can you listen to some broad do sports — especially when that broad not only isn't hot, but is the size of a house?

I never realized how much fun it was to travel with the Fink — who, I might add, introduced me to the Dairy Queen Blizzard — until my position forced me to travel with Vince. That was brutal. When we were on the road, I was attached to Vince's hip 24/7. Don't get me wrong — I'm not trying to paint a negative picture of the boss here — but it was taxing. You'd be working every passing minute, from the second you got in the car. Whether it was a 30-minute drive, or a four-hour road trip — you were talking wrestling. Not the wife, not the kids — they didn't matter. All that mattered was "the show." And the minute you fell asleep — the very second — he would take great joy in waking you up. At the end of every trip Vince would turn to me and ask, "Did I get it all?" (referring to my energy, my creativity — my entire life force). And I used to answer, "Every drop." In essence, Vince was the vampire and I was the poor, pale victim laying on the floor with the blood sucked out of his neck. The humor of it is that people actually used to envy me because I rode with Vince. *Envy me*? They could have him!

One of my funniest Fink moments came when we were doing a show in Detroit. Bruce Prichard — who always ribbed the Fink — sent referee Jack Doan out to the ring and instructed Jack to just take Howard down to the mat without warning. Well Jack, who knows some wrestling himself, took Howard down. Usually when something unexpected like this happens, when someone is the subject of a rib or practical joke, they don't sell it. The last thing the victim ever wants is to give the ribber the satisfaction of success. Well, Howard not only sold it — he sold it like Alec Baldwin in *Glengarry Glen Ross*. Like Jello in a tux, a wobbly Fink had to be helped to the back. Once backstage, Howard collapsed into a chair — I swear, you'd have thought he was *Scarface* after his last stand. Howard was sobbing — not crying, but sobbing. A grown man, sobbing. I went over to check to make sure he was all right, and I struggled to keep a straight face. Here's a grown man in a tuxedo sobbing because someone tackled him. Then Jerry "the King" Lawler came over. Lawler started to rub Howard's shoulders in an effort to console him. Howard's face was buried in his hands. Every few seconds, Lawler would look over at me with that !@#$-eating grin on his face, and every time I would lose it, blowing snot with every laugh.

After pulling myself together, I had to take care of Howard because we were traveling together. We're in the middle of downtown Detroit and Howard wants to go to the emergency room. I don't even know what hurts him at this point! So I take Howard to the emergency room — and there we are at 12:30 at night, the only white people in the joint. The guy to my left's been shot, the guy to my right has been stabbed, the guy across from me next to the water fountain is tripping on something and I'm sitting next to a grown man in a tuxedo, sobbing. Luckily I talked Howard into letting me bring him back to the hotel.

After picking up a bottle of Advil for the Fink on the way home, we drove back to our hotel and I walked Howard up to his room. Once inside Howard collapsed on his bed like Felix Unger after being dumped by Gloria. That sight has never left my mind. But hand it to the Fink, for everything they've put him through, to this day the guy remains loyal to the boss.

One of my other favorite people is the Ultimate Warrior. "Warrior" (now his legal name) may be *the* most intelligent person I've ever come across — in my life. Like Kevin Nash, even though Warrior is street-smart, he's also book-smart. He's on a different intellectual plane — and most of his knowledge is self-taught, from everything he can get his hands on. The writings of Warrior, based on his beliefs, are both enlightening and motivational. The man is not only a modern day poet, he's a genius. I've never met anyone with such strong ethical values and beliefs. And Warrior doesn't just talk a good game — he lives it every day.

Warrior bases his entire life on raw truth: calling a spade a spade, regardless of the consequences. I guess that's what drew me to him — his brutal, raw honesty. In a world laced with utter BS, Warrior stands tall, true in his beliefs and true to his word. Many people in the business call the Warrior a "freak," or even a "goof," and the simple reason is he plays on a different field than everyone else. They can't understand where he comes from because so many of them come from a plastic, phony world based on lies and deceit. My goal has always been to one day work with the Warrior and assist him in getting his word out. He is an individual who needs to be heard.

Chapter 51

OKLAHOMA

This is going to be a very interesting chapter, because I'm probably going to find out things about myself as we go along.

Jim Ross. Good ol' JR.

Man, I could use a shrink to help me write this, because after being removed from Titan Sports for a few years — I still don't know. Either JR is an !@#$% — or I'm an arrogant !@#$%. Or maybe it's a little bit of both.

Let's start at the beginning. I don't want to say I don't like Jim Ross, because I think I really do. I believe that my opinion of him has nothing to do with personal feelings — but rather professional experience. I did have some issues with JR and I believe those issues were due to what I believed were his shortcomings as head of talent relations.

You see, JR's role in the WWF was no different than the role a general manager plays for any professional sports team. I'm sorry, but I just can't see JR as the GM of the Dallas Stars. In my humble opinion, he may have been a little out of his league in his position, much like I may have been when I was hired as "editor" of the magazine. I just don't believe JR handled talent well. There was a difference in the way he treated rookies, mid-carders and main-eventers, and whether that's what that position calls for or not, I just didn't agree with it. He wouldn't give a D-Lo Brown the time of day, but he would have Stone Cold Steve Austin over his house for barbeques. . . .

I think that's wrong. Many people would disagree with me, saying that you have to "treat stars like stars." But I think you have to "treat people like people." And I believe the favoritism sent out a bad message to the boys. As I stated earlier, I treated Austin no differently whether he was Stone Cold or the Ringmaster. Today's jobbers (guys just starting in the business, who pay their dues by losing to *everybody*) might be tomorrow's stars. And many of the talents despised JR for showing favoritism. They might not have told him that to his face, because they were afraid of losing their jobs, but they told *me* on many, many occasions.

On top of that, as head of talent relations you need to be aggressive — you need to be shuckin'-'n'-jivin' from the minute you wake-up! Moving nonstop, almost like you accidentally got a spot of Ben-Gay inside your boxers. Look at Bischoff: with Eric around, there was a very competitive environment when it came to signing talent. And you know what Vince used to call JR behind the scenes? *Deputy Dog.* Yes, he wore that ridiculous cowboy hat 24–7. And even if Vince was kidding, you know there was something to it. Now, if you're a young talent with all the promise in the world, are you going to sign with a sharp, attractive, energetic go-getter like Eric Bischoff, or are you going to sign with a guy who's only worried about being on television, talking about a barbeque sauce that bears his name, and moves at the snail's pace of a laid-back, canine cartoon character?

When I was writing television, early on, and the ratings were just starting to reach the threes, every week I was looking at the same roster — the same names, over and over again. It's like you're managing a .500 team and you're not making any moves to bring that team up to the next level. Meanwhile, Eric Bischoff was signing *everybody*. When he inked the Ultimate Warrior, that was the last straw. *What is JR doing?* I would often wonder. *I need players!* At the time I told Vince that I would take 100 percent responsibility if the ratings didn't go up, however I needed some help — I needed some bodies! So screw it — if JR wasn't going to do his job, then I was going to do it for him. With Vince's permission, I started to personally recruit talent. JR couldn't have been happy about this, but then again, I really didn't care. All I was worried about was the company. So, I was instrumental in bringing Al Snow back to the WWF and introducing the Dudleys, Taz, Stevie Richards and Chris Jericho to the Federation before my departure.

I don't know about you, but I really don't like to talk. I like to get in and get out, say what I have to say then leave. That's another thing that used to drive me nuts about JR . . . he talked, and he talked, and he talked, and he talked, and he talked, and he talked and he talked some more. Again, in my opinion, when somebody may not be qualified to do what they do, they will talk your freaking ear off in an effort to try and convince you that they actually know what they're doing. After a while, I just flat-out refused to have *any* meetings with Jim. There just weren't enough hours in a day.

Look, in my opinion it breaks down this simply: all JR was ever interested in was being the best play-by-play man in the business. And to his credit, he was. But head of talent relations? To me that was another story. A little while back there was a company flight where two WWF wrestlers fought in mid-air. A commentator got knocked out cold by a wrestler, and then that same commentator had his hair cut by yet another wrestler. (At 30,000 feet!). All the while another WWF commentator was making out with a flight attendant in the back. And during the same flight, yet *another* wrestler took over the public address system and began to serenade his ex-wife. And, oh yeah, by the way, *Jim Ross*, the head of WWF talent relations, was on the plane! His job? His job was to police the boys. Even the real Deputy Dawg could have done better.

Need I say more?

Well, let's talk about *ego*. Man, I've got a story that's almost hard to believe — but again it demonstrates how, in the wrestling business, ego can take over like a cancer. After his second bout with Bell's palsy, JR was chomping at the bit to go back to television and do play-by-play. But after talking to Kevin Dunn, it was clear that there was no way on earth he was ready. The truth was, his face was still far from normal, and he noticeably slurred almost every word. Unfortunately, JR was lobbying the entire office, telling anybody that would listen how ready he was to be back. JR talked about it for weeks, but Kevin Dunn was telling me "No way." Then just as I feared, there we were the night before the next pay-per-view. And JR thinks he's going to do play-by-play, and nobody has told him differently. In the wrestling business, nobody wants to do the "dirty work." So, somewhere near the end of our production meeting, Jim Cornette gets up and says he thinks JR should do play-by-play the following night. All I could think was: "Some friend. How about we put you on TV looking like that?" But really, Cornette just didn't know any better. After Cornette's two cents, Vince and Kevin just looked at each other: "OK !@#$% — who's going to tell him?" Then Vince said, "Let me and Kevin talk about it, and we'll let JR know." They left the room.

With everybody gone, I knew I had to say something to JR I had to protect him from himself, because he just didn't see what I, the fan, was seeing. I'm not going to BS you — even back in his WCW days, I always thought Jim Ross was the best announcer in the game. I was a big fan. Forget professionalism, as a fan I could not let him go on national television that way. *Nobody* wanted to see him like that.

So I told him just that. I said I had always been a huge fan of his, and that I was speaking for all his fans. "Jim, they don't want to see you this way — this isn't the JR they know." I told him to give it a little more time and there was no doubt he was going to be back on the air. Throughout the entire plea, my voice was cracking like a woman's. I had to fight back the tears just to get the damn words out. After I was done pouring my guts out onto the floor, Jim thanked me.

Later that night I found out that following our conversation Jim went right to Kevin and Vince and *still* lobbied to go on the air the next day. That, my friend, is what ego is all about. Here is a wrestling legend, whose face is — let's say it — disfigured at the time, and he still wants to go out there in front of "his" fans.

I often think about another incident from JR's time away from TV. We were at the SkyDome in Toronto, in front of a pretty big crowd. JR took Vince to the side and asked if he could, "Just go out and wave to his fans before the show." I don't care how you look at it, that's scary. If it's that important for someone to be in the lime-light . . . I just don't know what else to say.

As Vince's television role grew, he brought in a Hollywood writer by the name of Ed Ferrara to help me. Over the past few years, Ed and I have had our differences. But I can never take this away from the guy — he was *extremely* talented. He easily could have been a stand-up comic. Not only does he look like a hedgehog, but the guy is just flat-out hysterical. Ed and I traveled everywhere with Vince, Shane and Stephanie, and during every trip he would entertain the troops. Even though Ed did many voices and characters, his staple was JR. Yes it was cruel, but Ed's imitation of JR during his Bell's palsy era was beyond words. I'm going to go to hell for saying this, but as a good writer, I need to properly set the scene. When JR was stricken a second time with the disease — every time he spoke, his tongue would pop out of his mouth and roll about like a lost slug looking for a cool rock to crawl under. Ed had this down to a science. Now — get over it — we weren't being deliberately cruel, we were just spending way too much time on the road. Yeah, we may all one day meet again at Satan's gate, but at the time it was freaking hysterical!

That's how Ed Ferrara playing WCW's Oklahoma came about. We did it as a rib on JR, and because we knew Vince would be dying on the inside, saying, "I can't believe those guys are doing that." Of course, the goodie-goodies at WCW made us kill the character because it may have insulted someone with Bell's palsy watching. . . .

But, you know what? With Vince, it was always that part of him that stood out the most. It was really my privilege at times to get that glimpse of the real Vince. At work, he was somebody else — he had to be. But when you could break down that guard, when you were able to get those special one-on-one times with him, it was almost like being with your best friend.

I miss those times.

● ● ●

Even after I first put this book to bed, I was forced to wake it up because of more asinine comments concerning yours truly. And they were made by good ol' JR.

Recently, during an internet interview, Ross stated that he couldn't "understand Vince Russo's logic." Well, Jimbo, let me make it simple for you. . . .

With Vince Russo writing: *Raw* ratings reach 7.1. (Obviously, I won't count the show following the tragic death of Owen Hart. However, if you wanted to count "Halftime Heat" during the 1998 Super Bowl, that would be an 8.4 — but I'll give *you* the benefit of the doubt, Hoss.)

Last week's *Raw* rating: 3.9. Let's see, that's a drop of 3.2, or 45 percent — pick your poison!

Oh, and one more thing, that was *with* competition (versus no competition). There's your *logic*.

I stated earlier that a large part of Vince McMahon's success can be attributed to surrounding himself with dedicated, hard-working people and then putting them in key positions. But then what happened with JR? How in God's name did he get to be the head of talent relations — perhaps the most important position in the company? I kept myself up many a night asking the same question, until Bruce Prichard supplied me with what may have been the answer.

As you know, JR was hired and fired by Vince — not once, but twice. Again what many don't know is that when Vince was being tried by the Federal Government, he had to prepare himself for a guilty verdict. Nobody really knew what the outcome was going to be, not even Vince himself. In putting his "yes-men in a row," so to speak, Vince once again needed the services of good ol' JR. But this time Jim was smart. According to Prichard — I don't know this to be a fact — Ross demanded and *got* a 10-year no-cut contract. Again, this is according to Prichard, so you have to take it not only with a grain of salt, but a whole sack of Morton's. . . .

I made the decision to print the JR log from two years ago in its entirety for a reason — to show, first-hand, exactly what a horse's ass I was. (God, I apologize now — that will be the last expletive in this book. There is just no other way to describe the type of human being I was toward JR.)

For those of you reading this who are in the wrestling business, it's unfortunate that you may look at the following as a "work," or a "swerve." That is part of being in the "wrestling bubble," and one of the reasons I finally decided to leave. But, to JR, who *I hope* is reading this, all I can do at this point is apologize for my actions toward you.

For whatever reason, call it stress, call it lack of patience, call it failure to understand — whatever you want to call it — I was *brutal* to Jim Ross. And for that I sincerely apologize. There was no reason, no justification — I was just caught up in something that was slowly but surely turning me into something I didn't want to be.

Why couldn't I put myself in JR's boots for just one minute? Why couldn't I understand what he was going through? His mom, who he was very close to, had just passed away; he had not one, but two, bouts with Bell's palsy and add to that the day-in, day-out stress of having to deal with Vince. . . . JR was at Vince's beck and call, even more than I was. I'll tell you why I didn't show him compassion — because at the time it was all about me, me, me. I am ashamed, embarrassed and again, I truly apologize to JR and his entire family — publicly.

Friends, that is why I no longer want to be a part of that world — and understand, I'm not just talking about the wrestling world, I'm talking about the *entire* world. Once you become a part of this world you have a tendency to be like everybody else. Your day is filled with gossip, deceit, negativity and hate. Your nights are overflowing with money, greed, lust and temptation — it's nothing more than Satan's playground. When Christ entered my life, I no longer wanted to be a part of that! Jesus showed me first-hand that it has *nothing* to do with this world, whatsoever — this is nothing but a temporary truck stop. Life should be all about God's eternal kingdom, a little place called Heaven. Once we set up our tents there, we no longer have to deal with the ugliness. No longer will the world rotate on an axis of hate — but instead spin on one of love. So, I've cashed in my chips. I'm not playing here anymore — I quit the game. My purpose here is to glorify God's kingdom, and bring as much of it as I can down from Heaven.

I have to say this, because I feel compelled to. . . . Just last night, I had a rather traumatic evening. About a week ago, I launched a Christian website, which I took extremely seriously. Without missing a beat, a number of wrestling fans, who unfortunately also reside in "the bubble," went on the site and stained it with wrestling reference after wrestling reference. Now, even though I didn't want to comment on this subject here — I feel I must, briefly. For the past few years I have heard nothing but rehash after rehash of the 2000 "Bash at the Beach" incident. Now, I'm not really going to get into it, because it isn't worth the ink on this page. But I will tell you this: that night, which no one seems able to let go of, was all about business, money, ego and greed — everything the wrestling world, and a good portion of the entire world, is built on.

Anyway, feeling somewhat distraught about what wrestling fans posted to my website, I left to teach my youth group at a local church here in Marietta. With my mind still reeling, I walked into an auditorium filled with 600 kids, all in middle and senior high, singing in harmony their praises and worship of the Lord. I stood in one spot, I closed my eyes, I listened . . . and I cried.

Now you tell me — which world do you want to live in?

Chapter 52

OWEN

Man, I wasn't looking forward to writing this — but it has to be touched upon. I loved Owen Hart. I'm not just saying that because that's what you say when somebody passes. I truly loved the guy: from the first time I ever spoke to him — that day at WrestleMania X — to the last time I ever saw him, Owen was my favorite.

I've got to be honest — as time went on I hated being on the road more and more. I hated leaving my family, I hated the politics that surrounded the business — it was getting to the point that I just hated everything . . . and everybody. But then when you walked into a building and saw Owen Hart, your face just lit up. Maybe it was because he was always smiling, always in search of that next practical joke. But whatever the reason, Owen was a constant reminder as to why I was still doing this — it was for people like him. Every chance I got, I used to call Owen from my office — just hearing his voice on the other end of the line would bring a smile to my face. He was simply a guy you had to love — a great father, a great husband, a great all-around human being.

Months before his death, Owen was partnering with Jeff Jarrett. One of the ideas I had was for Owen to fall head-over-heels in love with their manager, Debra. I don't know — just the thought of seeing Owen in love seemed like it would be great entertainment. I mean, he had that innocence about him. Even when he tried to be the tough guy — "I'm not a nugget!" — I just had to laugh. Now, this is the kind of guy Owen was: when I bounced the story past him, he didn't want to do it. He said that even though it was a work — his wife, Martha, would get upset. You had to respect that. So I told Owen, "No problem, we'll do something else." Owen is one of the few men I knew in the business who remained faithful to his wife and kids — that's especially honorable when you consider the hours, days and years he spent away from home.

With the Debra story no longer an option, I looked for other possibilities. I thought of the idea of bringing Owen's old character, the "Blue Blazer," a masked superhero, into the 21st century. Again, Owen, for me, was just a natural comedian — one of those guys who didn't realize how funny he was. Owen had no problem with this new idea — the only thing he suggested was that maybe the Blue Blazer could somehow, some way win the Intercontinental Title to gain credibility.

The night Owen died, he was going to be crowned the WWF Intercontinental Champion.

In the weeks leading up to the pay-per-view, Owen played the bumbling modern day superhero better than even Jim Carrey could. He was brilliant. I'll never forget the time when Owen was to make a spectacular entrance, via a cable wire from the ceiling, and then proceed to attack Steve Blackman. Well, as the script read, the cable got stuck about five feet from the ground and Owen hung there helplessly trying to free himself as Blackman pummeled him like a red, white and blue piñata. It was entertainment at its best and Owen seemed to be enjoying it. If he wasn't, he wasn't letting anybody in on it.

A few days before the pay-per-view I received a phone call from

Steve Taylor, who was the VP of Building Operations for the Federation. A WWF lifer, Steve told me that the people responsible for descending WCW's Sting on *Nitro* were going to be in Kansas City, and they wanted to show us what they could do. He asked me if we could use their services that night. After thinking about it for a few moments, I said to Steve, "Let's descend Owen. Why not let the Blue Blazer make another grand entrance?"

Up until that point Owen's descent had not been scripted. It was added after that phone call. Quite honestly, I never even thought twice about it. It had been done a million times before and it was just part of the show. But, let me make this point — it was not vital to the show. In other words, if Owen had balked — or didn't want to do it — it would have been scratched without even an afterthought.

The day of the pay-per-view was no different than any other. Hours before, I was running around the backstage area making sure everybody had their material. While making my rounds I ran into Owen, who had just finished practicing the descent. I asked him how everything went and he said, "Fine." He just had one request — could he be introduced first? Owen explained that once he was down, it took him a few minutes to take the harness off. If his opponent, the Godfather, was already in the ring, then he — in reality — would attack the blue Blazer before he was able to free himself. I told Owen no problem — we'd make the change. *Never*, at any time, did he tell me he didn't want to descend or that he was having second thoughts. Again, that would have been the end of it.

Let me make something perfectly clear — during the time I wrote television for both WWF and WCW, the idea of talent doing something they didn't want to do because they were afraid of losing their jobs was nothing more than an ol' rassler's tale. Never during my tenure as head of creative for either company did I pressure anybody into something they didn't want to do. And, I will also state, emphatically, neither did Vince. To this day Bret Hart says that Owen was "talked into doing a stunt he didn't want to do." I sure wish I knew who "talked Owen into it," because on the heads of my three children it was neither me nor

Vince. There was nothing to talk him into. The descent was an after-thought, not at all crucial to the match or the pay-per-view.

When I talk about not forcing somebody into doing something they didn't want to do, obviously I'm not talking about doing a job (getting pinned) — I'm talking about a story line, some dialogue, a dangerous bump or even a "stunt." As far as jobs go — everybody has to lose at some time or another in their career. Even Riff Raff occasionally got the duke over Underdog. But yeah — everybody had to do jobs whether they liked it or not. What I'm talking about is when one of the boys felt uncomfortable or unsure about doing something else.

The logic is simple — if a talent doesn't feel comfortable doing something and you force him to go out there and do it (which would never happen), that particular segment of the show is going to be a disaster. When a wrestler doesn't feel something, it comes across loud and clear over the boob tube. On top of that, why would you want to make somebody do something they don't want to do? It's wrestling . . . it's *fake*. There isn't a right way or a wrong way to do *anything*. There's a million different ways to do what needs to be done in the wrestling business. If a wrestler actually believes that insane folklore — that if you don't do what the booker tells you to do, you're putting your job in jeopardy — then it's just their paranoia talking.

Following the tragedy of that day, I heard a few people talk about "old-time rasslin." That Owen hadn't wanted to do the descent but was afraid to speak up. That is absolute nonsense. Vince and I never worked that way — with anybody. Owen knew that.

About an hour before show time, I again ran into Owen. He told me about the schtick he was going to do with the Godfather. It was hysterical — typical Owen. About 30 minutes before he went out, I saw him in a maintenance outfit — I guess he was going to wear that up to his spot in the rafters so nobody would know who he was. He was getting a cup of coffee. . . . That's the last time I saw Owen Hart alive.

It's funny, but looking back now it's still so vivid, seeing him that last time. Nobody else was around, and I was just watching him get coffee. It seemed like time froze. I even remember just looking at him and laughing to myself — it was just . . . Owen. When I was 18, I experienced something similar the last time I saw my grandmother. Something, or *somebody*, told me to get back to the house before my grandparents left, just to say goodbye.

Again, I wrote the above passage two years ago, and without even understanding why, I was talking about God. That last time I saw Owen was like the experience I had had with my grandmother. I knew that I was being told something — I felt it. And it's haunted me throughout the days and nights since Owen's passing.

Only a few days after Owen's death, I dreamt about him. All I can remember is him putting his hand on my shoulder and saying, "Vince, it's all right . . . I'm all right."

I now know that that was God speaking to me. I now know that God had much bigger plans for Owen Hart.

●　　●　　●

I was hovering around the gorilla position when Bruce Prichard started screaming, "Owen fell! Owen fell!" Bruce's face was as red as a stop sign. I don't know . . . it just didn't sink in at first. A few minutes later, paramedics raced to the ring. There was dead silence in the back — and it finally began to register. I couldn't even watch the monitor. The next thing I remember is the paramedics racing — with Owen laid out on a stretcher — from the gorilla position to a waiting ambulance. The Rock was alongside Owen's stretcher. I turned away because I didn't want to look . . . I just couldn't see Owen like that.

When the ambulance sped from the building, man, it just wasn't real. At first I guess it was instinct that made us go through the motions — go on with the show. I don't think anybody knew what else to do. In the back . . . we were all just zombies: breathing, but not living. Nobody said anything to anybody. Time stood still.

About a half-hour later, Shane McMahon whispered in my ear, "He didn't make it." Words can't describe how I felt. I was devastated.

This was Owen, man — Owen.

There were a lot of hugs that night and a lot of tears, from everyone who loved Owen: Triple H, the Rock, Chyna, Jeff. . . .

That night I went back to my hotel room and I called Amy, crying uncontrollably. All I could think of was Owen's wife Martha and his two kids — all the time he spent away from them to earn a paycheck to support them, and now he was never going to see them again. I thought of Amy and my own kids, and I cried out loud: "Why am I doing this? Why am I doing this?"

I seriously thought about going home that night — but I couldn't. I just had to be with the "boys," my other family, that following day.

The next day at TV, everybody was just beginning to come to grips with what happened. I remember it as if it were yesterday. Executive producer Kevin Dunn wanted to go on with Raw like nothing had happened. Even though I couldn't see it at the time, Kevin was just trying to do his job, trying to do what he did best. He couldn't have been thinking rationally — nobody was.

After Kevin made his pitch to Vince, I went into Vince's makeshift office, fighting back tears. I told Vince that if tonight's show wasn't some kind of a tribute to Owen, then I was going home . . . and I meant it. Vince and Kevin then made the decision to dedicate the show to Owen. A private set was made available for anybody who wanted to express their feelings. I never even thought about it. There is no way I could have got the words out. To this day I have never watched that show . . . it's just something I can't do. I don't want to ever remember Owen in death. I just want to remember that smile, that laugh.

I think about Owen frequently. He reminds me on a daily basis that nothing else really matters in this world except those you love . . . those you would give your life for. Thinking about Owen has helped me get through some tough days. His picture still hangs on the wall in my office — the only piece of wrestling paraphernalia I have. It's an autographed copy of the WWF *Magazine*. I'll never forget how thrilled he was to be on his first cover.

You know, sometimes, when all the negativity rears its ugly head — nonsense that just doesn't matter — I wish that people would just take the time to remember Owen Hart and all that he stood for. If they did, nothing else would matter.

I want to touch upon a sidebar to this tragedy, a question that is still asked today. Should Vince McMahon have allowed the show to continue after Owen's death? Well, what I can tell you is this — I was at the pay-per-view when Brian Pillman, a close friend of Owen Hart, had passed away just a few hours before the show. I clearly remember how the entire Hart family was scheduled to work that day. Well, minutes before the match I checked in on them to make sure that they were okay. Owen was sitting in the corner of the locker room lacing up his boots. He called me over.

"Vince . . . tell me that Brian's not really dead," he said.

"I'm sorry, Owen" was all I could say.

Moments later, Owen Hart went out through that curtain and gave a stellar performance. I know deep down inside that Owen did that in Brian's memory. The night he passed away I'm sure Owen would have wanted the same thing.

No matter where my life takes me from this point, I know that I will never meet another man like Owen. I was blessed by God to be able to call him "friend" during the time he was here.

God bless you, Owen. I will never forget you.

Subconsciously, the references to God were there. At this point he was perhaps working — slowly but surely — his way to my heart.

The week following the incident, when I got together with Vince to discuss the next *Raw* — he hit me with something I'll never forget. Vince brought up the idea of personally descending from atop the arena in an effort to demonstrate that the stunt, which cost Owen his life only seven days earlier was indeed safe.

In his defense, not only was Vince not thinking straight, but as he heard the words come out of his own mouth he realized what he had said, and said no more. And let me also add that on several occasions prior to Owen's death, I personally witnessed Vince attempt "stunts" before asking the talent to perform them — to make sure they were safe. Hours before the Bret Hart/Shawn Michaels Iron Man Match at WrestleMania xii, Vince actually did the Heartbreak Kid's Superman entrance, via rip cord, from the top of the arena to the floor. I can also remember an instance where Road Dog had to talk Vince out of being wheeled off the stage to the floor in a Dempsey Dumpster prior to Dog doing it.

As I sit here and write this, many years later, I think I know why Vince suggested repeating Owen's descent. Knowing Vince, I'm sure he felt horribly guilty that he hadn't tried it first. But again, none of us viewed the stunt as dangerous. It had been done many times before, and professionals were always involved in making it safe.

Chapter 53

MR. INVISIBLE

We were on top. Over a period of two years we had increased the ratings by well over five points. In the cable industry, that is unheard of. I was the golden boy *inside* Titan Tower. Those in the know were saying I was the person who'd saved the World Wrestling Federation. Vince, the Rock, Stone Cold Steve Austin and Chyna were all becoming media darlings. And Eric Bischoff? He was looking for a new line of work.

Throughout it all, I felt as if I was Vince McMahon's best-kept secret. I was Mr. Invisible. One part of me understood, but the other part was po'd. As a business man, Vince didn't dare let my contributions as a writer for the WWF be known, perhaps because there would then be some interest in me outside of wrestling. It was about this time that Kevin Dunn invited me to a brainstorming meeting with a bunch of programming execs who represented Studios USA, the syndication division of the USA Network. Among those present were Steve Rosenberg, the president of the division, and Richard Dominick, the executive producer of the *Jerry Springer Show*.

With that kind of audience, I knew that I almost had to get up on the table and do an Irish jig. And, I practically did. Rosenberg was from Long Island, so we hit it off immediately. Many times he would shush his own people so he could hear what I had to say. At the time, Studios USA was looking for a way to do syndicated shows with the WWF. They wanted ideas — and I fired them out almost quicker than my mouth could move. Man, I wooed them. When the meeting broke up they had to be saying, "Who is this guy — and where did he come from?" I saw that meeting as an opportunity to showcase my talents.

About a week later, I asked Kevin Dunn when we were going to meet with the Studios USA people again. Kevin said to me, "Don't worry about it — you don't need to be attending those meetings anymore."

What did you want me to think? I knew that Vince didn't want anyone to know about me. Another clue? The company was about to go public, so the PR department had a prospectus printed up showcasing the company and those who made it tick. "Key people in the organization," I think they called it. And there he was, in all his glory — Jim Ross. I even think he had his cowboy hat on. If Jim Ross was more valuable to Titan Sports than I was, then Michael Jordan was more valuable to the Chicago White Sox then he was to the Bulls. Ross and I weren't even on the same playing field — where he played the role of yes-man, I made a difference. You may be saying to yourself, "It sounds like part of this can be attributed to Russo's ego." You know what? You're probably right. But it was also about much more than that — it was about principle.

I've got to mention this. Just recently Vince did a PR tour of Australia where my name came up. In reference to my stint in WCW, Vince said something to the effect of "Vince Russo failed in WCW because he let his ego get in the way."

I want to comment on this. For starters, Vince has no idea what happened when I was with WCW. He doesn't have the first clue. If he wants to believe stories, from a fossil who has recently rejoined his organization — then he can knock himself out. But does Vince McMahon actually want to talk about somebody else's ego?

This is coming from the same guy who broadcast to the entire world that he, singlehandedly, was going to take down the National Football League with a little somethin'–somethin' by the name of the XFL; the same guy who seriously thought the American people would sit on the edge of their Lay-Z Boys every night while he gave his views on global issues; the same guy who has a *monstrous* self-portrait of himself hanging in his home in Greenwich, Connecticut.

Vince Russo has an ego?

Wow.

Looking back now — Vince wasn't the only one guilty of having an ego. . . . There I go again — talking about Vince having an ego and not me. Wait a minute . . . I have my *Webster's* right here — let me look it up.

Ego. 1: the individual as aware of himself. 2: conceit. 3: the part of the psyche which governs action rationally.

Wait . . . was number two "conceit"? Am I claiming not to have been "conceited"? Wasn't it all about me? *I did this, I did that?* Did I thank anyone else, *ever?*

You see, that's the beauty of Jesus. Once you accept him into your heart, it's no longer about you. If the next guy wants to take all the credit, let him. If it makes him feel good, give it to him. Why? Because once you are saved, there is only one person to please — the guy upstairs who made it all possible.

Man, every magazine with a picture of Vince made me want to vomit. The guy was taking credit for everything. And I was nowhere to be found — not even as a footnote. At first it wasn't a big deal — as long as Vince paid me. But the better we did and the more Vince talked about himself, the more despondent I became. Vince the genius — yeah, right. This was the guy that gave the go-ahead for Who's tag-team partner, What.

While a part of me was feeling slighted, another part was experiencing a sense of great self-satisfaction. Everything I had set out to do, I'd accomplished. I should have been on the high of my life, yet I was becoming more and more miserable, and it wasn't just about not getting the props. For starters, I no longer had a life. I had put so much energy into my job that my own family had become strangers. Amy and I were just so distant — and I felt like I couldn't fix it. It's almost as if I was embarrassed for choosing my profession over my wife, my only true love, and my three kids . . . my flesh and blood. And, I don't know, I was always thinking about Owen Hart. I thought about the way he dedicated himself to the wrestling business — all those days he spent on the road — and then one day, it was all over. No warning, no nothing.

What should have been the pinnacle of my career was turning into the lowest point of my life. I was tired, depressed and physically, mentally and emotionally worn-out. Vince had taken everything I had, and he was about to ask for more. Expect it, demand it.

There's something you really need to know to understand my mindset at that time. You see, outside of the ring I had other responsibilities — you know, weekly duties that are just part of everyday life. Cutting the lawn, going to the bank, helping my kids with their homework, getting the oil changed in my car — the things that just don't go away. My point is — when you're working 80 hours a week you still have to find the time to get all that other stuff done. That's something Vince can't relate to. He doesn't go to the bank. Doesn't go to Jiffy Lube. He has no idea which is more durable — the Snapper or the Lawn Boy — and he probably thinks Briggs & Stratton was an ECW tag team!

When Vince had down time it was just that — down time. I can remember one time during the holidays, Vince had a maintenance guy from Titan come to his house to put up his Christmas tree. Well, after putting up the tree, Maintenance Joe forgot to fold up the ladder and take it down. When I came back to Vince's house the following week the ladder was still in the same spot. Vince never even moved it.

God bless him, but when you make that kind of money you just don't live the same life everybody else does.

And even though I was making good coin myself, I never wanted to lose sight of who I was or where I came from. I wanted to be the same guy who used to sling textbooks for a whopping $14,500 a year. For some reason, I never wanted the money to change my life.... And it never did.

Looking back now, it was simply because the money never really mattered. Even though, at times, I felt like I'd become a prisoner to it, at the end of the day it was just never that important to me. I don't know.... Now that I had it... it just seemed like I didn't want it.

Chapter 54

SMACKDOWN

When the execs at TBS made the decision to add a two-hour wrestling show to their schedule on Wednesday nights, we were far from delighted. We knew that four hours of wrestling programming a week would kill not only the talent, but the product as well. It was *clearly* overkill, for everybody involved. But at the time, WCW was on a roll — and Turner wanted more, more, more. Now it was Vince's turn to want more, more, more.

I knew it was a mistake to add *Smackdown* to our programming schedule. It would just water down the product. But Vince — being Vince — didn't want to hear any of that. As I said earlier — nothing is ever enough for Vince. The guy just can't be happy and content. He's got to push all the time, and in the process, drive everybody working with him straight into the ground. Unfortunately, I was never asked my opinion. I was just told to write another show.

So, suddenly my workload doubled. Sure, I had Ed writing with me — but four hours of TV a week? Do you know how many writers it took to write a half-hour of *Friends* every week? And those writers weren't dealing with injuries. And I'm sure Jennifer Aniston never asked, "How is losing this match going to help *me?*"

I was now writing nonstop, 22 segments a week. Think about that. Think about *Frasier* as a four-hour marathon — every week. If I thought there was pressure before — what was this? To come up with a better show, not once a week now — but now twice — *!@#$% me!*

Like a match in a drizzle I was still burning, but barely. Man, I was on the verge of snapping. I can remember getting home at about nine o'clock one night, and just standing at the kitchen table cutting a promo (one-person dialogue) on everything and everybody. I was babbling — I didn't even know what I was saying. I remember ending the promo in a laughing rage — I was losing my mind.

Worse, I knew that there was no place left to go. We had already peaked. We had brought the ratings into the sevens — what else was there to prove? All that remained to be answered was how much more money could I make for Vince. This was BS — I was going to have a nervous breakdown or a heart attack. I needed a change. I needed something — I just wasn't sure what that something was.

Then came an offer I couldn't refuse.

Chapter 55

HOLLYWOOD

I'm bad with dates, but it was some time in the early summer of 1999 when Ed Ferrara introduced me to his friend, Theresa Edy. She was an executive vice-president for a production studio in Los Angeles by the name of Greenblatt-Janollari. An attractive, take-charge woman, Theresa had been speaking to Ed about developing a show based on professional wrestling. Ed was a little hesitant, but after telling me about the idea, I told him he should at least meet with her to see what she had to say. At the time, coming as a television writer from La-La Land, Ed was done with the town. Hollywood was just a memory as he looked to move on in his life. Me? I was coming from a totally different place. I always had a dream of being a cog in the Tinseltown wheel, and there is no doubt in my mind that if I hadn't been married at 22 — I would have been. Maybe this was my second chance.

Ed and I met with Theresa and her husband following a show we had at the Anaheim Pond. Theresa told us that at the time, sports entertainment was *it* in Hollywood. With the current success of the WWF, everybody was looking to hop on the bandwagon. Theresa then made her pitch to Ed, "Who better to write a pilot about professional wrestling than you and Vince?" Ed told Theresa he would think about it and let her know. I knew I was already in.

After the meeting, Ed and I went back to Stamford and worked on a treatment between writing *Raw* and *Smackdown*. Ed did most of the work. Being experienced in "real" TV, he knew what needed to be done. I pitched in where I could, just trying to learn every step of the way. After the treatment was finished, Ed began to get cold feet. Not only did he really not want to get involved in Hollywood again — he was also afraid of losing the job that had got him *out* of Hollywood. After various discussions, Ed made the decision to skip out on the project — but I was still determined to go spaldings-to-the-wall. So I called Theresa and told her I was going it alone. My chances of selling a pilot were now diminished because I no longer had Ed's Hollywood name and reputation — but I was still determined to give it a shot.

Within the next few weeks, Theresa set up a pitch meeting with the then-head of Fox, Sandy Grushow. In a matter of a month I was flying out to L.A. to pitch my idea, *Rope Opera*. Remember, this is now a few years ago — reality television was just beginning to see the light of day. One of the first series that played with the genre was *The Larry Sanders Show*, starring Gary Shandling, and to this day it stands out as one of the best in the history of television. If you're not familiar with it, *The Larry Sanders Show* was based on a late-night talk show, much like Leno. Only aside from seeing what happens in front of the camera, we were taken backstage and shown a glimpse of the "real" world of late-night television — what *really* goes on in putting a show together. This was my model for *Rope Opera:* taking the viewer behind the curtain of sports entertainment and showing them a world they'd never seen before. The whole thing would be seen through the eyes of the head writer, Sal Trucco — who was, of course, yours truly.

So I flew out to L.A. and I met with Sandy Grushow. What an experience. It was every movie concerning the "Hollywood Process" that I had ever seen. The best comparison I could make is to *Seinfeld*, when George and Jerry pitch their show about nothing to Hollywood executives. I swear to you, it was the same thing. Sandy's people laughed when Sandy laughed, they were silent when he was silent, and when he spoke, they all agreed — much like Vince's yes-men. The meeting was priceless. Once again, I sold my spaldings off, did the Irish jig on the coffee table, and by the time all was said and done, Sandy said . . . "Go write the pilot."

There was only one problem — Vince didn't know any of this was going on.

Theresa wanted to go public with the story in *Variety* — she wanted to make an official announcement, that Greenblatt-Janollari Studios had made a deal with WWF head writer Vince Russo. I begged Theresa, telling her, "You can't — not until I tell Vince." She agreed to give me some time.

Now understand — I was not under contract with the WWF. I was simply an employee who received a paycheck every two weeks. Even though I was hired as the editor of the magazine at $60,000 per year, and I was now the "head writer" of the creative team, making $350,000 per year, Vince, for whatever reason, never even brought up the notion of putting me under contract. And that was fine by me. I hate being bound by legalities. If I decided that I wanted to take my ball and go home, I wanted to have that freedom. So as far as my deal with Greenblatt-Janollari was concerned, as long as I worked on my own time there was nothing Vince could do about it. The truth was, I didn't even have to tell him — but I didn't work that way with Vince, I was always honest with him. There was a side of me that wanted his blessing. I was really growing tired with our product — and I felt this opportunity could once again stir my creative juices.

So I met with Vince and told him of my opportunity with Greenblatt-Janollari. At that point I hadn't signed a legal, binding contract with Theresa either. To be honest — I didn't know how

Vince was going to react. I had been his best-kept secret for so long, and now people on the outside — Hollywood people — were beginning to take notice. No, I didn't know what Vince was going to say, but my mind was made up — I was writing *Rope Opera.*

To my surprise, Vince took the news well and seemed very supportive. Common sense would tell you that it was in his best interest to keep me happy — and working on my own project would do just that. Vince loved the idea of *Rope Opera*, and asked me to give him a treatment of the show — just so he could take a look. I've got to tell you, the meeting went better than I ever dreamed. After I left Vince's office, I called Theresa and told her it was a go. I gave her the green light to get the word out via press release, or whatever Greenblatt-Janollari had in mind.

The next day I dropped off the treatment in Vince's office. A few days later I was called up by Beth, Vince's assistant, who told me Vince wanted to see me. When I walked into his office, I could see *Rope Opera* on his desk. It was marked up.

"Vince, I read your treatment," he said. "I like the idea . . . but I would make some changes." Vince than proceeded to give me *his* spin on *Rope Opera*, how he would do it. Again — it was typical Vince — in my opinion he turned my Shakespearian work into some sophomoric, *Three Stooges* BS. I hated his ideas — but I didn't say a word. Then Vince said, "Vince — forget this Hollywood studio you're dealing with. I don't think you're seeing the big picture. I want the World Wrestling Federation to be an entertainment conglomerate. I want to do music, movies and television shows, and I want you to be a part of it. Let's take this *Rope Opera* and let's do it together."

I hated what Vince was saying — I hated every word. Excuse me, did I say Vince? Oh, I'm sorry I meant *Ted Turner!* Here he was again, attempting to become something he wasn't. But you know what? Whatever floats his boat. If Vince has all these dreams and ambitions, good for him, go for it. But in just one 30-minute conversation, *Rope Opera* went from mine to *ours.* No! Vince didn't own me, and I was going to do this project myself. I left McMahon's office with him thinking we had a deal. But believe me, there was no "deal" — I just didn't know what to do.

As I look back on that meeting now, I view it much differently. At the time, I had been with the WWF for about five years. As the cliché goes — I had seen it all. My heart had become so hard, so calloused, that I just didn't believe anybody — not even Vince, a man I once trusted. Without realizing it, the wrestling business had turned me into something I never wanted to become. I was just as paranoid as the boys. For all intents and purposes, Vince might have been sincere. He might have honestly been trying to help me. But again, I'd become jaded by being in the "bubble." In my mind there was no way Vince was working *with* me — he was definitely on the "other side," even though he was only protecting his own interests.

Meanwhile, I was getting pressure from Theresa. Fox wanted me to start on the pilot and I still hadn't signed a contract with Greenblatt-Janollari. I told Theresa about my conversation with Vince, and she was more determined than ever to get me to sign. Man, I didn't get much sleep. Talk about being caught in the middle. But then again, I knew what I wanted to do. I'm the kind of guy who has to move on. After I've been there, done that — it's on to the next project. That's what I'm talking about when I say money don't mean squat. I was making $350,000 with Vince, and that wasn't even part of the equation. I knew what I had to do. There was going to be a showdown. And it was going to happen the next day.

The only problem was . . . Vince beat me to the punch.

I guess after my conversation with Theresa she became nervous. She decided to issue a press release: that Greenlatt-Janollari had signed the head writer of the World Wrestling Federation, Vince Russo. Well, as soon as it went out, Vince somehow caught wind of it. I got a call from him the next morning, telling me that he wanted Theresa's name, the name of her firm, and her telephone number because he was going to call her up and put an end to this. I'm thinking, "What am I, 11? I'm almost a 40-year-old man — if anybody's going to call Theresa it'll be me." And screw that — I wasn't putting an end to anything. I wanted to go forward with *Rope Opera* with Greenblatt-Janollari! So I told Vince I'd take care of it and hung up.

It was back to the drawing board. I wasn't going to take care of anything — I was going to continue with *Rope Opera*, even if it meant my job at the WWF. I had to tell Vince this — take the spaldings in hand one more time.

So I met with him yet again. I told Vince that, first of all, I didn't agree with his revisions. I saw *Rope Opera* a certain way and I wanted to stick to my vision. Vince said that if I was going to write a show based on the likenesses of WWF characters, then it was his responsibility to get involved. The conversation was going nowhere, until Vince said, "You know what you should do, Vince? You know what you're talking about? Forget Hollywood — I already have a publishing deal in place. What you should do is write a book about your experiences as head writer of the WWF — and I'll let you say whatever you want." He then went on to say that he would call the publisher personally and get the ball rolling.

I'm thinking, "What is this guy smoking?" Do you really think that Vince would have given his blessing to the kind of book I wanted to write? Vince then said in so many words that he didn't want to talk about the Greenblatt-Janollari deal again — it was a dead issue. So I left his office with him now thinking I was writing a book.

No way. I wasn't writing a book, and I wasn't killing any deal I had in place. Vince didn't own me. Maybe he owned others, but not me. Days turned into weeks as I agonized. At this point, I not only started hating my job more and more — I started hating my whole existence. Vince McMahon and the WWF had a stranglehold on my life — I no longer had any control. At that time Vince also wanted me to have a cell phone on me 24/7, so he could reach me at all times.

Was he kidding me? I'm at the movies with my kids on a Saturday and Vince is going to call me during *American Pie* so we can talk about what Austin was doing on the next *Raw*? Screw that.

I used to have to drive into the city with Vince, when he would get his hair cut at some posh hotel, so we could talk about *Raw* during the 45-minute limo ride. That was messed up. I don't even make my kids sit there while I got my hair cut. But I sat — like some jabeep — waiting for Vince. What an idiot I was.

Something had to give. Amy was miserable — giving me the "single parent" BS, and I just didn't want to hear it anymore. And on top of all that — I was now writing *Smackdown* as well as *Raw*, and Vince wasn't paying me one cent extra. He'd doubled my workload and I wasn't given one thin dime. Can you imagine the NBC execs telling Jerry Seinfeld, "Yeah, Jerry. We want you to write a spin-off — *The Newman Show* — but we aren't going to pay you any money for it. All right? Good." I might also add that at this point my partner Ed was gone, mentally and emotionally, and barely there physically. Vince had already succeeded in driving him over the edge. He'd only stayed with the WWF because I begged him to — and Vince doubled his salary at my request.

You know, you simply can't understand just by reading this, but McMahon was just so overbearing. Everything was about the company; every day, every hour, every minute, every second. After a while that wears on you. Subconsciously, I wanted out so bad — fired, quit, whatever it was. I was at the end of my rope.

And all it would take would be one phone call for it to finally snap.

A few days prior to my last meeting with Vince, I had just finished writing *Raw* and *Smackdown* when I called Steve Austin to go over the script. At the time, Austin had a boo-boo and claimed he couldn't do certain things. Whatever.

So I call Steve at home, and he's telling me he can't do what I had written because he was "hurt." Meanwhile I could hear him with his hunting buddies, drinking and having a good time. Okay — you're making somewhere about five million dollars a year, you're hurt so you can't perform on TV — but you're well enough to be out drinking and playing Ted Nugent. It was just a small incident — it had happened a million times before — but this time it pushed me off the deep end.

Chapter 56

MY LAST MEETING WITH VINCE

I was so unhappy that, as I stated earlier, I probably wanted to be fired. I didn't have the spaldings to quit. Let's face it — you're talking about walking away from $350,000 here. Unless *Rope Opera* took off, there was a good possibility I'd never see that kind of money again. But at that point, money was secondary. What really mattered was my well-being and my family. So I set up another meeting with Vince, only this time I was just going to throw everything at him, hoping he'd say, "This guy's fried — it's bye-bye time."

It's ironic, but seeing those words I feel like God was beginning to get more heavily involved in my life right at this point. Notice that what was once important to me, no longer was. And what once took a back seat was quickly moving to the forefront. There is no question in my mind that this was the start of my journey. No sane person ponders walking away from $350,000 without there being a faithful force behind him. It's just something that, in "this world," we do not do.

God was clearly putting my priorities in the proper order. He was at work showing me what truly was important. Unfortunately, even at this point I would waste another two-plus years.

When I sat down to square off with the boss this time, there was no plan. No script was necessary. I was just going to reel off everything that was weighing heavily on my mind, in whatever order it flew out. This wasn't one of those "take your spaldings in your hand" kind of moments, because this time I honestly didn't care what the outcome was.

That last line is exactly what I was talking about in my last "revelation."

I had been in that office so many times before — same 42nd Street red, same zebra stripes. For whatever reason, my mind flashed back to the first time Tom Emanuel had brought me there. Man, I'd been so nervous, sitting there in my little black suit, voice trembling like a timid child. Who was that? Vince and I had come so far in just over two years, it was odd to think I was once nervous talking to him. But wait, this feeling *was* familiar. It was as if I was back at the beginning again. I don't know, in my mind I just felt as if this could be it. The laughter, the heartache, the good times, the bad, mocking JR . . . was this the way it was going to end?

In opening the conversation, I expressed my concern about my hectic schedule: I was never at home anymore, and Amy was more or less raising the kids on her own. I then told Vince that I wanted the option to be able to move, so that Amy could at least be closer to her family. Being on the road so much now with the two shows, I would see Vince at least three days a week anyway. If it had to be more than that, fine. I would fly in and out of Stamford, but I had to think about Amy and the kids — she was miserable.

After giving it a moment's thought, Vince looked me dead in the eye and said something I'll never forget, "Vince, I don't know what the problem is. You make enough money now. Why don't you just hire a nanny?"

That was it — all those times I was wondering if Vince truly cared about me — I was just given my answer. With such a cold, callous response I knew that he didn't give a !@#$ about Vince Russo or his family — all he cared about was his ratings, his money and his company. I was crushed. My feelings towards Vince and his family were always sincere. I truly cared about them. They had become a part of my life . . . a part of me. It used to really bother me not knowing how Vince felt — but now I knew.

After that, I just didn't care. I knew in my heart that it was over. Amy, Will, VJ and now Annie had paid enough. And for what? For me to be sitting at a table with a guy who is telling me to hire a nanny to raise my kids? That's what it all came down to. Reading this you may think it was no big deal, but to me it was. How can you BS somebody into thinking you're sincere for so long? How can all that matters to you in your life be money, greed and power? I'm sorry — I just can't relate to that. As I've said 100 times, my real motivation was to help the McMahons because of my sincere feelings for them. If it were all about money would I have been sitting there in Vince McMahon's office increasing my chances of losing this God-forsaken job by the second?

But if Vince wanted to make it about money, then I'd make it about money. So from there, I steered the conversation toward the almighty greenback.

"Vince," I said, "in 15 months I am going to be 40 years old. I promised myself and my family that at 40, I was walking away from this business. The past five years have taken 10 off my life. I knew when I first got into this that it was going to have a shelf life. Well, the clock is ticking. For the next 15 months I want . . . one million dollars, then after that, I'm done."

As much as he always protects his hand, Vince couldn't this time. His facial expression dropped his cards all over the table. He was shocked.

"Well, that's an awful lot of money," he said.

"Is it, Vince?" I answered. "You think I don't know what my creative contributions have meant to this company financially? You think I don't know what this company makes? What Steve Austin makes?"

"Well, that just seems like an astronomical amount of money," he said.

"Vince — I know what I'm worth. That's what I want."

I left Vince's office with him telling me he'd "think about it."

Almost two weeks passed — I didn't hear a word. During those two weeks nothing had changed — it was the same old BS. I was still working around the clock and there was still no motivation for me, not even the money. I knew in my heart that even if Vince came back with the million dollars, it wasn't going to matter. I was spent on all levels. Forget my kids — I was the one who needed a nanny!

Well, I'm not one to wait around. I'm one to make things happen. Knowing Eric Bischoff had just recently been released from his duties, and knowing what my value would have been to WCW — it was a no-brainer. But even more appealing to me was the challenge. At the time WCW was foundering — they had hit rock bottom, much like we had only two and a half years earlier. This was my chance to prove myself all over again — only this time without Vince McMahon.

So I made the call to WCW. Two days later I had the job.

You know, in going to WCW, a lot of people have said to me, "But Vince, what was the difference? You were going to have to put the same amount of time in." The difference was: *there was no Vince*. Again, I'm not running down the boss in any way, but unless you'd been in my shoes you just couldn't fathom how taxing it was. Monday ran into Sunday and every day was more stressful than the last. At WCW, there'd be no more trips to the salon in the city, no more phone calls on Saturday afternoon, and no more 7:30 a.m. meetings the morning following *Raw*. On top of that, I was also allowed to sleep in the car, I didn't have to miss any more Giants playoff games — and yes, it was okay to be sick!

In coming to an agreement, I informed wcw that I was going to put a staff in place —so that my actual presence wouldn't be needed 100 percent of the time. In other words, if I was to miss a *Nitro* or *Thunder* taping, the earth wasn't going to come crashing down.

Another key factor in the negotiations was that the wcw would allow me to go through with my *Rope Opera* deal. That was really the key for me. Even though at that point I knew I'd had my fill of wrestling, at least now I had the freedom to work on outside projects.

But let's be real — I was jumping from the fire into the towering inferno, and I knew it. My objective was to hold on for two more years. And I almost did . . . but that's a story for another book.

Chapter 57

SAYING GOODBYE

I accepted the job as wcw's Creative Director on Sunday night, October 2, 1999. Vince was expecting me at the Meadowlands in New Jersey for *Raw* the following morning. I flew out of Atlanta that night and had to change planes in Philadelphia. It was about 10:30 p.m. — this was my only opportunity to call.

I dialed Vince at home in Stamford, Connecticut, and he answered the phone. When he realized it was me he gave me his familiar, "Hey pal, how's it going?"

My heart was wedged so tightly in my throat, I thought I was going to gag. With my voice cracking I said, "Vince . . . I just accepted an offer from wcw. I'm starting with them next week."

"What?" Vince answered — so I repeated myself.

"You're ribbing me, right? This is a rib?"

"No, Vince," I said. "I just got back from Atlanta."

"Why, Vince? Why?" he asked.

"I have nothing left to give you, Vince," I said. "You took everything I had."

Now that it was starting to sink in, Vince became hot. "You know I'm going to go after them?" he said. "You know I'm going to come after you!"

"Vince — there's nothing to come after. I never had a contract with you. I'm sorry, Vince."

Vince then said some things in an attempt to make the conversation ugly. He wasn't anticipating this and he didn't quite know how to deal with it. He never saw it coming. At one point he fired me up a bit, and I think I rambled on about not getting any credit for the success of the WWF. But then I caught myself. It was pointless . . . it was over. I wasn't going to let my last conversation with a man who was an idol to me when I was younger — and later, a mentor — end in an argument. I told Vince I wasn't going to allow him to make our last conversation an ugly one. I'd simply made the best decision that I could for me and my family. With my parents living in Florida and Amy's in Indiana, Atlanta was smack in the middle. If nothing else — Amy would be able to see her parents more and the kids, their grandparents.

"I didn't know I was such a bad person, Vince," McMahon then said.

"You're not Vince — I never said that. I just have nothing left to give you. I love you and I love your family, but my tank is on empty."

"Vince . . . this is the most devastating phone call I've ever received," he said. "I just want you to know, I was going to give you the money."

"It was never about the money," I said.

The last thing I said to Vince was that everything was in place. He clearly had momentum and was riding a wave he could coast for at least a year. I assured him that I had done all I could, and it was just time for me to move on.

Vince's last words to me were, "I hope one day our paths will cross again."

To this day I've never forgotten those words.

You know, after writing nearly 100,000 words, I've come up with the same answer — I still don't know. . . . Part of me really hopes our paths do cross again, while another part of me says, "Thanks, but no thanks." It was just that statement about my kids and the nanny. In just eight words Vince told me exactly what our relationship had meant to him — what I'd meant to him. It was all about *his* company, *his* greed, *his* success and *his* money. To this day that rips my heart out. My feelings towards the McMahon family never had a single thing to do with how much money they were paying me.

But in hindsight, I'm a different animal. I'm not from that world, and I never was. I was just a man trying to make a living to support his family. Nothing else ever really mattered.

Wow, wow and wow again. I don't even remember writing that sentence. . . .

"But in hindsight, I'm a different animal. I'm not from that world, and I never was."

Wow. What world was I talking about? Was I talking about the world of sports entertainment, or was I talking about "the world"? I am so blessed that I have these words to go back to. How many of us have the opportunity to look at our lives through a microscope prior to being saved by the Lord, Jesus Christ. Those words I wrote two short years ago provide so much insight into what was going on at my very core: some sort of a transformation that I wasn't even privy to at the time. This book has such purpose — such meaning for those who are now at the place where I had lived. A place with no God — nothing.

Lord, I give you absolute praise in enabling me to share this story with others. In enabling me to show firsthand who I was . . . and what I have become.

• • •

It's October 15, 2004. What I'm writing now, I'm writing for the first time. Certain circumstances arose after I wrote the original manuscript — circumstances that are pertinent to this book. . . .

It's so difficult to assess Vince McMahon — maybe because you just can't. I sit here listening to, and drawing inspiration from, the television — yes it still inspires me, only differently. (What would once have been Howard Stern, is now Joel Osteen, an extremely gifted pastor from Houston.) But there is one thing that remains precisely the same. I still don't know the real Vince.

Without going into detail (I will in the next saga), I had the opportunity to meet with Vince one last time in July, 2003. There was just something calling me back to him — a sense of unfinished business. I flew to Stamford for the encounter I'd known one day would come.

I'll never forget the feeling of going back to the house; it was just so surreal. As I sat waiting for Vince, every part of my relationship with him passed through my mind in vibrant colors — from the laughter, to the tears, to that final phone call. Sitting there, I felt like I had never left.

But I had, and though I was now a different person, in my heart I knew I was still looking for the answer to the question that continues to haunt me to this very day — did Vince, or did he not, really care about Vince Russo, the human being? Still living in "this world" at that time, his acceptance, or approval, was just so important. Ironically, in a lot of ways I must have been feeling like Shane — just wanting to see Vince's soft side, his human side. I needed that.

When Vince finally came down the stairs, I'd be lying if I said I didn't get choked up. I was happy to see him. I needed to see him. After a friendly embrace, Vince and I sat down and began to talk.

In what was a long time coming, I finally got the chance to explain to Vince face-to-face why I left. I hadn't really had the opportunity before and I was grateful to have it now. I told Vince that I was troubled because in my heart I really cared about him, and after working closely with him for more than two years — I'd never known if the feeling was mutual. Vince looked at me and said, "Vince, when you work that closely with someone, you *have to* care about them."

Fourteen words and twenty-three months later — I still knew nothing more — or less.

I haven't seen Vince since, and I'd be lying to you if I said I didn't miss him. The funny thing is, I really don't know why. For some reason beyond my comprehension, there has been a sense of unfinished business since I left. I don't know what the connection is. I have to believe that God does; I have to believe that he brought these two individuals together, from two completely different worlds, to reach great levels of professional success for a reason — a reason that to this day I've yet to understand.

I hope that one day I will.

Chapter 58

AND IN THE END . . .

What a great Lennon/McCartney line: "And in the end, the love you take is equal to the love you make."

I wish I could say that about the wrestling/sports-entertainment business, but I can't. I gave and I gave, and I feel like I got very little back. But as I stated earlier, that's the nature of the beast.

So here I am, in the back of my CD Warehouse — rednecks shopping, butt-cracks popping — as I come to the end of an unforgettable journey. Whatever happened to *Rope Opera*, you ask? Well, my masterpiece was placed in the hands of, again, two feminine males — not that there's anything wrong with that — who just didn't understand the concept. To them, sports entertainment was a hysterical slapstick comedy starring guys in their underwear who hit each other over the head with chairs. Guess what? Vince McMahon has a script to sell you. Me? I refused to alter my vision to fit theirs. I was never ashamed to be in the business, and the last thing I was going to do was make a joke out of it.

So, what it all comes down to is this: to this day, I still am just a man trying to make a living to support his family. Whether it was at my peak of $535,000 per year at wcw, or my current salary of $250 per week, the money never really mattered. What matters now is every Friday night after me and my two boys, Will and VJ, close the store, count the money, turn off the lights and lock the door behind us, together we go to Applebee's and eat $3 chicken wings. We'll stay there til well past midnight, reciting movie line after movie line. And that's simply what it's all about.

Do I still watch the World Wrestling Federation? No — I can't, and I can't even tell you why. But I will say this — it's just not the same. It never will be.

Bizarroland was a place I will never forget. There were some good times, there were some bad — but if you'd ask me if I'd have done anything differently, if I could trade it all in, would I? The answer is . . . *no*. It is a part of me that will stay with me forever. It was a five-year run that helped me put everything into its proper perspective — career, money, family. In the end, it was all about my wife Amy and my three kids. All the money and success in the universe weren't worth my time away from them. Even though it hurt at times, I learned first-hand what really mattered most.

It was the best of times, it was the worst of times.

!@#$% me — it was only the beginning.

See you in the sequel.

THE END.
(I love writing those two words!)

Chapter 59

STILL TO COME

(Written October 16, 2004)

That was the end of my original manuscript. The turn my life has taken since I typed the last word has been an incredible journey — the kind of journey you only read, or hear about. Definitely somebody else's ride . . . the ride that "could never happen to you."

But, it did. And today I live it every second.

I want to take this opportunity to set the record straight on a few things. If I offended anybody in this book, with God as my witness, I apologize from the bottom of my heart. My intention was to hurt no one, that's why I spent months going through the original manuscript to assure that the severe ugliness was eliminated. However, the story was kept intact because I had to matter-of-factly show you Vince Russo, the old creature, for you to fully understand the transformation to this new life — my life today. I have no bitter feelings towards anybody I ever worked with in the wrestling business — not one — not even those from whom I've suffered great personal hurt. Today, thanks to what God has instilled in me, my heart is overflowing with love. I just wish that the wrestling business in general could somehow, in some way, experience what I have experienced over the past year.

It pains me deeply to pick up books written by other wrestlers whose main agenda is to put themselves over while tearing down everybody else along the way. I just don't understand it. In such a tight-knit fraternity, why is there such hatred, such jealousy, such deceit? My prayer is that one day, everybody in the business will care about those they are working with — care about their families, their well-being, their feelings and their lives. I almost sound like Martin Luther King here, but one day . . . well, I'll continue to dream, anyway.

As I finish up the final chapter of this book, I look forward to following it up with others where I can complete my journey in my own words. Yet to come are my struggles — mental, emotional and physical — with WCW, and the love/hate relationship with a friend at TNA, but most importantly what happened from there — the miracle in my life known as Jesus Christ, to whom every word I write is dedicated.

I look forward to sharing that story with you in the future, but for now, I'll leave you with some advice . . . my favorite quote from the Bible. . . .

"At once they left their nets and followed him." (Matthew 4:20)

It's that simple. See you on the second half of the journey.